IN THE NAME OF

ALLAH

THE ALL-COMPASSIONATE, ALL-MERCIFUL

An Inspired Life

***The Prophet Muhammad* (ﷺ)**

- Title: AN INSPIRED LIFE — The Prophet Muhammad
- Author: Abbas Tawfiq
- English Edition 1 (2010)
- Layout Design: IIPH, Riyadh, Saudi Arabia
- Filming and Cover Design: Samo Press Group

An Inspired Life

The Prophet Muhammad (ﷺ)

وما ينطق عن الهوى
النبي محمد (ﷺ)

Abbas Tawfiq

الدار العالمية للكتاب الإسلامي

INTERNATIONAL ISLAMIC PUBLISHING HOUSE

King Fahd National Library Cataloging-in-Publication Data

Tawfiq, Abbas

An Inspired Life - The Prophet Muhammad. / Abbas Tawfiq; .- Riyadh, 2010

320 p ; 21 cm

ISBN Hardcover: 978-603-501-079-5

1- Prophet Muhammad life 2-Muhammad, Prophet
I- Title

239 dc 1431/4631

Legal Deposit no. **1431/4631**
ISBN Hardcover: **978-603-501-079-5**

International Islamic Publishing House (IIPH)
P.O. Box 55195 Riyadh 11534, Saudi Arabia
Tel: 966 1 4650818 / 4647213 — Fax: 966 1 4633489
E-mail: iiph@iiph.com.sa — iiphsa@gmail.com
www.iiph.com.sa

Contents

Arabic honorific symbols used in this book

(سبحانه وتعالى): *Subḥânahu wa ta'âlâ* — 'The Exalted'

(صلى الله عليه وسلم): *Ṣalla-Allâhu 'alayhi wa sallam* — 'Blessings and peace be upon him'

(عليه السلام): *'Alayhis-salâm* — 'Peace be upon him'

(رضي الله عنه): *Raḍiya Allâhu 'anhu* — 'May Allah be pleased with him'

(رضي الله عنها): *Raḍiya Allâhu 'anhâ* — 'May Allah be pleased with her'

Pronunciation and Transliteration Chart

Arabic script	Pronunciation	Transliterated as:
أ	short ‘a’, as in *cat*	a
آ – ى	longer ‘a’, as in *cab* (not as in *cake*)	â
ب	/b/ as in *bell*, *rubber* and *tab*	b
ت	/t/ as in *tap, mustard* and *sit*	t
ة	takes the sound of the preceding diactrical mark sometimes ending in h (when in pausal form): ah, ih, or ooh; or atu(n), ati(n) or ata(n) when in uninterrupted speech	h or t (when followed by another Arabic word)
ث	/th/ as in *thing*, *maths* and *wealth*	th
ج	/j/ as in *jam*, *ajar* and *age*	j
ح	a ‘harsher’ sound than the English initial /h/, and may occur medially and in word-final position as well	ḥ
خ	as in *Bach* (in German); may occur initially and medially as well	kh
د	/d/ as in *do*, *muddy* and *red*	d
ذ	as in *this*, *father*, and *with*	dh
ر	/r/ as in *raw*, *art* and *war*; may also be a rolled r, as with Spanish words	r

Arabic script	Pronunciation	Transliterated as:
ز	/z/ as in *zoo*, *easy* and *gaze*	z
س	/s/ as in *so*, *messy* and *grass*	s
ش	as in *ship*, *ashes* and *rush*	sh
ص	no close equivalent in English, but may be approximated by pronouncing it as /sw/ or /s/ farther back in the mouth	ṣ
ض	no close equivalent in English, but may be approximated by pronouncing /d/ farther back in the mouth	ḍ
ط	no close equivalent in English, but may be approximated by pronouncing /t/ farther back in the mouth	ṭ
ظ	no close equivalent in English, but may be approximated by pronouncing 'the' farther back in the mouth	<u>dh</u>
ع	no close equivalent in English: a guttural sound in the back of the throat	'
غ	no close equivalent in English, but may be closely approximated by pronouncing it like the French /r/ in 'rouge'	gh
ف	/f/ as in *fill*, *effort* and *muff*	f

Arabic script	Pronunciation	Transliterated as:
ق	no close equivalent in English, but may be approximated by pronouncing /k/ farther back in the mouth	q
ك	/k/ as in *king*, *buckle* and *tack*	k
ل	/l/ as in *lap*, *halo*; in the word *Allah*, it becomes velarized as in *ball*	l
م	/m/ as in *men*, *simple* and *ram*	m
ن	/n/ as in *net*, *ant* and *can*	n
هـ - ه - ـه	/h/ as in hat; unlike /h/ in English, in Arabic /h/ is pronounced in medial and word-final positions as well	h
و	as in *wet* and *away*	w
و (as a vowel)	long u, as in *boot* and *too*	oo
ي	as in *yet* and *yard*	y
ي (as a vowel)	long e, as in *eat*, *beef* and *see*	ee
ء	glottal stop: may be closely approximated by pronouncing it like 't' in the Cockney English pronunciation of *butter*: *bu'er*, or the stop sound in *uh — oh!*	' (Omitted in initial position)

Diphthongs:

Arabic script	Pronunciation	Transliterated as:
أَوْ ، و	Long o, as in *owe*, *boat* and *go*	au, aw, ow
أي ، يَ	Long 'a', as in *able*, *rain* and *say*	ay, ai, ei

Diacritical marks (*tashkeel*):

Name of mark	Pronunciation	Transliterated as:
ـَ fatḥah	very short 'a' or schwa (unstressed vowel)	a
ـِ kasrah	shorter version of ee or schwa (unstressed vowel)	i
ـُ Dammah	shorter version of oo	u
ـّ shaddah	a doubled consonant is stressed in the word, and the length of the sound is also doubled	Double letter
ـْ sukoon	no vowel sound between consonants or at the end of a word	Absence of vowel

About the word 'Lord'

The word *lord* in English has several related meanings. The original meaning is 'master' or 'ruler', and in this sense it is often used to refer to human beings: 'the lord of the mansion' or 'Lord So-and-So' (in the United Kingdom, for example). The word *Lord* with a capital L is used in the lexicon of Islam to refer to the One and Only God — Allah. In Islam, there is no ambiguity about the meaning of this word. While it is true that one may occasionally use the word *lord* (whether capitalized or not) to refer to a human being, in Islamic discourse the reference of this term is always clear from the context. Whereas for Christians, Hindus and other polytheists, the word *Lord* with a capital 'L' may refer to Allah, to Jesus or to some imagined deity, for Muslims, there can be no plurality of meaning. Allah alone is the Lord, and the Lord is Allah — not Jesus, not Rama, not any other being.

The Editor

Publisher's Note

All praise and thanks belong to Allah alone, the One, the Almighty, and All-Merciful. Blessings and peace be upon Prophet Muhammad, the last of His Messengers and Prophets, and upon his family, his Companions and all those who follow in his footsteps until the end of time.

Perhaps no human being has had his life story told and retold as much as the Prophet Muhammad (ﷺ) has. There are several reasons for this, and perhaps the most obvious one is that Muhammad ibn 'Abdullah has touched the lives of more people than any other human being in history. Most biographies in English of this great man were translated from Arabic or other languages. *An Inspired Life* has been compiled from Arabic sources, but written in English, by a bilingual academic scholar. Dr. Abbas Tawfiq, like so many before him, was motivated by his deep love and respect for the Messenger to write this biography of him, with a view to helping English-speaking readers to know, understand and thus learn to love the Prophet of Allah.

May Allah accept the efforts of all those who contributed to the production of this book, and may it be acceptable to Him, *âmeen.*

Muhammad ibn 'Abdul Mohsin Al-Tuwaijri

Managing Director
International Islamic Publishing House
Riyadh, Saudi Arabia

Preface

The advent of the first Islamic State in Madinah transformed Arab society. The new Muslim community was a system organised and cultured by the introduction of new values, and it caused the Arabs to witness the renewal of spirituality on a grand scale. It also provoked a considerable change in the geographical balance of power. This colossal shift was ascribed to the mission that was divinely assigned to the prophet of Islam, Muhammad (*ṣalla Allâhu 'alayhi wa sallam* — blessings and peace be upon him). Ever since, special attention has been paid to his life, the details of which were instrumental in facilitating the understanding of the new religion and in providing exemplary guidelines for those who believed in his message.

Most of the relevant information was transmitted orally to the successive generations and almost a century intervened between the occurrences themselves and the time of their compilation into detailed scholarly works. Combined with this, the phenomenon of a number of fraudulent sayings that were attributed to the Prophet (ﷺ) for political and sectarian reasons played a prominent role in sullying this important Islamic source. Had it not been for the critical methodology adopted, particularly by the scholars of Hadith [statements or actions of the Prophet (ﷺ)], who singled out false expressions and individual frauds, the reality would have been lost and Islamic law confused. The greatest attention has been paid to the reported speech and actions of the Prophet (ﷺ) due to their religious importance, while some historical narrations may still require further scrutiny to identify and remove any remaining erroneous material.

This work intends to depend only on authentic hadiths and historical books in order to draw a clear biographical picture of the Prophet (ﷺ) and to outline the lessons that can be learned from his treatment of people and his general behaviour. This work does not provide all the details produced by other writers nor does it generally engage in debates concerning their approaches to the life of the Prophet (ﷺ). The methodology of this book has been adopted in order to allow the reader to follow the sequence of events in the Prophet's life without the distraction of side issues and discussions. For this same purpose, the description of matters not directly related to his life has also been avoided, despite the historical relevance of such matters to the general study of the movement of Islam.

This biography begins with an overview of geographical, social and religious aspects of the Arabian Peninsula. The focus then narrows to examine Makkah, the hometown of the Hâshim family, from whom the Prophet (ﷺ) descended. The spotlight then shifts to the scant information that is available concerning the years from the Prophet's birth until the time he started receiving revelation. For the earlier period, I have concentrated on his strategy of preaching Islam, calling people to the Right Way,[1] and the internal and external consequences of the mission prior to the emigration of the first Muslims to Madinah. Then I highlight the unique power of the Prophet (ﷺ) in developing the first Islamic State, bringing the population and its diverse faiths under one umbrella and effectively practising tolerance. In addition, the emerging power of Islam was obliged to engage in many situations and battles until the death of the Prophet (ﷺ). The present work focuses on a variety of occurrences during the Prophet's lifetime, their causes and effects, and the lessons that Muslims learned from them to guide their lives both at that time and in the future.

CHAPTER ONE

The Arabian Peninsula

Location and nature

The Arabian Peninsula is situated in southwest Asia. It is bordered by the Arabian (or Persian) and Oman Gulfs in the east, by the Red Sea in the west, by Iraq and Syria in the north and by the Arabian Sea or Indian Ocean in the south. It lies at a strategic point between the East and the West. At the time in history under discussion here, the Arabian Peninsula was located between two major world civilisations, namely the Persian Empire that stood for Eastern civilisation and the Roman Empire, which represented the West and Christianity.

Despite the fact that the Arabian Peninsula is part of Asia, it is also close to Africa and Europe and plays a connecting role between these different parts of the world. This position was of importance to the ancient powers who attempted to dominate the Arabian Peninsula as a part of their belligerent political struggles. However, these bids for control usually failed despite the fact that some world powers did extend their influence into several of the surrounding areas. The unique position of the Arabian Peninsula did provide the opportunity for settlers and others to engage in trade.

The land of the Arabian Peninsula is mainly a desert, and this inevitably shaped the lifestyle of its inhabitants. Only a minority of the population formed the urban community, which lived and traded in the major towns of the Peninsula, such as Makkah, Yathrib, Ṭâ'if, Ḥeerah and so on. The Bedouins constituted the majority of the population, and they were found scattered all around the desert of the Peninsula. As the area was arid, people faced hardships in providing for their basic needs and this meant that they were spread out into scattered tribal groups wherever water and grassland were available. It was not unusual for two tribes to share a fertile location, but there were specific agreements whereby the 'guest' tribe must be the first to move on when water and grazing became limited. An ousted group would seek a new environment: a process that was repeated continually as homelands were sought to meet the needs of the people and relationships with others were shaped to create mutual benefits.

To maintain the safety of trade caravans, agreements were made with the tribes through whose land the caravans passed. This generally involved financial payments or other types of compensation. The tribe's leader was the person authorised to make treaties and the tribe's people had to abide by all his agreements. This convention, however, was nearly always a result of general consultation among the family members and relatives of the leader.

In those times, a tribe was an independent unit, with factors such as free will, sustained loyalty and a sense of identity linking its members and shaping their various dealings.[1] Still, Arab tribes also used to invade one another, plunder possessions and enslave free members of the invaded tribe.[2] Such skirmishes occurred between groups that were not allied through treaties, or when one side had broken the conditions of their mutual agreement.[3]

Social life

The nature of social life in the Arabian Peninsula during the pre-Islamic period was characterised by the same features that coloured social life in other parts of the world at that time, though each was stamped to differing degrees by the dominant cultures of that period.

Arab society was run according to a class system that consisted of free people and slaves. The former were constantly vulnerable to enslavement if their own tribe was defeated by invading tribes. Although this risk can be deduced from examining Arab history, a clear illustration is provided in the statement of al-Mugheerah *ibn*[4] Shu'bah when he was received by Rustum, the Persian commander: "We the Arabs do not enslave each other unless there is a war."[5]

The second social class consisted of slaves who had been purchased, subjugated in war or who became enslaved due to being isolated for some reason from the protection of their own tribe. In order to be released, a slave had to reach an agreement with his or her master in order to buy liberty. Alternatively, the slave could wait in the hope of being released during a subsequent counterattack by his or her fellow tribesmen. Counterattacks were important in upholding the honour of Bedouins in the eyes of other tribes, especially if they had forfeited female prisoners. Moreover, if an enslaved female bore a child to her enemy, for instance with her master who had captured her, then the ignominy would cling not only to herself and her children, but also to the whole of her original tribe.[6] This dreaded fate, in addition to the fear of poverty, underpins the fact that many Bedouins would feel ashamed if they produced a female child, and would hasten to bury her alive. The Noble Qur'an mentions this in the following verses:

﴾And when the news of [the birth of] a female [child] is brought to any of them, his face becomes dark, and he is filled with inward grief! He hides himself from the people because of the evil of that of news. Will he keep her with dishonour or bury her in the earth? Certainly, evil is their decision.﴿ *(Qur'an 16: 58-59)*[7]

﴾And kill not your children for fear of poverty. We [Allah] shall provide for them as well as for you. Surely, the killing of them is a great sin.﴿ *(Qur'an 17: 31)*

In contrast to this darker aspect, the urban women in particular enjoyed high status within their families and had a degree of freedom in many aspects of their lives. They contributed to society in terms of trade, war and other essential matters, and shared and participated in their spouses' daily affairs and concerns,[8] although the men alone retained positions as head of the household.

The relationship between the two genders was based on various types of marriage. Referring to a quotation from 'Â'ishah[9] (raḍiya Allâhu 'anha — may Allah be pleased with her), Bukhari, a great scholar of Hadith, defined four kinds of marriage current at that time. One was similar to modern marriage, whereby the man asked the parents or guardian of the woman for permission to marry her and offered her a dowry. Another type of coupling occurred when a husband asked his wife, after her menstruation ended, to seek someone to copulate with her in order to beget a noble child. The husband then separated himself from her until they were sure that she had become pregnant by this third party. Once they were certain of this, the husband might resume intercourse with his wife if he so wished. The third kind of marriage was when a group of up to ten men copulated with one woman. After the birth of a child, the woman had the final word in choosing the man to whom she wished to attribute her child. The fourth kind of union occurred when a prostitute had intercourse with a large number of men. After her baby was born, a specialist in recognising familial resemblances was sought and a suitable man was chosen to give his name to the baby. Islam annulled all but the first type of marriage.[10]

In addition, there existed the practice of 'wife swapping', where payment was offered for the exchange,[11] and the practice of a man offering his daughter in marriage to someone if he could marry the other man's daughter in return, without a dowry.[12] The latter was known as *ash-shighâr.* Moreover, in the pre-Islamic period, a man could marry his father's widow, or he could be married to a woman and her sister or her maternal or paternal aunt at the same time. In fact, a man could have as many wives as he wished.[13] All of these practises were subsequently abolished by Islam.[14]

Some of these types of marriage were unjust for women, such as the combination of marriage to a woman and her close relatives. In addition, there would be insult caused by a husband taking many wives, as this would reduce a woman's status. This is why Islam nullified several of these types of marriage and restricted the number of wives to a maximum of four at any one time, on condition that equality and justice is applied in the treatment of each of them.

Religious life

The majority of Arabs were polytheists prior to the rise of Islam. They worshipped a number of idols: the most well known being al-'Uzzâ, Hubal, Manât, Isâf and Nâ'ilah. During the time of Ismâ'eel (Ishmael) (*'alayhi as-salâm* — peace be upon him), many of the Arabs had been monotheists, worshipping the one true

Creator, Allah (*Subḥânahu wa Ta'âlâ* — Glorified and Exalted is He), and had transmitted this faith down the generations. However, they eventually began to deviate from this path.

Ibn Hishâm,[15] who compiled the most authentic biography of the Prophet (ﷺ), mentioned that paganism infiltrated the generations of Ismâ'eel (عليه السلام) when they began to leave Makkah and settle in the surrounding areas. As a result of their reverence of the Ka'bah,[16] on their departure, each group would take a stone from Makkah and set it where they lived, glorifying and circling around it as an example of the Ka'bah itself. As time passed, they began to forget its significance and continued to bow to the stone for its own sake.[17] At the same time, Ibn Hishâm quoted from Aktham ibn al-Jawn al-Khuzâ'i's narration that the Prophet Muhammad (ﷺ) dreamt of a man named 'Amr ibn Luḥay who was in hell. The Prophet (ﷺ) stated that this man was the first to introduce idolatry into the religion of Ismâ'eel's descendents.[18]

Despite reverting to polytheism and paganism, the Arabs retained certain aspects of the religion of Ibrâheem [Abraham (عليه السلام)] and Ismâ'eel (عليه السلام), though in a distorted form. For example, they still adhered to glorifying the Ka'bah by walking around it, making major or minor pilgrimages to it, and performing sacrifices in its vicinity. However, they corrupted these practices by circumambulating the Ka'bah while naked, and by declaring, "O God! Here I am at your service. You have no partner but a partner that is yours, whom You possess..."[19] when the correct statement to utter was, "O God! Here I am at your service. No partner do You have..."

After this, polytheism remained the predominant tenet of the Arabs, although a few people persisted throughout history in believing in the Oneness of Allah, maintaining it in their hearts and incorporating it into their lives. These people were known as the

Ḥunafâ', or 'Orthodox', and some of them were known by name, such as Zayd ibn 'Amr ibn Nufayl and Quss ibn Sâ'idah.[20]

A few of the Arabs tribes followed other religions. A number of Jewish tribes migrated to the Arabian Peninsula after 70 CE,[21] following the Roman occupation of Palestine, and settled in Yathrib, Khaybar and Taymâ'[22] before spreading out until there were over twenty Jewish tribes in the Arab lands.[23] When the Prophet Muhammad (ﷺ) emigrated to Madinah, there were noticeable Jewish clans there, such as Khaybar, Banu[24] an-Naḍeer, Banu Quraydhah, and Banu Qaynuqâ'.

As for Christianity, the Arabs knew of it because of the occupation of some of their regions by Abyssinian and Roman forces[25] on the one hand, and from coming into contact with some charismatic individuals on the other.[26] The Arabs in Syria and certain tribes, like Taghlib and Ṭayy', had also embraced the Christian religion. Because of his faith in Christianity, Abrahah had built a great church in Sana'a and intended to instruct Arabs to make pilgrimage to it instead of to Makkah,[27] as will be discussed further.

There might also have been followers of other creeds, such as Magians and Sabians; however, there is little information available[28] to describe their influence, if any, on the Arabs before Islam. Neither Judaism, nor Christianity, nor any other religion was so effective that it was able to convert the Arabs from heathenism, the formal faith of the Arabian Peninsula at that time. This was possibly due to a failure on the part of their followers to consider the spread of religion as a holy obligation.

Makkah

Makkah is the town where the Prophet Muhammad (ﷺ) was born. It is midway between the Sarawât Mountains and Tihâmah and located in the west of the Arabian Peninsula approximately fifty miles from the eastern edge of the Red Sea and three hundred meters above sea level.[29]

Historically, this area was just a barren desert and mountainous area. It was uninhabited until Prophet Ibrâheem (عليه السلام) received a command from Allah (سبحانه وتعالى) to bring his wife Hâjar and their child Ismâ'eel to dwell there. This event happened at some point in the nineteenth century BC.[30] The Noble Qur'an omits the precise date, but records this occasion in the following verse:

﴿Our Lord! I have made some of my offspring to dwell in an uncultivable valley by Your Sacred House [the Ka'bah at Makkah] in order, our Lord, that they may establish regular prayers. So fill some hearts among the people with love towards them, and provide them with fruits so that they may give thanks.﴾ *(Qur'an 14: 37)*

When Ismâ'eel (عليه السلام) and his mother had exhausted their provisions, water gushed out to nourish them at the place that would be forever after known as the Zamzam well.

Later, people of the nomadic Jurhum tribe passed nearby and noticed signs of life. They found the water of Zamzam, and with the consent of Hâjar, they settled and shared the land with the small family. Hence, Ismâ'eel (عليه السلام) grew up in an inhabited area, took a wife from among his new neighbours and generated the new Arabs (*al-'Arab al-Musta'ribah*).[31] This appears to be the reason for Ibn Hishâm's belief in the Arabs being the descendants of both Ismâ'eel and Qaḥṭân. Some Yemenis, however, assert that even

Qaḥṭân was engendered from Ismâ'eel, who then consequently was the only father of the whole Arab race.[32]

At any rate, Ismâ'eel (ﷺ) and his progeny after his death took care of the Ka'bah. Eventually, the different families of his descendants tried to keep the service of the Sacred House to themselves and this became a cause of contention and conflict between them. Some historians refer to Khuzâ'ah as the controlling family of Makkah and the Sacred House[33] at the end of the third century CE,[34] but as a result of further struggles, control of Makkah was finally transferred to the Quraysh, under the leadership of Quṣay ibn Kilâb.[35] He organised the running of the region and decided to impose various duties on the different tribes in Makkah, so that they could all have a share in its governance. He divided Makkah into plots and distributed them among the clans of Quraysh. His progeny and subsequent inhabitants also adhered to this plan.

Still, Quṣay ibn Kilâb retained control of all the activities that related to serving the Ka'bah and to the crucial issues of Makkah itself. For example, he retained the keys of the Sacred House so that no one could enter without his permission.[36] He also supplied people with the water from Zamzam, or from other wells after Zamzam was filled in with earth by the Jurhumis when they were obliged to evacuate Makkah. He provided water[37] mixed with honey, milk or raisins, and maintained the duty of offering food to pilgrims.[38]

On the demise of Quṣay, these duties were bequeathed to one of his descendants, Hâshim ibn 'Abd Manâf, and under his leadership they became public activities while Hâshim worked in a supervisory role. He received ingredients for preparing food for this purpose,[39] a hall that served as a deliberation chamber (*Dâr an-Nadwah*) for the discussion of major issues and a banner (*al-*

Liwâ') which would be raised only by officials during battle.[40]

His children continued these duties after he died, but they soon clashed as each group wanted to take sole possession of these honours. This new situation resulted in destroying not only the unity of the Quraysh but also the unity of other Arab tribes. Each group of Quṣay's descendents was supported by a specific tribe and they were on the verge of war to impose their demands until, for some unknown reason, they finally reached a compromise.[41] The solution was simply to divide all of the aforementioned duties among Quṣay's descendants. So, the line of 'Abd ad-Dâr took responsibility for the keys to the Ka'bah, the banner and Dâr an-Nadwah, while the line of 'Abd Manâf, represented by Hâshim ibn 'Abd Manâf, oversaw the preparation of food and drink for the pilgrims.[42] This compromise endured until the rise of Islam and later. As descendents of Quṣay, the Prophet's uncle al-'Abbâs ibn 'Abdul-Muṭṭalib and his progeny were responsible for these matters, and until the present day they continue to own the keys to the Sacred House and welcome the visitors and dignitaries who are allowed to enter inside of it.

It was clear that Makkah had become a great religious centre for the Arabs, since the Ka'bah was located there, and in financial terms, Makkah also became a commercial centre. The esteem in which the other Arab tribes held Makkah because of the Ka'bah reflected upon their attitudes towards its inhabitants, since they were the people who devoted themselves to serving the Sacred House. The religious faith of Makkans was not pure in its devotion to Allah. It was similar to that of the rest of the Peninsula, apart from the fact that it was devoid of Judaism. Only a very few people believed in Jesus (عليه السلام) and there was a small but notable number of people known as Aḥnâf who followed the religion of Ibrâheem (عليه السلام). However, the majority of Makkans continued as idolaters.

Most of the people of Makkah were related through their ancestors. Nevertheless, as the centuries passed, they created different tribal groups and it became common for them to either conflict with each other or form alliances to strengthen themselves against predicted events. Of all tribes, I wish to focus on the Hâshemite family from whom the Prophet Muhammad (ﷺ) descended.

Banu Hâshim

This family obtained its name because of its attribution to Hâshim ibn 'Abd Manâf whose line hailed from 'Adnân and then Ismâ'eel ibn Ibrâheem.[43] Genealogists agree upon the accuracy of the chain up to 'Adnân and prefer not to continue it further due to uncertainty regarding the line between 'Adnân and Ismâ'eel.[44] The Prophet himself (ﷺ) mentioned his ancestry briefly: «Allah the Great and Almighty had selected Ismâ'eel from the children of Ibrâheem, Kinânah from the children of Ismâ'eel, the Quraysh from Kinânah, the generation of Hâshim from the Quraysh and selected me from the children of Hâshim.»[45]

Hâshim's actual name was 'Amr. Hâshim was just a nickname which reflected the fact that he had assumed responsibility for providing food and drink for the pilgrims to the Sacred House, often at his own expense. People, therefore, gave him this nickname, which is indicative of his generosity to the pilgrims.[46] In addition, it was said that he introduced to the Quraysh the two annual business caravans, one in the winter and one in the summer.[47] Thus, he was well qualified to occupy his position of leadership in the region. However, there is little further information available about this important figure apart from the fact that he married Salmâ bint[48] 'Amr, from the family of 'Adi ibn an-Najjâr in Yathrib, which resulted in the birth of Shaybah, who was later known as 'Abdul-Muṭṭalib.[49]

Upon Hâshim's death, his position was transferred to his youngest brother, al-Muṭṭalib, who was also a noble and generous man.[50] When he died, the honourable duty descended to Shaybah, that is, 'Abdul-Muṭṭalib,[51] who was also the grandfather of the Prophet Muhammad (ﷺ). He took his responsibility seriously and was elevated to a position that far surpassed that of his predecessors. During his lifetime, many important events occurred which made a crucial impact on life in Makkah.

'Abdul-Muṭṭalib

Zamzam is the well that sprang up under the feet of Ismâ'eel (عليه السلام), which as previously mentioned, had been destroyed by the Jurhumis when they had to leave Makkah. Since then, the Arabs had depended again on their local wells for their own water supply and for supplying pilgrims. Ibn Hishâm described the names and locations of these wells,[52] which were all far from the Sacred House.[53] The distance made it difficult to supply pilgrims with water, especially as the size of the Makkan population and the number of pilgrims increased. Historians relate how 'Abdul-Muṭṭalib dreamt that he received an order to dig for the Zamzam well. He responded positively to the order and started work with his only son at that time, al-Ḥârith. A short time after beginning his endeavour, he discovered the original fountain of Zamzam. Two golden gazelles, some swords and body amour were also buried in the well. He constructed a gate for the Sacred House using the swords and decorated it with the golden gazelles.[54]

'Abdul-Muṭṭalib also made a vow to Allah to slaughter one of his sons if He granted him ten male children, provided that they lived and grew to an age at which they could defend him. When his request was granted, 'Abdul-Muṭṭalib drew lots to decide which one of them to sacrifice. The lot fell on his youngest and most beloved son, 'Abdullâh, who later became the father of the Prophet (ﷺ). 'Abdul-Muṭṭalib intended to slaughter his son but the people prevented him and suggested that he should pay blood money instead, which he did, according to the requirements at the time.[55]

A third important event in the life of 'Abdul-Muṭṭalib was the attempted invasion of the Ka'bah led by Abrahah al-Ashram, the governor of Yemen, on behalf of the king of Abyssinia. Abrahah had built a great temple in Sana'a and intended to divert the Arabs to make their pilgrimages there rather than to Makkah. This news spread quickly and a man from the tribe of Kinânah became furious about it and decided to show his disrespect towards the temple and went and soiled it. Upon discovering that the temple had been soiled by a nomad, Abrahah was inflamed with rage and swore not only to alienate people from the Sacred House but also to raze it. This was, at least, the apparent motive for his campaign. He also possibly wanted to convert people to Christianity, the religion he had embraced, and to create political as well as military problems for Persia in this part of the world, since it was in continuous conflict with Rome, which was Christian. Whatever the case may be, Abrahah concentrated his forces on achieving his goal and supplied them with a huge elephant.[56] It was mentioned that there may have been as many as thirteen elephants among his troops.[57]

As the leader of Makkah at that time, 'Abdul-Muṭṭalib went to meet with Abrahah. 'Abdul-Muṭṭalib asked Abrahah to return the two hundred camels that had been looted by his troops. Abrahah was surprised by this demand, as Makkah itself was in great danger, while its leader was thinking only of his own personal property. 'Abdul-Muṭṭalib, as a true believer in Allah the Almighty, replied that he was the owner of the camels and therefore he should ask for their return, while Allah is the owner of the Sacred House and He would defend it.[58] Still, the people of Makkah were in no position to withstand an attack from Abrahah's army. On the advice of 'Abdul-Muṭṭalib, the Makkans retreated to the mountains.[59]

On the day that Abrahah started his attack, his elephant knelt down and refused to advance on Makkah, even though it would happily go in any other direction. Allah the Almighty defended His Sacred House by sending small martins and egrets from the coast, holding little stones in their beaks and feet to smash the invading forces of Abrahah and cause their absolute defeat. This event was so important that the Arabs adopted it as the starting point for their dating system.

The Noble Qur'an mentions this event and draws the Arabs' attention to the crucial victory that Allah (ﷻ) had granted His House, in order that they should believe in His Oneness and in His Messenger Muhammad (ﷺ). This short chapter of the Qur'an is entitled *al-Feel,* or *The Elephant*:

﴿Have you not seen how your Lord dealt with the owners of the elephant? Did He not make their plot go astray? He sent against them birds, in flocks, striking them with stones of baked clay; and He made them like an empty field of stalks [of which the corn has been eaten up by cattle].﴾ *(Qur'an 105: 1-5)*

Ibn Hishâm narrated from Ibn Is-ḥâq that measles and smallpox had not been known in the Arab land previously, but in that year,[60] Allah the Almighty sent an epidemic in order to protect His House.

This extraordinary event made a special impact on the Arabs' attitudes towards Quraysh, the inhabitants of Makkah. The Arabs started to show greater respect to the people of Makkah, claiming that Allah's standing up for them reflected their unique position with Him. Perhaps in order to clarify this point, Ibn Hishâm quoted verses composed by poets from various districts.[61] At any rate, the level of the Arab's glorification of the Ka'bah had increased and their recognition of its special religious position had deepened. The critical victory that Allah the Almighty granted to His Sacred House was just a miraculous introductory sign of the Prophet's upcoming mission.[62]

'Abdullâh ibn 'Abdul-Muṭṭalib

Following 'Abdullâh's salvation from being slaughtered, described above, his father decided to have him marry one of the best Qurayshi women at that time, Âminah bint Wahab ibn 'Abd Manâf. The linage of both, 'Abdullâh and Âminah, joined together at the level of Kilâb, who was Âminah's fourth grandfather and 'Abdullâh's fifth. The Prophet Muhammad (ﷺ) was a product of this marriage. There is no clear reference to the time of this marriage and little information about other aspects of 'Abdullâh's life. 'Abdullâh died and was buried in Madinah,[63] probably due to a malarial infection, after he had returned from Syria in a trade caravan.[64] Ibn Hishâm mentioned that 'Abdullâh had passed away when his wife was still pregnant with the Prophet (ﷺ)[65], and aṭ-Ṭabari noted from another narration that the Prophet (ﷺ) was twenty-eight months old when his father died.[66] The Prophet's mother, Âminah bint Wahab, later died in a place called al-'Abwâ', between Makkah and Madinah, when the Prophet (ﷺ) was only six years old.[67]

CHAPTER TWO

The Prophet's Early Life

Birth

Biographers concur that on a Monday in the month of Rabee' I in the Year of the Elephant, the Prophet Muhammad (ﷺ) was born. The majority of biographers refer to the date as the 12th of Rabee' I.[1] The invasion of the elephant occurred in 570 or 571 CE. In converting the date of the Prophet's birth from the Arabic lunar calendar to the Gregorian solar calendar, one may deduce that the nearest day to the 12th of Rabee' I coincides with the 22nd of April 571 CE. The Prophet (ﷺ) was born in the Banu Hâshim area of Makkah. His birth marked the start of substantial changes in the whole situation of the Arab Peninsula.

Ibn Hishâm narrated that, during her pregnancy, Âminah, often dreamt of good omens that indicated that the child she was carrying was unique. Her dreams also inspired her to name him Muhammad, which means 'praiseworthy'. After his birth, Âminah sent news to his grandfather, 'Abdul-Muṭṭalib, who happily came to welcome him and agreed with the name given in Âminah's dream.[2] This suggests that Muhammad's father was absent at that time, either away on a caravan trip or already deceased.

His nursing

'Abdul-Muṭṭalib took over responsibility for the baby and following the Arab tradition, he began looking for a wet nurse from the desert to care for the child and ensure that he grew up in a healthy area and built up a powerful body and strong character. A woman named Ḥaleemah as-Sa'diyah from the Banu Sa'd tribe was chosen to suckle him. Some of the other wet nurses had spurned taking him because he was an orphan, as they thought a grandfather would not reward them as much as a child's father would.

The biographers mentioned that the district of Banu Sa'd at that time was subjected to such severe drought that even the breasts of the wet nurses were drained. Despite this, Ḥaleemah as-Sa'diyah's breasts flowed copiously with milk and her surrounding region became green and productive immediately after she agreed to nurse Muhammad (ﷺ).[3] He remained under her care for two years and then was returned to his mother who asked Ḥaleemah to continue to nurse him to maintain his good health.

A few months later, Muhammad (ﷺ) was with his foster brother and playmates when the Archangel Jibreel (Gabriel) (عليه السلام) came and washed his heart. According to Muslim, the great scholar of Hadith, the Prophet (ﷺ) narrated this occurrence and stated that Jibreel (عليه السلام) cracked open his chest, took his heart out and removed a clot of blood from it, saying that it was the share of Satan in him. Jibreel (عليه السلام) then washed and mended his heart and returned it to its correct position. His foster brother and playmates hastened to seek help from his nurse as they thought that the man dressed in white had killed him. Ḥaleemah and her husband rushed to the child and found that he was very pale.[4] He (ﷺ) told them what had happened and because the event lay beyond their comprehension, they decided to return him to his mother.[5]

The Prophet (ﷺ) returned to the arms of his mother and was raised by both her and his grandfather, 'Abdul-Muṭṭalib, until he was six years old, at which time his mother took him to visit his maternal uncles in Madinah. They stayed there for a month, and on their return journey to Makkah, the Prophet's mother died in a place called al-Abwâ'.[6] His grandfather loved him deeply and kept the young orphan under his wing until he died two years later when the Prophet (ﷺ) was just eight years old.[7] Responsibility for the Prophet's care was then transferred to his uncle, Abu[8] Ṭâlib. Ibn Hishâm justified 'Abdul-Muṭṭalib's decision to entrust the Prophet (ﷺ) to him because both Abu Ṭâlib and his brother 'Abdullâh, the father of the Prophet (ﷺ), had the same mother.[9] The Prophet (ﷺ) remained with his uncle until he reached adulthood.

Two points need to be noted in this regard. The first is the clear ancestry of the Prophet (ﷺ) which can be traced back to Ibrâheem (عليه السلام). This thwarts those who would reject his prophecy by trying to weaken his position in the lineage of the great prophets and those who would discredit his holy mission by accusing him of inferiority. The second significant point is that, as an orphan, the Prophet (ﷺ) did not have the strong influence of parents or grandparents, only that of his uncle Abu Ṭâlib and society in general when it came to morals and religious beliefs. Abu Ṭâlib later died after the Prophet (ﷺ) had started calling the people to Islam and refused, at least apparently, to embrace the new religion. Under such circumstances, no one could suspect that the Prophet's close relatives had any impact on his message or that the story revolved around tribal, familial or leadership issues.[10]

Furthermore, being an orphan meant that the Prophet (ﷺ) had no one on whom to depend other than Allah (سبحانه وتعالى) and himself. This enabled him (ﷺ) to build up the distinguished personality that was necessary to fulfil the immense role of prophet. Allah the Almighty had paved the way for him from the very beginning; He showed signs of His protection of and His attention to the Prophet (ﷺ) from childhood, some of which were apparently unpleasant, such as his being orphaned.

Other signs were auspicious, like the light that his mother observed when she gave birth to him and which illuminated the palaces of Syria for her.[11] There was also the sudden emergence of plenty that prevailed in the house of his wet nurse as well as the gush of fertility in the region while he (ﷺ) resided among them. These signs drew the attention of others towards the Prophet (ﷺ) during his early years and this is why his nurse's husband told her, "O Ḥaleemah! By God, you have taken a blessed person." She replied, "By God, I think so."[12] In addition, his mother and grandfather used to say that he would undoubtedly possess a distinguished prestige.[13]

As for the Prophet himself (ﷺ), he found blessing and peace in his heart. This is utterly clear from the narration cited by aṭ-Ṭabari, which details the opening and cleansing of his heart. In this narration, the Prophet (ﷺ) said that he did not feel any pain from the Archangel and when his heart was impressed with an illuminating seal, he continued to experience a sense of peace for a long time afterwards.[14]

Meeting with Baḥeerâ (Sergius)

It is probable that an account of the above events had been circulated within the family and Abu Ṭâlib, who became the Prophet's guardian, noticed his nephew's special nature. He kept the child close to him, developed a strong relationship with him, and used the phrase 'my son' whenever he wished to address him.

When the Prophet (ﷺ) was just nine or twelve years old, he showed a deep desire to accompany his uncle on his business trips to Syria. Abu Ṭâlib consequently decided to take him along. When they reached Buṣrâ, they passed, as usual, the cell of a Christian monk named Baḥeerâ (Sergius). Baḥeerâ noticed how the Prophet (ﷺ) was shaded by a cloud as he moved and how a tree's branches drooped over so that he could sit in their shade. As a result of these miracles, Baḥeerâ desired to observe the child more closely. The monk offered a feast for all the members of the caravan. Everyone attended except the Prophet (ﷺ), who was still very young for such revelry. When Baḥeerâ did not find him among the guests, he insisted that the child be brought to join them.

Baḥeerâ carefully looked for the signs he had learned in his scriptures regarding the coming of a major prophet, and he was soon convinced that this child was indeed the one who had been foretold. After everyone had eaten, Baḥeerâ said to the Prophet (ﷺ), "I adjure you by al-Lât and al-'Uzzâ (two of the Arabs' great idols) to answer what I am going to ask you." Muhammad (ﷺ) answered, "Do not ask me by these. By Allah, I do not abhor anything more than I abhor them." Baḥeerâ then adjured him by Allah, and the Prophet (ﷺ) said, "Ask me about whatever you like." The Prophet (ﷺ) answered his inquiries and finally Baḥeerâ looked for a particular birthmark that he knew a prophet of Allah would have, and he found it between the boy's shoulder-blades. The monk was convinced that he really was in the presence of the next prophet.

Baḥeerâ went to Abu Ṭâlib and asked him, "Who is this child with you?" Abu Ṭâlib replied, "My son." Baḥeerâ commented that he could not be his son as his father should not be alive! Abu Ṭâlib admitted the child was his nephew. Baḥeerâ advised him to take the child back home and warned him about the

Jews, swearing that if they discovered what he himself had already recognised, they might try to harm him. Abu Ṭâlib then finished his business promptly and returned to Makkah with Muhammad (ﷺ).[15] This is the core of the story, although some of its details may vary from one narration to another.

Many Orientalists denied the validity of this narration. Other Orientalists used it as evidence that, during this meeting, Muhammad (ﷺ) learned the teachings of Judaism and Christianity and integrated them later into the new religion.[16] Both groups of Orientalists failed to demonstrate a real scientific approach towards this narration. While the first denied the story without actual justification, the second unwisely assumed that the Prophet (ﷺ) had learned the whole of Judaism and Christianity from Baḥeerâ in just a few hours and had kept this in mind for approximately twenty-eight years before reproducing it as a new religion!

There is no difference between denying the prophecy of Muhammad (ﷺ) and attributing whatever came down in his religion to his supposed knowledge of Judaism or Christianity. The only difference lies in the tools used to justify the position. There are many demonstrations of the validity of Islam as a divine religion not discussed here since this is a historical biography of the Prophet (ﷺ) rather than a treatise on the creed of Islam, so I am not inclined to accept this story as an important proof of the authenticity of the Prophet's mission. There is no report in the Hadith literature that the Prophet (ﷺ) ever referred to this event nor did he go on to remind his uncle or his people of it when he invited them to become Muslims. Moreover, the Prophet (Blessings and peace be upon him), as we will see later, undertook Khadeejah's (رضي الله عنها) trade in Syria without heeding the monk's warning. Thus, the actual historical accuracy of the Prophet's meeting with Baḥeerâ bears little relevance to the message of Prophet Muhammad (ﷺ).

However, the people of that time were waiting for a new divine message that had been prophesied in the Torah and the Bible. It is well known that Jews were awaiting a prophet. Ibn Hishâm also quoted the story of four people who sought to follow the religion of Ibrâheem (عليه السلام). One of them, Zayd ibn 'Amr, contacted people from previous divine religions to direct him towards the right path. In Mayfa'ah, a place in Balqâ', he met a priest who told him that the religion he sought would appear soon in his own homeland.[17] The Prophet Muhammad (ﷺ) was also mentioned as Munḥamannâ in the Syriac copy of the Bible and as Paracletus in Latin, and both of those names mean the same as the name Muhammad in Arabic.[18] Some narrations from Salamah ibn Sallâmat ibn Waqsh, Ka'b al-Aḥbâr, and Salmân al-Fârisi had clearly described the distinguishing features of the coming prophet which matched the features of the Prophet Muhammad (ﷺ).[19] Likewise, Bukhari quoted from 'Abdullâh ibn 'Amr ibn al-'Âs (رضي الله عنه) the similarity of the Prophet's characters and features in the Torah and the Noble Qur'an [20]. Ibn Taymiyah referred to a copy of the Book of Psalms which included a clear statement about the prophecy and the name of the Prophet (ﷺ), although a different copy failed to include it. Hence, he concluded that some copies of previous scriptures might contain his (ﷺ) description, while others were devoid of them.[21]

<u>Lessons to be learned from this story</u>: Muhammad (ﷺ) was bright and strong, even in his youth, otherwise his uncle would not have allowed him to travel so far with him. Also, he (ﷺ) recognized the futility of idol worship, even at his early age, and he was strong and confident enough to express his view on that.

His work

In his early years, the Prophet Muhammad (ﷺ) tended sheep for his people to provide financial support for his uncle who was not wealthy and had a large family. In one of his sayings, the Prophet (ﷺ) referred to the tending of herds as a task of every prophet at some point in their lives: «The Prophet (ﷺ) stated: There was no prophet that did not shepherd sheep and goats. His Companions asked: What about you? He (ﷺ) replied: I used to shepherd the flocks of the people of Makkah...»[22]

This hadith reveals that Allah (ﷻ) led His Messengers to experience the task of shepherding at some stage in their lives in order to teach them how to increase their patience, compassion and leadership while promulgating the divine revelation.[23] Moreover, the followers of the Prophet (ﷺ), at that time and in the coming generations, would copy him and work to earn their livelihoods. Muhammad S. R. al-Booṭi noted another important advantage of the Prophet's being a shepherd: it was appropriate for the Prophet (ﷺ) to sustain himself by depending on his own efforts so that he would not be indebted to anyone, a position which might hinder him in his task. This meaning, of course, had not come to the Prophet's mind when he was tending his herds, but it was Allah's choice to save His Messenger (ﷺ) from any inappropriate situation which might affect his prospective mission.[24]

While the Prophet (ﷺ) was still young and attending the herd, he showed an interest in youthful pleasures. He once asked another shepherd to look after his livestock so that he could go into Makkah. While he was there, he heard the music of a wedding celebration and took pleasure in listening in to it, but he fell asleep and did not wake until the following day while he should have returned much earlier to care for his flock. Again he asked his companion to look after his livestock, but this also ended with the same regrettable consequences. The Prophet (ﷺ) said that ever since he never again tried to do a bad action.[25] Through the repetition of the situation, he realised the unsuitability of following evil and useless inclinations and the necessity of not repeating his mistakes.

Furthermore, this incident shows us the human side of the Prophet's nature and how Allah the Almighty saved him from indulging in unacceptable activities, on the one hand, and how the Prophet (ﷺ) deciphered the matter and transformed his perception into practical action. This gave the people some insight into the character of the man whom they followed. He was neither a divine being nor an angel; he was just a man like them, with desires and shortcomings. As a result, they found it possible to follow his way in order to refine their souls and nature.

The Prophet (ﷺ) tended herds for a while and also participated in commerce and the clothing trade.[26] People found him so honest and fair in the handling of his business that they used to call him '*aṣ-Ṣâdiq al-Ameen*' which means 'the truthful, honest and reliable'. It was a nickname that stuck with him even when his mission was being denied.

The sacrilegious war

During this time, the Prophet (ﷺ) participated in what was known as the Sacrilegious (*al-Fijâr*) War which broke out among certain Arab tribes. It was so called because it included the fact that the enemy tribes had contravened the rules of the sacred months.[27] Biographers and historians are not certain how old the Prophet (ﷺ) was when this event occurred, but they estimate that he must have been either fourteen, fifteen[28] or twenty years old.[29] The Prophet

(ﷺ) said that he repelled and collected the enemy arrows for his uncles, and subsequently the Quraysh and their allies were victorious.[30] Although contribution in this war might seem to be based on tribal position, the real incentive to fight was the violation of the sacred months by certain Arab tribes.

Apart from the motivation for this war and its results, it seems that the populace of Makkah was aware of the necessity of ensuring peace, quiet and justice so that those who wished to perform the pilgrimage could do so safely. The prominent Qurayshi leaders therefore met in the house of 'Abdullâh ibn Jad'ân and concluded an agreement whereby they swore to champion the cause of any seriously wronged person who entered Makkah and to enable the person to regain his or her rights. Historically this agreement was known as Ḥilf al-Fuḍool.

In spite of the fact that the Prophet (ﷺ) was just about twenty years old at that time, he was one of those who drew up and witnessed the agreement.[31] To be involved in such a declaration at such a young age reflected his upstanding character and the respect he enjoyed among his peers. His wish to establish justice was his motivating factor in participating in the Sacrilegious War and in working with others to bring about the aforementioned agreement. It was also narrated that his praise of it demonstrated his readiness to respond positively if he were to be called during his prophethood to enter into something similar.[32]

Marriage to Khadeejah

Aṣ-Ṣâdiq al-Ameen, 'the truthful, honest and reliable one', was the title of the Prophet (ﷺ) and people increasingly turned to him and entrusted him with their possessions or business dealings.

Khadeejah bint Khuwaylid (ﭐ), an affluent widow of Makkah who was said to have been forty years old, was known as a noble and pious woman. She wished to benefit from the Prophet's reliability, and she asked him to conduct business in Syria on her behalf.[33] At this time, the Prophet (ﷺ) was twenty-five years old. Without hesitation, he consented as this meant he could help support himself and his uncle and he could increase his experience in trade with foreign lands. He left Makkah accompanied by Maysarah, a servant of Khadeejah, sent to cater for his needs on the journey.

He fulfilled his new role with excellence and he generated huge profits, thought to be double what was expected, and handed them all over to Khadeejah (ﭐ). She was very impressed, not only by the unusual financial returns, but also by Muhammad's character (ﷺ) and the extraordinary incidents witnessed by her astounded servant during the trip.[34] Khadeejah transmitted all the information to her cousin, Waraqah ibn Nawfal, seeking an explanation from him. Waraqah, who was a pious Christian and had knowledge of the scriptures, notified her that if the news were true, Muhammad (ﷺ) would be the anticipated prophet of his people.[35]

Impressed with Muhammad (ﷺ), Khadeejah (ﭐ) conceived the idea of marrying him. She demonstrated her desire either directly to the Prophet (ﷺ)[36] or through a female friend named Nafeesah bint Munayyah.[37] The Prophet (ﷺ) mentioned the matter to his uncles, who agreed to the marriage, and Ḥamzah, the youngest of them, accompanied him when he became betrothed to Khadeejah via her uncle, 'Amr ibn Asad.[38] This marriage resulted in seven children: three boys named al-Qâsim, aṭ-Ṭayyib and aṭ-Ṭâhir, and four girls named Ruqayyah, Zaynab, Um Kulthoom and Fâṭimah (may Allah be pleased with them). All of his sons died a few years after they were born and before he started receiving divine revelation, but his daughters survived to hear it and all believed in his message. With the exception of Fâṭimah (ﷺ), all of them died during his lifetime.[39] Many biographers of the Prophet (ﷺ) refer to two boys rather than three and state that aṭ-Ṭayyib and aṭ-Ṭâhir were nicknames for his second son, whose name was 'Abdullâh.[40]

Despite the fact that the Prophet (ﷺ) was fifteen years younger than Khadeejah, he never took another wife throughout their time together, which lasted for about twenty-five years. In the history of Islam, this conjugal lifestyle became a shining model of the ideal family that united its members with deep and mutual love and respect. Even after her death, the Prophet (ﷺ) continually cherished her memory, praising her and sending presents to her female friends. He preserved her memory to such an extent that his subsequent wife, 'Â'ishah (ﷺ), declared that she was not jealous of any of the Prophet's other wives except for the deceased Khadeejah (ﷺ). Bukhari narrated numerous hadiths that reflected her special status in the Prophet's life.[41]

It is worth mentioning that the Prophet (ﷺ) was not polygamous until he reached his fifties and then there were also specific juristic, social, tribal or political reasons for his other marriages. However, he was not blessed with a child from any of his other marriages except for Ibrâheem, a son he had with Mâriya al-Qibṭiyah (ﷺ); however, the Prophet's son Ibrâheem died at the age of two.

The rebuilding of the Ka'bah

The Arabs intended to renovate the Ka'bah, which had been damaged by erosion. They planned to demolish it, rebuild it and add a roof. To ensure that all the Arab tribes and families of Makkah shared in this sacred work, it was decided that each of them would bear the expenses equally and not contribute any impure funds. Each of the four sides of the Ka'bah was consigned to a number of families to work on.[42] We can infer from the relevant narrations that the Arab clans of Makkah cooperated with each other more than usual to accumulate the material required for rebuilding the Sacred House and then participated in the chore alternately.

The families of 'Abd Manâf and Zuhrah, to which the Prophet (ﷺ) belonged, were charged with the side of the Ka'bah which included the door. The Prophet (ﷺ) was at that time thirty-five years old.[43] He worked actively with the other members of his family in collecting stones, but unlike his relatives, he did not lift up his clothes to his shoulders and neck and render his lower body naked to protect himself from being scratched by the stones. His uncle al-'Abbâs advised him to prevent these scratches by imitating the others. As soon as he followed this advice, he fell down and asked for his clothes to cover himself.[44] The event reminded him of the incident in his youth when sleep fell upon him to protect him from carrying out an inappropriate act and drew his attention to the unsuitability of being immodestly dressed, which did not befit his standing. Thus, he (ﷺ) carried on working in his own modestly dressed way.

The people of Makkah had adopted a cautious approach when it came to sharing the responsibility for rebuilding the Ka'bah by dividing up the work on its four sides. Their wisdom failed, however, when they reached the moment of putting the Black Stone[45] back in its place. Each tribe wanted to have the honour of performing that task. There was only one Black Stone and no tribe was ready to give up this honour for the sake of another. These conflicting wishes brought all of them to the edge of warfare. They even formed alliances in anticipation of a bloody outcome. One of the elderly people of Quraysh, thought to be Abu 'Umayyah ibn al-Mugheerah,[46] suggested that they should consent to the arbitration of first person who entered the Ka'bah area from a specific door.

The first person to enter by that door happened to be the Prophet (ﷺ). The people all exclaimed, "It is Muhammad the Honest, and we are pleased it is he."[47] As a matter of fact, this collective agreement on his judgement and personality reflected the high rank he held in their eyes. They were satisfied with his impartiality and never thought that he might be inclined to give preference to his own tribe or family. They described the crisis to him and he judiciously solved it. He simply asked for a piece of cloth, put the Stone on it and then invited representatives from every tribe to take hold of the cloth together. When they raised it to the level of the Stone's position, he took the Stone and set it in its place.[48] Thus, he not only avoided bloodshed but also considerably increased his status in their hearts.

CHAPTER THREE

Religious Tendency and Prophecy

Virtuousness

The scant information that is available about the Prophet's early adulthood shows his respect for the sacrosanct issues that had been drawn up in the monotheistic faith of Prophet Ibrâheem (ﷺ).

The families of Makkah considered themselves more distinguished than the other Arab tribes and decided to protect this alleged prestige by abandoning some of the traditional rites when performing pilgrimages, like departing on the hajj[1] from Mount 'Arafât, and by introducing other restrictions for themselves during pilgrimage. They considered themselves a special class of people which they called *al-Hums*, meaning the Inhabitants of the Holy Land in Makkah. Although the tribes composing al-Ḥums were aware of the original hajj rites, they adhered to the changes they had drawn up to differentiate themselves from the other Arabs.[2] The Prophet (ﷺ) continued to follow the religion of Ibrâheem (عليه السلام) closely and ignored the changes his people had effected. Regardless of the fact that he was from Makkah, he stood on Mount 'Arafât and set off from there on the pilgrimage that he performed.[3]

There is no doubt that the Prophet (ﷺ) rejected his community's distorted religion, but with the exception of the common knowledge he had about Ibrâheem's true religion, he did not know any alternative way of worshiping his Lord. However, as a few other Qurayshi people used to do, he started to spend time alone in spiritual retreat occasionally, sometimes for a whole month. For this purpose, he chose a cave called Ḥirâ' which is just two miles from Makkah, and he chose the month of Ramadan to be his period of full isolation. He was used to being surrounded by his family,[4] but as the cave was only large enough to accommodate one person, his family used to stay close to the Ḥirâ' grotto, while he was worshiping Allah and meditating on His creation alone inside the cave.

In fact, reflecting on one's environment and reflecting on the cosmos are essential activities for those who desire to bring about any fundamental change within themselves and their societies. Purifying one's heart of any flaws is necessary in order to achieve successful reform within the community.[5] Social success is based on personal prosperity. Moreover, this kind of rational isolation is helpful for implanting in the heart the idea of love and adoration of Allah in order to progress not only in adhering to His orders but also in striving to spread His teachings.[6] Muhammad (ﷺ) began this custom a few years prior to being invested with prophethood, possibly because of some extraordinary occurrences.

Ibn Hishâm narrated that before Muhammad (ﷺ) started receiving revelation, he would pass by trees or stones and receive the greeting, "O Messenger of Allah! Peace be upon you!" He used to look around to find the greeters but could only see trees and rocks.[7] Muslim, the great scholar of Hadith, narrated that the Prophet (ﷺ) referred to how a stone in Makkah used to salute him before his call to prophethood.[8] In addition, the Prophet's wife 'Â'ishah (ﷺ) stated that his inspiration started with true visions: whatever he saw in his dreams came into reality.[9]

These facts, in addition to the aforementioned points regarding his childhood, illustrate the Prophet's awareness of his preparation for a special role, despite its nature remaining unclear until Archangel Jibreel (ﷺ) descended to give him (ﷺ) revelation. In addition, the Prophet (ﷺ) described his accurate dreams as inspirations,[10] and he (ﷺ) later stated that the accurate dreams of virtuous individuals comprise one forty-sixth part of prophethood.[11] Thus, it is reasonable to assume that he had at least some vague idea about his future role though he did not recognise the nature of his mission nor know how he could translate it into action.

The beginning of revelation

The Prophet (ﷺ) detected his prominent role, but as he could not understand it clearly, he was shocked when it was first revealed. Although he of all people was prepared to accept such a task, he did not imagine that the revelation would be as awesome and powerful as it was. The unexpected way the revelation came to him was part of the reason why he felt astonished and frightened. Indeed, the prophets are the first of the people to fear Allah and recognize His supremacy, and they are the first to submit themselves completely to their Creator and Provider, Allah the Almighty.

When the Prophet (ﷺ) had reached the age of forty, while he was in seclusion in the cave of Ḥirâ', Jibreel (ﷺ) came down to him and asked him to read. The Prophet (ﷺ) replied, "I am not a reader," meaning 'I am an illiterate', or possibly 'What should I read?' It is reported that the Prophet (ﷺ) said: «The angel took me in his arms and pressed me hard until I could not bear it anymore, and then he released me and said: Read! I told him I am not a reader, so he took me once again in his arms, pressed me hard until I could not bear it anymore. Then, he released me and said: Read! I replied: I am not a reader. He took me in his arms for the third time, pressed me hard, then released me, and said: ﴿Read! In the name of your Lord Who has created [all that exists]. He has created man from a clot [a piece of thick coagulated blood]. Read! And your Lord is the Most Generous.﴾ *(Qur'an 96: 1-3)*"»[12]

According to Bukhari, 'Â'ishah (رضي الله عنها) narrated that, after this first revelation, the Prophet (ﷺ) returned home trembling and informed his wife Khadeejah (رضي الله عنها) of what had happened. His wife soothed his fears and reminded him that he was a good man with a noble character and that Allah would surely not disgrace him. After Khadeejah's cousin, Waraqah ibn Nawfal, heard the whole story, he informed the Prophet (ﷺ) that this was the same angel that Allah had sent to Prophet Moosâ (Moses)[13] (عليه السلام), and he warned him of the adversity he would face. In some reports, Waraqah also then kissed his head.[14]

This divine light of revelation started some time in Ramadan,[15] in August of 610 CE. It is interesting to note that the above verses of the Qur'an, the first verses ever revealed, focus on reading and knowledge. This is a clear reference to the scientific methodology of Islam in inviting people to the path of Allah and in following this way of life. According to Abu al-Ḥasan an-Nadawi, this is the secret behind the huge scientific movement that emerged in the early history of Islam, which is incomparable in the history of other religions and nations.[16]

The Prophet (ﷺ) was frightened by what occurred, and the first human to whom he turned was his wife, Khadeejah (﵂), who assuaged his concerns.[17] The Prophet's behaviour towards Khadeejah is actually a demonstration of the high position of women in Islam. This status is also proved by the fact that another wife of the Prophet (ﷺ), 'Â'ishah (﵂), was one of the main narrators of Hadith, the secondary source of Islamic legislation. Attributing such high rank to women has been a point of pride for the promotion of Islam.

A further point that can be raised from the Prophet's description of the revelation relates to the fact that he was pressed hard by the Angel Jibreel (ﷺ) and released three times. The resulting exhaustion can be interpreted as a symbol of the difficulties that the Prophet (ﷺ) was expected to face. It is as if Jibreel wanted to instil into him the power to accept the revelation and bear the difficulties that would accompany his prophetic role.

Receiving this message from Allah (ﷻ) through Jibreel (ﷺ) marked the end of groping for the true way of worshiping Allah and was a starting point for more clarity. The period of Muhammad's prophethood is divided, according to 'Â'ishah (﵂), into two phases: visions and revelation. I referred to the first phase earlier, but the second phase was a mixture of visions and revelations. Throughout the rest of his life, the Prophet (ﷺ) made many references to his dreams which continued to be proven true. Some of these references in different circumstances will be pointed out later in this work.

The Prophet (ﷺ) was so overawed by this initial revelation that Jibreel (ﷺ) stopped descending from the heavens for a time[18] in order to help him to absorb the new situation and to prepare himself to receive further revelation. The exact length of this quiescence remains a disputed issue.[19] This does not mean, however, that Muhammad (ﷺ) was in any sense deserted; soon Jibreel (ﷺ) did again appear to him. When the Prophet (ﷺ) informed his Companions about that period, he said: «While I was walking, I heard a sound from heaven, and looked up to see the same angel who had come to me in Ḥirâ' sitting on a chair between the sky and the earth. I was frightened of him, and I went back home and said: Wrap me! Wrap me! Then Allah the Almighty sent down the verses: ﴾O you enveloped in garments! Arise and warn! And magnify your Lord [Allah]! And purify your garments! And keep away from the idols!﴿ *(Qur'an 74: 1-5)*»[20]

The stage of calling to Islam in secret

Here was a clear instruction to the Prophet (ﷺ) to call people to the Oneness of Allah. The Prophet (ﷺ) started with his own small family who all believed in his Message. The biographers mentioned the following individuals who embraced the new religion: the Prophet's wife Khadeejah, his cousin 'Ali, his foster child Zayd ibn Ḥârithah,[21] and all of his daughters[22] (may Allah be pleased with them). Outside the family, he notified his close friend, 'Ateeq ibn Abi Quḥâfah, who was two years younger than he, and was later known as Abu Bakr aṣ-Ṣiddeeq (رضي الله عنه). Without hesitation, Abu Bakr embraced the new religion and converted to Islam.[23]

Abu Bakr began preaching the new faith to his household and his friends who, without exception, became Muslims. Abu Bakr's amicability and sound knowledge of local history, along with the fact that he was a magnanimous merchant, had attracted people either to ask him about the past or to engage in business dealings with him. He explained Islam to those whom he trusted,[24] and within a short period, he had led prominent people of different ages and from different tribes to believe in the Messenger of Allah (ﷺ). Examples of these include 'Uthmân ibn 'Affân, who was aged thirty-four, Ṭalḥah ibn 'Ubaydillâh, who was just thirteen years old, az-Zubayr ibn al-'Awwâm, 'Abdur-Raḥmân ibn 'Awf and Sa'd ibn Abi Waqqâs (may Allah be pleased with them). All of these, including Abu Bakr, shared some lineage, as they were descendents of Murrah ibn Ka'b ibn Lu'ay,[25] albeit to more than one phratry.

This group formed the main base of the new religion at its inception. The Prophet (ﷺ) worked to build up the number of firm believers and performed his missionary activities secretly. This way of preaching Islam lasted for three years, during which time the number of believers increased to approximately fifty. Some of these were slaves and people from families in the lower classes, but the majority belonged to noble families.[26]

This early phase was based on three policies. First, there was the goal of educating the followers in a clear conception of the Oneness of Allah and the human being's mission in life. The revealed verses of the Noble Qur'an[27] were the fountain from which the Prophet (ﷺ) drew the theoretical foundation of Islamic education. At the same time, his followers were highly compliant with his teachings, so they had two sources to help them understand their role: the Qur'an and the instructions and example of the Prophet (ﷺ), which is also known as the Prophet's *Sunnah*.

Secondly, the Prophet (ﷺ) realised, as the number of Muslims increased, that gathering such a number of people continuously in one place would attract the attention of the pagans, and this was a worrying issue. To avoid the negative reactions of the pagans, he (ﷺ) divided his followers into small groups consisting of two to four people, and instructed them to meet each other in order to recite the verses already revealed, think about their meaning and absorb them, and to perform their prayers together, as praying was obligatory twice a day at that time.[28] This type of meeting was possibly held on a daily basis. This pairing or grouping of the believers in Makkah helped to reinforce the brotherly connections among the Prophet's followers and can in some ways be compared to the brotherly relationships that the Prophet (ﷺ) later organized in Madinah between the immigrants and the believers of Madinah who helped them.[29]

About two years after the start of the mission,[30] the Prophet (ﷺ) arranged for occasional meetings to bring all of the believers together. For this purpose, he chose the house of al-Arqam ibn Abi al-Arqam. In choosing this place for meeting, the Prophet (ﷺ) demonstrated his insight and alertness. Since the house was on aṣ-Ṣafâ Mountain and its owner belonged to the tribe of Banu Makhzoom which was in competition with the Prophet's own Banu Hâshim tribe, it was not prone to doubt. If there were any suspicion of irregular activities which might attract the attention of the pagans based on tribal criteria, it would not be turned to this particular house.[31]

The Prophet's third policy was to include people from different tribes and integrate them within the new, growing community. The Prophet (ﷺ) himself was from Banu Hâshim and started calling to Islam within his own household. Then, he spoke to Abu Bakr who was from Taym and the other callers to Islam were sent to a variety of clans and nations[32] to show that Islam was not a religion for Makkah alone.[33] Having faithful believers in different tribes also ended up helping the new Muslim community as it prevented the Arab tribes, who were controlled by their tribal traditions, from acting in collusion against the Prophet's clan. The Prophet (ﷺ) worked to remove erroneous beliefs from the hearts of his followers and implant correct concepts there instead. He concentrated upon the unity of human beings' origin. As they all generated from Adam (ﷺ), they were therefore brothers and sisters, even though they belonged to different tribes and clans. Their distinction from each other could thus only be based upon piety, and that prepared the groundwork for establishing a new life, free from injustice, persecution, and adoration of anything except Allah.

This dogma, therefore, had many benefits. It saved people from going to hell due to their unawareness of the correct path. It cemented the relations between the believing groups, so that they would not deal with each other according to their previous positions, such as being either free or enslaved. It also paved the way for the believers to feel pity for those who deviated from the Straight Path. Thus, the believers were extracted from their un-Islamic social constraints and integrated into a new sense of humanity.

Moreover, the Prophet (ﷺ) at this stage concentrated on spreading the message of Islam among young people because their hearts were generally more open to rejecting the ingrained pagan traditions[34] and more capable of bearing the hardships that were anticipated to befall the path of the new faith. A quick glance at the ages of the earliest followers shows that fifteen of them were under twenty years old and twenty-one were less than thirty, while the total number of converts was about fifty.[35]

Despite the fact that the Prophet (ﷺ) and his followers were on their guard, the Quraysh had managed to obtain some information about the new creed. Three years of secret missionary action was a long period through which it was possible for them to get hints about the new belief. The Muslims used to pray in the mountain passes of Makkah twice a day, so they ran the risk of being seen by others.[36] The Qurayshi people, according to

Muhammad al-Ghazâli, had misgivings about the situation, but they did not take any action because they thought that this was just another kind of worship similar to some ways that were already followed by some of them and they did not realize that the Prophet (ﷺ) had rejected their idols.[37] Other historians are less certain that the Quraysh had misgivings about the known practices of the early Muslims. Ibn Hishâm declares that the people of Makkah did not boycott the Prophet (ﷺ), nor did they reject his views even after he announced his missionary work, but they took this decisive step only after he openly censured and criticised their 'gods'.[38]

Although the Prophet (ﷺ) was entirely confident of Allah's support and protection, he inspiringly chose to preach his message secretly in the early stages. The fact that he (ﷺ) adopted this policy teaches the succeeding callers to Islam to balance out their dependence upon Allah with the cautious implementation of their calling, when a situation reasonably necessitates caution.

The stage of open preaching

The Prophet (ﷺ) continued to move his mission forward and began declaring it overtly in response to divine order. Ibn Hishâm links this open proclamation of Islam to the following three revealed verses:

﴾Therefore proclaim openly [Allah's Message of Islamic monotheism] that which you are commanded...﴿ *(Qur'an 15: 94)*

﴾And warn your tribe [O Muhammad] of near kindred, and be kind and humble to the believers who follow you.﴿

(Qur'an 26: 214-215)

﴾And say [O Muhammad] I am indeed a plain warner.﴿

(Qur'an 15: 89)

﴾And warn your tribe...﴿ is the first verse in this regard that came down to the Prophet (ﷺ).[39] It appears in *Soorat ash-Shu'arâ'*[40] which contains the stories of the previous prophets who called their people to the Right Path but were denied and accused of lying, and who, thanks to the support of Allah, were eventually victorious. Here, Allah the Almighty acquainted Prophet Muhammad (ﷺ) with the sort of responses that His previous Messengers had received, in order to inform him about the arduous task with which he was entrusted and the harsh rejection that he was destined to face. Thus, the verses in this chapter of the Qur'an prepared the Prophet (ﷺ) and his followers for these expected tribulations.

The Prophet (ﷺ) conveyed his message to his close relatives first. Then he (ﷺ) gathered his clan, the children of 'Abdul-Muṭṭalib, together with certain other individuals from among the children of 'Abd Manâf. He presented his message to them, asserting his truthfulness and honesty to them, but his uncle Abu Lahab strongly resisted him. The main reason for his rejection depended on their tribe's inability to oppose the other tribes of Quraysh and Arabia, in case it came to conflict, as according to Arab custom the tribe must protect one of its own.[41] In contradiction to Abu Lahab's position, another uncle, Abu Ṭâlib, who was the chief of the family, was supportive of Muhammad (ﷺ), despite the fact that he personally did not submit to Islam.[42] Although the discussion led the family, excluding Abu Lahab, to take a pledge to support the Prophet (ﷺ), they refused to change their heathen faith. Thus, the Prophet (ﷺ) obtained the protection of over forty backers who did not believe in his prophecy, a point that reflects Allah's protection of him as well as his genius in conducting the affairs of the Islamic community at this critical juncture.[43]

The support of his clan paved the way for him (ﷺ) to widen the scope of his calling. He began this stage by the customary tradition of summoning others to an assembly. People came to him, along with prominent individuals in the area or their representatives. He stood on top of a small mountain and started by asking them if they would trust him if he informed them that cavalrymen were approaching up the side of the mountain to attack them. They all admitted his truthfulness and that they had at no time ever heard him utter a lie. Then, he declared his mission and forewarned them of the coming retribution of those who continued to worship other than Allah. No one responded to him positively, and indeed his uncle, Abu Lahab, launched a severe verbal attack on him.[44]

Hence, these two steps taken by the Prophet (ﷺ) had outwardly failed to convince others to convert to Islam, although in fact they were crucial and triumphant achievements. While the first meeting with his own family gained their protection over him, the second event put the word out and made Islam a public matter so that every tribe, or rather every person, became engrossed in discussing it. From the viewpoint of spreading information about Islam, this declaration was made at a critical and appropriate time.

The noble verses, which resulted in the stepping up of the Islamic movement, implied that the Prophet (ﷺ) should first warn his tribe of near kindred. A question might arise about this distinction and the universality of the message of Islam. To answer this question, it is necessary to understand the hierarchical configuration of responsibility. As an individual, the Prophet (ﷺ) required some time in which to absorb the prophecy he was receiving, to familiarise himself with the inspiration and adapt himself to the new principles and values. Once his own soul was fully strengthened, he moved on to start with the people closest to himself, that is, his immediate family and closest friends. Then he (ﷺ) spread the message to the rest of the relatives in his clan. This is the natural order for humans' responsibility towards their relations. Every Muslim first accommodates himself or herself to follow the religion with full trust, and then progresses to taking an active part in transferring that knowledge to his or her relatives. The next level is to take up the responsibility of guiding the whole community or nation to the Right Path.[45]

Another point that can be deduced from the Prophet's actions involves his persuading the people to use their intellect when dealing with general life issues. This is why the Prophet (ﷺ) pushed the people to avow for his honesty and trustworthiness before he gave them the news of Islam. They would be contradicting themselves by agreeing to his credibility and then rejecting his message. Moreover, the protection which was offered to the Prophet (ﷺ) by his tribe, and his acceptance of it while they preserved their own faith, means that is it permissible for Muslims to enjoy protection from non-Muslims provided that it is not at the expenses of their Islamic faith.

Opposition to the Call

The Quraysh drew up a strategy to oppose the new religion. Their first scheme was to ignore it and to consider the Prophet (ﷺ) and his followers just like other pious people in Makkah who devoted themselves to their own ritual obligations. This step can be derived from a statement made by Ibn Is-ḥâq:

> When the Prophet (ﷺ) declared his mission in response to Allah's command, his people did not move away from him nor did they retort until he mentioned and censured their gods. When he did so, they regarded it as a serious and

objectionable action and (consequently) they agreed upon dissenting and antagonizing him.[46]

However, this policy did not last long and showed how the Quraysh failed to extinguish the power of the divine light of Islam.

Their second tactic was to contact Abu Ṭâlib, the Prophet's uncle (ﷺ) and defender as well as leader of Banu Hâshim, in order to obtain his help in preventing the Prophet (ﷺ) from propagating the new faith. To achieve this purpose, the Quraysh formed a lobby group of ten chosen people from the different tribes and granted each of them immunity. The group went to Abu Ṭâlib and appealed to him as a fellow religionist. They reminded him that his nephew was criticising their polytheistic faith of worshipping various gods. They asked him to either employ his authority to prevent the Prophet (ﷺ) from continuing his preaching of Islam or to release himself from the protection that he had granted the Prophet (ﷺ), so that they could tackle the case without breaking Abu Ṭâlib's word. The delegation failed to realise its objective. Abu Ṭâlib spoke to them gently and repelled their suggestions calmly.[47]

Meanwhile, the Prophet (ﷺ) continued his efforts to enlighten the people about the purpose of their existence, namely to devote their lives to the service of the one and only God, and he informed them of their religious obligations. This resulted in increasing the discord and enmity between the idolaters and the Muslim believers. The new religion represented a threat to the Quraysh. To guard their existing sense of prestige, they felt that they had to squash the growing faith. Consequently, they directed their struggle against Islam towards other crucial areas.

Considering Abu Ṭâlib a part of the Islamic bloc, the delegation returned to him with the following options. Either he forced the Prophet (ﷺ) to stop his propagation of Islam or he would place himself and his whole family in a position of conflict such that surely one of the opposing parties would perish.[48] Both of these choices weighed heavily on Abu Ṭâlib; he did not wish to betray the Prophet (ﷺ) nor did he find it easy to oppose his nation or to stir up their enmity. He summoned the Prophet (ﷺ), explained the situation to him, and then asked the Prophet (ﷺ) to save them all.

The Prophet (ﷺ) understood the issue underlying this request, which was to give up his missionary work or lose the protection of his uncle, but as he (ﷺ) was actually relying on Allah the Almighty, he pronounced a very indicative phrase that reflects his determination to go ahead with his preaching of Islam and his readiness to face all difficulties in his path. He replied to his uncle that if they put the sun in his right hand and the moon in his left to abandon Islam, that he would not abandon it until Allah granted it victory, or he died in the attempt.[49] In admiration of this fortitude, Abu Ṭâlib reiterated his advocacy of the Prophet (ﷺ).

Next, the Quraysh offered Abu Ṭâlib the strongest and most handsome Qurayshi youth, a young man named 'Umârah ibn al-Waleed, whom he could adopt as his own son and whose intellect and acclaim would strengthen Abu Ṭâlib's family. In return, they requested that the Prophet (ﷺ) be handed over to them to be killed! This proposal divided the tribe of the Prophet (ﷺ) and a section of it, led by al-Muṭ'im ibn 'Adi ibn Nawfal ibn 'Abd Manâf, deemed this a plausible offer and urged Abu Ṭâlib to agree to it. However, Abu Ṭâlib rebuffed this vehemently and lost the support of that group of his extended family.[50]

The conflict between the Quraysh and the Prophet (ﷺ) continued and the inimitable verses of the Noble Qur'an constituted the Prophet's main support during this time of tribulation. The Quraysh decided to wreak their wrath upon his followers. Each tribe started torturing their members who were believers. The aim was to force them back to their previous creed. The pagans thought that if the Muslims suffered they would abandon their Messenger (ﷺ), leaving him isolated, in which case he would be easily destroyed. At the same time, non-Muslims would think twice about converting to Islam lest they receive similar punishment.

The methods of torture that were inflicted on the Muslims were absolutely savage and brutal. One of the believers, Khabbâb ibn al-Aratt (رضي الله عنه), mentioned that he was taken and placed on a fire that had been kindled for him. To make it worse, someone placed a foot on his chest to press his flesh into the fire; to prove this, Khabbâb showed his scarred back to the people.[51] 'Ammâr (رضي الله عنه) and his parents were another example. Their ally tribe, Banu Makhzoom, abandoned his father, Yâsir (رضي الله عنه), and his mother, Sumayyah (رضي الله عنها), in the desert in the excessive midday heat for insisting on belief in Islam. Sumayyah was bound to two camels and someone said that Abu Jahl, one of the biggest enemies of Islam, stabbed her in her private parts with his bayonet and killed her.[52] Bilâl (رضي الله عنه), who was a slave, was taken by his master, 'Umayyah ibn Khalaf, to the desert in the severe heat and was laid down with a huge stone on his chest. He was told that this torture would continue until he rejected the faith of Muhammad. His response was to say "One! One!",[53] a declaration that there is only One God, Allah the Almighty. Ibn Katheer narrated how the idolaters used to condemn converts, attempt to diminish their honour, ruin their trade if they were merchants and destroy their wealth.[54] The torture was so severe that some Muslims ostensibly acquiesced to the demands of the pagans just to escape the agony.[55]

The Quraysh incited the lowliest of their people to go around accusing the Prophet (ﷺ) of insanity, bewitchment, divination and poetising.[56] In addition, the Prophet's uncle, Abu Lahab, used to follow him wherever he went to preach his mission and would publicly berate him and accuse him of lying.[57] The Prophet (ﷺ) did not respond to him, but Ḥamzah, the Prophet's uncle and foster brother, was stirred up with anger when heard what Abu Lahab was doing. Ḥamzah (رضي الله عنه) was not satisfied with merely avenging the Prophet (ﷺ); he enraged the Quraysh by declaring that he too believed in Islam.[58]

Returning to diplomacy, the Quraysh sent one of its prominent figures, 'Utbah ibn Rabee'ah, one of the Prophet's uncles, to speak with him (ﷺ). Politely, 'Utbah conversed with the Prophet (ﷺ). 'Utbah considered the Prophet's mission a divisive issue for the nation. He therefore asked the Prophet (ﷺ) to reflect on certain matters:

> If your goal is to gain money, we will contribute towards your funds from our own until you become the wealthiest of us. If you seek dignity, we will make you the leader whom we consult before taking any action. If you wish to reign by this issue, we will make you our ruler. If the one who comes to you (to give you this revelation) is a jinn (demon) but you are unable to repel it, we will seek to help you and we will sacrifice our wealth in order for you to be rid of it.[59]

It is clear that 'Utbah and his people were unable or unwilling to perceive the revelation and prophecy as a divine message for rectifying human life. This is why 'Utbah envisaged the case of the Prophet (ﷺ) as a matter of health, requiring treatment, or as a matter of personal ambitions to obtain authority in society and sovereignty over the people. The Prophet (ﷺ) was sure of his holy mission. All the most sought-after worldly aspirations were within his reach, but his ambition was not worldly. His ambition was the eternal salvation of human beings. Hence, in response to these propositions, the Prophet (ﷺ) recited the whole of *Soorat al-Fuṣṣilat*.[60] This chapter of the Qur'an[61] includes words for the Prophet (ﷺ) to use in advising the pagans and descriptions of the power of Allah with reference to some of the previous Messengers and the end consequences for those who rejected them, as well as the rewards the believers receive in this life and the hereafter.

'Utbah returned to his companions who swore that his face was not the same as before he went to meet the Prophet (ﷺ). Besides commenting appreciatively on the verses of the Qur'an and rejecting the new religion until his last breathe, he predicted that the Islamic mission would have a huge impact. He suggested that the Quraysh leave the Prophet (ﷺ) to call to his religion freely: either the other Arabs would stop him if his preaching reached their lands, or if he were successful, the Quraysh, his tribe, would benefit. The Quraysh, however, rejected these options.[62]

The offers 'Utbah proposed to the Prophet (ﷺ) were offered once again by a delegation of Qurayshi leaders. In return, the Prophet (ﷺ) simply asked them to believe in the Oneness of Allah and the teachings of Islam, but they vehemently refused to do.[63] On another occasion, some prominent people of Makkah suggested to the Prophet (ﷺ) that they would worship Allah if he would also worship their idols! He, of course, refused.[64]

To examine the truthfulness of the Prophet (ﷺ), the Quraysh decided to send two of his worst enemies to Madinah to question the rabbis about him, as the rabbis were the people of the old scriptures and might have a better understanding of him. The rabbis informed the delegation about three questions that only a true prophet would be able to answer: what had happened to a number of young people in ancient times, what was the story of the man who had travelled to the East and the West, and what is the Spirit?[65] The answer to these questions was revealed in *Soorat al-Kahf* (the Chapter of the Cave) in the Holy Qur'an. Still, despite receiving the correct information in respect to these three matters, the arrogance of the Quraysh prevented them from submitting to Islam. Instead, they intensified their torture and persecutions of the Muslims.

The revelations of the Noble Qur'an, however, continued to comfort the Prophet (ﷺ) and the Muslim believers and empowered them to firmly resist the various methods employed by the Quraysh to persecute them. In the Qur'an, there are detailed stories about the wrongdoings committed against Allah's prophets and the brutal oppression of their followers, while on the other hand, there are also stories about the believers in Allah who had been outstandingly brave in bearing their suffering with fortitude and who had been increased in their ability and strength to resist the pagans. In the past, some of the prophets and their followers had been tormented, burnt and even killed. However, eventual victory was predestined for those who professed the Oneness of Allah.

The Noble Qur'an invites believers to know that this is the manner in which many of the faithful have been afflicted in the past and will be afflicted again in the present and future. Establishing the correct way of life is a huge responsibility, which doubting individuals cannot implement. It must fall on the shoulders of true and sincere people. The affliction that they face, therefore, is just a refining tool for isolating true and false personalities from each other. The Qur'an openly urged the Muslims to be steadfast and patient and to embody these values. It also revealed in other cases that the enmity that they might encounter was not always a result of a desire to oppose the new faith, but that it also might be due to the jealousy that others felt towards Muslims. The story of Prophet Yoosuf (Joseph) (عليه السلام) and the grief he suffered from his stepbrothers is a good example of this.

Another method used in the Qur'an to comfort the Muslims was showing them the consequences of belief and disbelief, both in this current life and on the Day of Judgement. Besides straightforward instruction to the Prophet (ﷺ) and his followers, the stories about previous prophets in the Qur'an were lessons for the believers to increase their strength and faith. The Qur'an also praised the followers of the Prophet (ﷺ), and this praise urged Muslims to sacrifice their souls for the sake of elevating Islam. In *Soorat al-Kahf*, there is an example that may cover all these points.

﴿And keep yourself patiently with those who call on their Lord [your companions who remember their Lord with glorification, praising in prayers, and other righteous deeds] morning and afternoon, seeking His Face; and let not your eyes overlook them, desiring the pomp and glitter of the life of the world. Obey not him whose heart We have made heedless of Our remembrance, and who follows his own lusts, and whose affair [and deeds] has been lost. Say: The truth is from your Lord. Then whoever wills, let him believe; and whoever wills, let him disbelieve. Verily, We have prepared for the *dhâlimoon* (polytheists and wrongdoers), a fire whose walls will be surrounding them [the disbelievers in the Oneness of Allah]; and if they ask for help [such as relief or water], they will be granted water like boiling oil, that will scald their faces. Terrible is that drink, and an evil dwelling place [it is]! Verily, as for those who believed and did righteous deeds, certainly We shall not make the reward of anyone who does his [or her righteous] deeds in the most perfect manner to be lost.

These! For them will be *'Adn* [Eden] Paradise [everlasting gardens of bliss]; wherein rivers flow underneath them. There they will be adorned with bracelets of gold, and they will wear green garments of fine and thick silk. They will recline there on raised thrones. How good is the reward, and what an excellent dwelling [and resting] place!❳ *(Qur'an 18: 28-31)*

Regarding the moral battle waged by the Quraysh against the Prophet (ﷺ), the Noble Qur'an refuted their accusations in several verses. One example is found in *Soorat adh-Dhâriyât*:

❲Likewise, no Messenger came to those before them but they said: A sorcerer or a madman! Have they [the people of the past] transmitted this saying to these [Quraysh pagans]? No, they are themselves a people transgressing beyond bounds [in disbelief]!❳ *(Qur'an 51: 52-53)*

Another example is from *Soorat al-Anbiyâ'*:

❲No, they say: These [revelations of the Qur'an which are inspired to Muhammad (ﷺ)] are mixed up false dreams! No, he has invented it! No, he is a poet! Let him then bring us an *âyah* [sign as a proof] like the ones [prophets] that were sent before [with signs]! Not one of the towns, of those which We destroyed, believed before them [though We sent them signs]. Will they then believe?❳ *(Qur'an 21: 5-6)*

Apart from these examples, the Quraysh themselves were aware of the false accusations they had imputed to the Prophet (ﷺ). Abu al-Ḥasan al-Wâḥidi narrated that al-Waleed ibn al-Mugheerah asked a few of the Qurayshi leaders, "You claim that Muhammad is a madman; have you ever seen him became insane?" They answered, "No by God!" He asked, "You allege he is a soothsayer; have you ever found him soothsaying?" They answered, "No by God! He does not have the murmuring and rhyming of soothsayers' speech." He asked, "You claim he is a poet; have you ever heard him composing a single verse?" They answered, "No!" He asked, "You claim he is a liar; have you ever caught him saying a lie?" They answered, "No, but (give us a suggestion) what should we say then?" He answered, "Say he is just a magician and what he says is magic!"[66]

Emigration to Abyssinia

The Prophet (ﷺ), as the Muslim leader, was engaged in finding a safe place to protect his followers from the extreme punishment that they were receiving from the Quraysh and their pagan relatives. In the fifth year of his prophethood, he directed some of his followers to emigrate to Abyssinia since it was ruled by the Negus (meaning 'judge') Aḥḥamah and was a Christian country. As a land of a divine religion, it would be safer to worship Allah there. The Prophet (ﷺ) planned for them to stay in Abyssinia until Allah the Almighty had dispelled their fear and grief.[67]

Abyssinia was also a centre for the Quraysh's commerce,[68] and it had a temperate climate.[69] Several of these features were present in places such as Syria, which was also a centre for Qurayshi trade and a Christian land. Although living among people of a divine religion seems to suggest a more comfortable environment than that of heathen territory, the Prophet (ﷺ) did not neglect Syria arbitrarily in favour of Abyssinia. Syria was a centre of different religions, including paganism. There were also conflicting policies between the Syrian clans and the tribes of the Arabian Peninsula, and Syria was a land lacking in justice.

We may find in contemporary studies further rationalisation of the Prophet's choice. Sayyid Quṭub, for instance, believed that the Prophet (ﷺ) was looking for another base for his mission. To support this view, he points out that the majority of immigrants were noble and free Qurayshi people who enjoyed the protection of their families against persecution and torture. They were not forced to leave Makkah due to their weak status, as were slaves, for example, or individuals who sought to better their lot by expatriating.[70] Other researchers concurred with this notion and considered the immigration to Abyssinia as a strategic step in finding an alternative starting point for the Islamic movement.[71] However, there is no support for this theory in the Prophet's (ﷺ) own sayings. Moreover, there is no information that the Prophet (ﷺ) ever instructed his followers to propagate the call to Islam in Abyssinia. In fact, when they returned to Madinah years later, their number had increased only due to the children they bore there and a Yemeni group that arrived in Abyssinia by accident.[72] Furthermore, looking for a substitute region for preaching Islam required that the Prophet (ﷺ) himself, as the receiver of the divine revelation, emigrate to ensure the continuity of his message.

The emigration to Abyssinia reveals the significance of the possibility that Muslims should ask for protection from non-Muslims if necessary. This juristic point was also derived from the protection, as mentioned earlier, that the Prophet (ﷺ) was granted by his uncle, Abu Ṭâlib, and from other similar events.[73] The condition of such protection is that it should not prejudice Islam or causes change in its rules or silence it regarding illegal issues from the Islamic viewpoint.[74]

Furthermore, from events which occurred while some of the Muslims were in Abyssinia, several scholars have deduced that being unacquainted with an Islamic ruling is an excuse for being acquitted of the sin of not performing a religious duty. Ibn Taymiyah mentioned that the prayers had been changed in terms of their timing and numbers, but that the immigrants to Abyssinia had received no information about that. They continued performing their prayers according to the earlier practice, that is two units of prayer twice a day, and the Prophet (ﷺ) did not order them to repeat or make up their prayers.[75]

In any case, the first immigrant group consisted of fourteen people, ten men and four women.[76] Later, other groups left Makkah and joined them, and their number reached eighty-three in total, not including their children who accompanied them.[77] When they learned of the Muslims' departure, the Quraysh tried to bring them back. This task fell on the shoulders of 'Abdullâh ibn Abi Rabee'ah and 'Amr ibn al-'Âṣ, who both became Muslims a few years later. They took many gifts to the Negus, the king of Abyssinia, and to his patriarchs. They explained the motives for their visit and, through the words they chose, tried to enrage the king against the people who had come to his land. They said:

> A number of foolish persons from among our people have migrated to your country. They rejected the religion of their nation and did not embrace yours; they produced a heretical religion which neither we nor you know anything about. The noblemen of their families and tribes sent us to you to turn them back.[78]

The king dealt with the matter wisely. He decided to call the Muslims and hear their side of the story. He also asked them about their new religion. Ja'far ibn Abi Ṭâlib (رضي الله عنه), the cousin of the Prophet (ﷺ) and the representative of the immigrants, briefed the king about their heathen background and the severe punishment that they received from their people for following the Prophet's honesty, nobility, and sublime teachings. To escape from torture they eventually were obliged to seek protection in Abyssinian territory. Ja'far recited part of the Noble Qur'an, which influenced the king greatly and resulted in his rejection of the Quraysh's request.[79]

This marked a success for the Muslims, but 'Amr ibn al-'Âṣ devised a plot to try to have them uprooted. He returned to the king and told him that the Muslims alleged that Jesus (ﷺ) was just a human being. The king then asked the Muslims about their view of Christ (ﷺ). Ja'far (ﷺ) replied that, according to the teachings of the Prophet (ﷺ), they considered Jesus "the servant and the Messenger of Allah, His Word which He bestowed on Maryam (Mary) the Virgin."[80] The king accepted this description, agreed with it, and gave the group full freedom to practice their region. He returned to the Quraysh the presents they had brought and refused their demands to expel the Muslims.[81]

Ibn Hishâm narrates a story concerning the secret conversion of the king into Islam,[82] kept secret probably in order to retain his power. Bukhari also transmitted a few hadiths about the death of the king which caused the Prophet (ﷺ) to lead the Muslims in a special prayer for the deceased in absentia.[83] This supports the idea of the Negus embracing the faith of Islam.

Ḥamzah and 'Umar become Muslims

In Makkah, the number of Muslims was increasing, and two of the most powerful and prominent Makkans declared their belief in the Prophet (ﷺ). These were Ḥamzah ibn 'Abdul-Muṭṭalib (ﷺ), the uncle and foster brother of the Prophet (ﷺ), and 'Umar ibn al-Khaṭṭâb (ﷺ), who later came to power as the second orthodox caliph in the history of Islam. With the support of these two men, the small Muslim community acquired an essential crutch that enabled its members to reveal themselves and perform their prayers openly at the Sacred House in Makkah.[84] Moreover, Islam began growing into one of the strongest tribes in Arabia.[85]

These combined developments enraged the Quraysh, who became convinced that as the Muslims' strength increased, their own decline was being accelerated. They relinquished some of their tribal traditions and began to attack the Prophet (ﷺ)[86] despite the protection that he had been granted by his uncle, Abu Ṭâlib.

Meanwhile, in Abyssinia, the Muslims there received exaggerated and false news of many improvements in Makkah, suggesting that all of the Quraysh had now embraced Islam. A group of thirty-three of them began to return home since they thought that the major cause of their departure had been removed. As they approached Makkah, they learned that the news they had received was unfounded. They found themselves in a critical situation; they either had to return to Abyssinia or enter Makkah.[87] The first option seemed impractical, both economically and politically, particularly if the Quraysh were already aware that they were close to Makkah. They knew what would happen if they fell into their enemies' hands and hence had no choice but to adopt the second option and enter Makkah secretly or under the protection of people from specific tribes.

CHAPTER FOUR

Tribulation and Comfort

Boycott of the Muslims

As has been shown, the Quraysh wanted to strengthen their position and stifle the Islamic faith in Makkah. Their previous attempts to stop the Prophet (ﷺ) from proclaiming his religion and attempts to convince his uncle, Abu Ṭâlib, to hand him over proved ineffectual. They, therefore, decided to kill the Prophet (ﷺ)[1] in the seventh year of his prophethood.

Abu Ṭâlib summoned the family of 'Abdul-Muṭṭalib, the Prophet's family, and asked them to bring the Prophet (ﷺ) within their gates and guard him. They responded to his command positively, either as a reflection of their belief in the Prophet (ﷺ) or out of respect for their family. So, all of them, regardless of their attitude towards Islam, participated in this protection.[2]

Hence, the Quraysh were determined to isolate the entire tribe of Banu Hâshim, including its al-Muṭṭalib branch. They decided to put into affect a full boycott of them and refrain from business transactions, intermarriage, and any form of association with them, unless they extradited the Prophet (ﷺ) to them to be killed.[3] The aim was to let them choose between expelling the Prophet (ﷺ) or destroying themselves. To confirm their adherence to all of these measures, the Quraysh recorded their agreement and preserved the document inside the Sacred House. The besieged people sided with Abu Ṭâlib and congregated in the mountain pass where he dwelt. The only person excluded from this accord was the Prophet's uncle, Abu Lahab, who sided with the Quraysh.[4]

The siege was one of the most severe ordeals that the Islamic mission underwent in Makkah. It lasted three years, a very long period in a desert land, where survival depended on trade rather than agriculture. The Quraysh did not allow even a small amount of nourishment to reach the besieged people. They hastened to purchase any kind of victuals that came to Makkah, even at a high price, to prevent the blockaded people from buying any of it and to leave them suffering from hunger that would perhaps compel them to relinquish the Prophet (ﷺ).[5] A few people brought the boycotted tribe secret assistance;[6] but this was ineffective in relieving their situation, which was so severe that they were coerced to eat even leaves and animal skins in order to survive and their women and children were groaning with hunger.[7]

In addition to these stern economic and social circumstances, Abu Ṭâlib still feared that the Prophet (ﷺ) might be killed by the pagans. To avoid this, after everyone had gone to bed at night, Abu Ṭâlib would order one of his sons, nephews or cousins to exchange beds with the Prophet (ﷺ), to confound any intending assassin who might manage to infiltrate the camp.[8]

The end of the siege

Despite the unbearable severity of this siege, the Prophet (ﷺ) and his followers adhered wholeheartedly to their religious duties. They continued carrying out their tasks, calling others to the Oneness of Allah and liberating them from paganism and its obligations.

After three years of the solid boycott, towards the tenth year of the divine revelations, the Prophet (ﷺ) informed his uncle about specific damage that had been caused to the document that outlined the clauses of the boycott agreement. He told him that Allah the Almighty had caused white ants to gnaw away everything in the document except for the name of Allah. His uncle transmitted this information to the Quraysh and asked them to bring the document forward to examine the accuracy of this information. If true, it would be a sign that God rejected this boycott and it should be lifted; otherwise, he would deliver Muhammad (ﷺ) to them to treat as they wished. They agreed to this proposal and brought the document out in public. They were truly astonished at the accuracy of the Prophet's description of the document[9] and did not expect such an internal blow. To avoid confessing defeat, they refused to fulfil their promise and instead increased their persecution[10] of the Muslims and the tribe of Banu Hâshim.

However, a few individuals led by Hishâm ibn 'Amr ibn Rabee'ah discussed the circumstances of the siege as well as those of the new agreement about lifting it which had been broken by the Quraysh. They admitted that they had behaved unjustly and ruthlessly towards the Prophet (ﷺ) and the people supporting him and that they must desist in this behaviour. This created dissension among the Quraysh and resulted in the suspension of the boycott.[11]

Punishing people with a boycott was an unfamiliar action in the Arab region. This fact is helpful in understanding why news of the boycott spread throughout the Arabian Peninsula. In turn, this news provided Islam with publicity since it necessarily contained information about the Islamic mission and the divine revelation of the Prophet (ﷺ). Moreover, people were filled with admiration for the steadfastness of the Prophet (ﷺ) and his supporters, and this stimulated them to think about the tenets of faith which the Muslims held dearer than life. In contradiction to the Quraysh's plan, the boycott proved effective in spreading the news of Islam everywhere.[12]

Similarly, the disbelievers in the Prophet's message, who had still guarded him during the siege out of family loyalty,[13] had the opportunity to come into close contact with the new religion, investigate its teachings, and be influenced by the ideals of life practised within the Muslim community. Furthermore, they shared the suffering of the Muslims and consequently felt sympathy with those who followed the new religion. This emotional connection paved the way for the majority of them to subsequently embrace the Islamic creed. Hence, while the boycott caused great suffering for the Muslims, it ultimately proved beneficial to them.

Deaths of Abu Ṭâlib and Khadeejah

Shortly after the termination of the exhausting blockade, the two main supporters of the Prophet (ﷺ), namely his uncle, Abu Ṭâlib, and his beloved wife, Khadeejah (رضي الله عنها), passed away.[14] Narrators vary concerning who died first and the interval between the two deaths, but it is agreed that they both died in the same year,[15] which was the tenth year of Muhammad's prophethood, sometime in 620 CE. Although there is no reference linking these deaths to the boycott, it is likely that the severe siege had affected these two people, particularly due to their advanced age, and they may have found the famine and the continuous worry intolerable. Khadeejah was sixty-five years old, and Abu Ṭâlib was eighty.

It is worth mentioning at this point that Abu Ṭâlib adhered to polytheism until his death, despite the great protection and defence he offered his nephew. The Prophet (ﷺ) was eager to have him embrace Islam and made a final attempt to convince Abu Ṭâlib as he lay on his deathbed, but he refused lest he cause shame to his predecessors, who had been polytheists, or people thought that he had changed his religion purely out of fear of death.[16] The Prophet (ﷺ) promised to ask Allah to forgive him, unless he was ordered by Allah not to do so.[17]

Through the loss of these two sympathetic and compassionate people, the Prophet (ﷺ) lost reliable pillars within his immediate family and within his tribe and Makkah. He mourned for them, and that year became known by the name 'the year of grief'.[18] Biographers explained this designation with regard to the pain he endured upon their deaths.[19] Muhammad S. R. al-Booṭi interpreted this description of the year differently, and considered it not as a result of great sorrow from their deaths, although the Prophet (ﷺ) was saddened by this loss, but because the many methods the Prophet (ﷺ) had employed to save his uncle had been rejected when he died refusing to proclaim a belief in Islam.[20] His grief, therefore, was for the sake of the mission rather than the sake of his beloved relatives. The Prophet (ﷺ) submitted to the will of Allah and was not expected to exceed the natural limit of human grief in the case of death, but he was filled with distress about calling people to the path of Allah and failing to elicit a positive response.

Banu Hâshim, the tribe of the Prophet (ﷺ), did not now provide him with the same protection that he enjoyed during the life of Abu Ṭâlib, particularly since the leadership of the tribe had transferred to his hostile uncle, Abu Lahab. After the Prophet (ﷺ) was forced away by the people of Ṭâ'if, when he tried to bring them into the fold of Islam, he (ﷺ) sought support from a variety of tribes.[21]

In several verses of the Noble Qur'an, revealed both before and after Abu Ṭâlib's death, Allah the Almighty advised the Prophet (ﷺ) not to become dispirited by the pagans' rejection of Islam. The Prophet's grief reflected his attitude towards his mission and his eagerness to rescue people from going astray. The following verses provide two examples of this:

﴾Perhaps you would kill yourself [O Muhammad] in grief, over their footsteps [for their turning away from you] because they believe not in this narration [the Qur'an].﴿ *(Qur'an 18: 6)*

﴾We know indeed the grief which their words cause you [O Muhammad]. It is not you that they deny, but it is the verses [of the Qur'an] of Allah that the *dhâlimoon* [polytheists and wrongdoers] deny. Verily, [many] Messengers were denied before you, but with patience they bore the denial; and they were hurt, until Our help reached them, and none can alter the words [and decisions] of Allah. Surely, there has reached you the information [news] about the Messengers [before you].﴿

(Qur'an 6: 33-34)

At this time, the Quraysh seized the opportunity to increase their hostility towards the Prophet (ﷺ) and their persecution of his followers. Ibn Katheer quoted a hadith from al-Bayhaqi that says: «The Quraysh stayed cringed until Abu Ṭâlib died.»[22] He also quoted from Ibn al-Jawzi that in the wake of the deaths of Abu Ṭâlib and Khadeejah (رضي الله عنها), the Prophet (ﷺ) stayed at home and rarely went out.[23] This was likely due not to his grief but part of his plan for the future and his intention to reduce the Quraysh's chance to harm him.

The Prophet (ﷺ) was physically threatened. Bukhari cited two narrations regarding this. The first occurred when the Prophet

(ﷺ) was prostrating himself in worship. 'Uqbah ibn Abi Mu'ayt brought a slaughtered animal's innards and threw them on his back. The Prophet (ﷺ) did not raise his head from his prostration until his daughter Fâṭimah (رضي الله عنها) had come and removed it.[24] The second also involved the same attacker, 'Uqbah. He saw the Prophet (ﷺ) praying close to the Ka'bah and tried to strangle him using his clothing. He might have succeeded had Abu Bakr (رضي الله عنه), the Prophet's friend and later the first orthodox caliph, not rescued him from the miscreant.[25]

We find further information about attacks on the Prophet (ﷺ), but Allah the Almighty continued to protect his Messenger (ﷺ). For example, Abu Jahl, one of the most hostile enemies of Islam, decided to tread on the Prophet's neck as he was prostrated in prayer. When he approached the Prophet (ﷺ) to carry out this threat, however, he recoiled and shielded himself with his hands. When asked why he had acted in this way, he replied that he had seen a ditch of fire, a terrifying sight, and wings preventing him from reaching Muhammad. The Prophet (ﷺ) commented that if Abu Jahl had approached him further, the angel Jibreel (عليه السلام) would have pulled his organs out one by one.[26]

Despite Allah's protection of his life, the Prophet (ﷺ) sometimes suffered physically in order to provide an example for his followers, both in his own time and subsequently, of bearing everything for the sake of the principles in which one believes. Allah's intervention to protect him reflects a similar wisdom; it is a miracle which may convince doubters of the veracity of his mission, in order to cause them to support him (ﷺ) and the other Muslim believers. The verses of the Noble Qur'an frequently explain Allah's ways with His creation, and more people were converting to Islam. Both of these facts brought great comfort to the Prophet (ﷺ) and his followers.

Visit to Ṭâ'if

The Prophet (ﷺ) concluded that the people of Makkah were strongly restricted in their attitudes and that the ten years he had devoted to inviting them to Islam had not succeeded to the degree he had hoped. The assistance from his tribe had diminished, but the concept of the Oneness of Allah had been circulated throughout the Arabian Peninsula, and some of the Arabs believed in it. In order to gain independence and predominance, the religion required crucial elements, like settled circumstances and a secure place to live and practice the faith, and Makkah did not fit that criteria.

The Prophet (ﷺ) therefore started considering the surrounding areas to find a new home to achieve his goals. There were a few possibilities in the area, but they were not sufficiently strategic to enable him to face the Quraysh or other prominent tribes. Abyssinia also was not an ideal choice, neither for the Prophet's dwelling place nor for the centre of his religion, for it was a Christian territory. He (ﷺ) had a delegation there, which was secure, but this was not adequate reason to move the entire Muslim community there. The Prophet (ﷺ) preferred to try to seek local support, perhaps to keep himself working within the framework of the Qur'anic verse which he had received:

﴾And warn your tribe of near kindred.﴿ *(Qur'an 26: 214)*

The Prophet (ﷺ) decided to investigate the possibilities in Ṭâ'if, located approximately sixty miles from Makkah, since it was a key spot for the Quraysh, too. The Quraysh would have sought to control it had it not been for its alliances with other tribes.[27] So, it is also possible that the people of Ṭâ'if might support the Muslims with the aim of weakening the Quraysh. If the people of Ṭâ'if embraced Islam, there would be further benefits for them and for the young Muslim community. The Prophet (ﷺ) seems to have made his journey to Ṭâ'if alone,[28] but several biographers mention that he was accompanied by his adopted son, Zayd ibn Ḥârithah (رضي الله عنه),[29] without stating the source of this information. This trip took place in Shawwâl, three years prior to the famous Muslim migration to Madinah, or sometime in May or June of 620 CE.

The Prophet (ﷺ) met the prominent people of Ṭâ'if and presented to them his message, but they violently rejected it and incited the impudence of their people to curse and cry out against him in such a way that he was obliged to hide in an orchard to escape them.[30] The situation was serious and represented one of greatest dangers that he ever faced. He referred to this experience when his wife 'Â'ishah (رضي الله عنها) asked him if he had ever experienced any day as hard day as the day of the Battle of Uḥud.[31] The visit to Ṭâ'if, thus, proved fruitless and the Prophet (ﷺ) was saddened by this outcome, but Allah the Almighty provided him with three events to mitigate his sorrow. One of them was visible to certain people, the second was visible to the Prophet (ﷺ) alone and he informed us about it, and the third was invisible even to him, but the Noble Qur'an explained it to us.

The first event occurred when the Prophet (ﷺ) hid in an orchard which was owned by two brothers from the Quraysh. They asked their farm manager, a man named 'Addâs, to offer some grapes to the man who had taken refuge in their grove, a man whom they did not recognize. 'Addâs placed the grapes in front of the Prophet (ﷺ) and was surprised when the Prophet (ﷺ) mentioned the name of Allah over the food before he began to eat it: «'Addâs said to the Prophet (ﷺ): The words which you pronounced are not known to the people in this area. The Prophet (ﷺ) enquired about his religion and his homeland; he replied that he was a Christian from Nineveh. The Prophet asked: The town of the righteous man Yoonus son of Mattâ (ﷺ)? 'Addâs replied: How do you know about Yoonus son of Mattâ? The Prophet (ﷺ) said: That is my brother! He was a prophet and so am I. 'Addâs knelt down before him, and kissed his head, hands and feet.»[32]

'Addâs' employers were astonishment at his behaviour, and they asked him on his return about his reason for it. He replied that their visitor had told him something that no one knows except a prophet. They doubted and warned him, saying, "Addâs, be cautious lest he turn you aside from your religion; for your religion is better than his!"[33] Still, at least the Prophet's journey resulted in winning one convert.

Regarding the second event, the Prophet (ﷺ) informed his wife 'Â'ishah (رضي الله عنها) about the affliction he felt when he was repulsed in Ṭâ'if. He said that he wandered aimlessly and did not become alert until he was in Qarn ath-Tha'âlib: «I raised my head and saw a cloud shading me. I looked at it, and unexpectedly, I saw Jibreel (ﷺ) in it. He called to me and said: Allah has heard what the people said to you and how they repulsed you. He sent to you the angel who is responsible for the mountains to order him to do whatever you wish. So, the angel (of the mountains) called and saluted me and said: Do you wish me to raze al-Akhshabayn (the two great mountains in the area) down upon them? The Prophet (ﷺ) answered: I would rather that Allah multiplies (the number of those) who worship Allah alone and do not take anything into partnership with Him.»[34]

The third event occurred on the Prophet's return trip to Makkah. He (ﷺ) had passed by a place known as Nakhlah, a valley situated a few miles from Makkah. While performing his night prayers, a number of the jinn heard his recitation of the Noble Qur'an, and they stopped to listen to it. They embraced Islam and returned to their families to inform them of the new religion. The Qur'an registered this event in the following verses:

﴾And [remember] when We sent towards you [Muhammad] a group of the jinn, [quietly] listening to the Qur'an. When they were in the presence of it, they said: Listen in silence! And when it was finished, they returned to their people, as warners. They said: O our people! Verily, we have heard a Book [this Qur'an] sent down after Moosâ [Moses] confirming what came before it. It guides to the truth and to the Straight Path [of Islam]. O our people! Respond [with obedience] to Allah's caller [Allah's Messenger Muhammad], and believe in him [and believe in that which Muhammad has brought from Allah and follow him]. He [Allah] will forgive you of your sins, and will save you from a painful torment [in the Hell-fire].﴿ *(Qur'an 46: 29-31)*

Superficially, the visit to Ṭâ'if could seem a failure, but the aforementioned events provided the Muslims with symbolic meanings of those methods that were adopted by the Prophet (ﷺ) in preaching the Islamic Message. The prominent feature in this regard is that the Prophet (ﷺ) embodied mercy towards humanity in such a way that, instead of seeking revenge when the angel offered to punish the dissenters in Ṭâ'if, he hoped that they or their offspring would eventually come to obey Allah. This means that he was preparing himself for a very long period of calling to Islam. Even though his contemporaries might not accept the invitation, he set his hopes on the coming generations. Therefore, mercy, carefulness and patience were his tools, and they should represent the main tools of callers to the principles of Islam, as this event reveals.

As for the gardener and the believing jinn, their belief symbolises the universality of the Islamic mission. Islam has not been sent to humans only but also as a religion for the jinn to follow. In addition, this incident reveals that the Prophet (ﷺ) had a notion about recruiting believers from both the seen and unseen worlds, even though the tribes that he had visited in Ṭâ'if had rejected him brutally.

Prior to re-entering Makkah, the Prophet (ﷺ) complied with the tribal traditions and asked some well-connected individuals to grant him the protection that would enable him to travel in safely. Two out of the three people with whom he communicated refused his request, but the third, al-Muṭ'im ibn 'Adi, to whom the Prophet (ﷺ) was very grateful, agreed to protect him. Thus, the Prophet (ﷺ) was able to re-enter Makkah and continue his work.[35]

The Prophet's behaviour with al-Muṭ'im was also clarified in another of the Prophet's teachings, as he (ﷺ) stated: «He who does not thank the people does not thank Allah.»[36]

The Prophet (ﷺ) repeated his gratitude years later, after the Battle of Badr, and showed his followers the necessity of appreciating even the kindness of a pagan. He (ﷺ) said: «If al-Muṭ'im ibn 'Adi were alive and interceded for these war captives, I would have released them for his sake.»[37]

Therefore, many lessons can be learned from this experience in the life of the Prophet (ﷺ). The first is for those who perform the duty of preaching Islam, who should remain enthusiastic in the face of any kind of difficulties they might encounter: this implies the necessity of patience and continuous entreaty to Allah for His help, presenting grievances to Him alone. Another lesson is to believe in the existence of the jinn, although they are invisible. A Muslim's faith in the unseen world is strengthened and confirmed by this story illustrating the Prophet Muhammad's (ﷺ) belief in the existence of the jinn. Unbelievers, on the other hand, often only trust in what they can see, though an inability to see objects does not mean that they do not exist.

Night Ascension to the seven heavens

Soon after the return of the Prophet (ﷺ) from Ṭâ'if, a miraculous journey occurred. He (ﷺ) was taken to Jerusalem and ascended into the heavens. There are many narrations of this event. They all agree upon the content of the journey, although they vary somewhat in respect to the manner in which it unfolded. Sometime between the Prophet's night and dawn prayers, Jibreel (عليه السلام) came and took him on this unique voyage.

First, Jibreel (عليه السلام) slit open the Prophet's chest, washed his heart and filled it with belief obtained from a golden basin. This was the Prophet's second experience of this nature, the first one being while under the protection of his foster mother, as described earlier. Then, an animal named al-Burâq was brought to him. It was, according to the Prophet (ﷺ), smaller than a mule but larger than a donkey, and he (ﷺ) rode it on his night journey.

In Jerusalem, the previous prophets, including Ibrâheem, Moosâ and 'Issâ (Jesus), (peace be upon them) lined up behind Muhammad (ﷺ), and he led them in prayer. He (ﷺ) was offered two cups, one containing milk and one containing wine. He (ﷺ) chose the milk and drank it, which Jibreel (عليه السلام) interpreted as another sign that Prophet Muhammad (ﷺ) and his followers had been guided to keep to the pure innate nature of human beings to worship One and only one God.

The Prophet (ﷺ) ascended to heaven and passed through the seven heavens. In each level, he met a particular prophet until he emerged from the seventh heaven, where the Muslims were ordered by Allah the Almighty to perform fifty prayers each day. On his descent from the seventh heaven, he met Moosâ (عليه السلام), who asked him about the obligation under which he had been placed. Moosâ appealed to him to request that Allah reduce the number of obligatory prayers. The Prophet (ﷺ) made the appeal and ten prayers were removed, but Moosâ (ﷺ) encouraged him to try for a further reduction. This appeal was repeated until the number of prayers was set as five each day. Moosâ (ﷺ) still urged the Prophet (ﷺ) to attempt to reduce the number of prayers even further. He justified his encouragement by his own experience with his people and the fact that they were reluctant to adhere to that even that small number of prayers, but the Prophet Muhammad (ﷺ) explained that he was too shy to ask for more reduction. At this point, he was informed that the reward for those five prayers would be as great as if fifty prayers had been performed. In addition, he viewed many images of Paradise and its luxury as well as Hell and its punishments. On his return to Makkah, he passed by some caravans on their way to Makkah, too.[38]

Allah mentions this incredible experience in the Noble Qur'an:

﴿Glorified [and Exalted] is He [Allah] Who took His slave [Muhammad] for a journey by night from the Sacred Mosque [in Makkah] to the Farthest Mosque [Masjid al-Aqṣâ in Jerusalem], the neighbourhood of which We have blessed, in order that We might show him [Muhammad] of Our *âyât* [proofs, evidences, lessons, and signs]. Verily, He [Allah] is the All-Hearer, the All-Seer.﴾ *(Qur'an 17: 1)*

Scholars disagree over whether the journey was just a vision, considered as a revelation to the Prophet (ﷺ) or whether it happened while he was conscious. Evidence has been provided to support both views, but the majority believed that it occurred when the Prophet (ﷺ) was awake. The main justification for this preference is the pagans' accusation that he was lying when he informed them about it. If it were a dream, no one would have accused him of that.[39]

Another point of disagreement is whether or not the Prophet (ﷺ) actually saw Allah during the night ascension. The evidence can support differing analyses. While some scholars admitted his visual sighting of his Lord and displayed relevant proof, others preferred to think that he saw only the light of Allah, and others believed the sighting to be purely in his heart.[40]

At first, the Prophet (ﷺ) disclosed part of his experience to the people of Makkah. He informed them of his journey to Jerusalem but said nothing about his ascension into heaven. They derided him and disapprovingly asked him how it was possible to complete such a journey in a single night. To expose him, they asked him to describe Jerusalem to them.[41] It was narrated also that Abu Bakr (رضي الله عنه) was the person who asked him to describe Jerusalem just to show the pagans the truthfulness of his claim.[42] Responding to this challenge, he gave a precise portrayal of Jerusalem, in spite of the fact that he had never visited it before and, during his visit, his entry and departure from it had occurred at night. Regarding this point, he disclosed another miracle that Allah the Almighty granted him; he (ﷺ) said: «Allah manifested Jerusalem for me and I began looking at it while I was informing them about its signs.»[43]

People commented that his depiction was completely accurate,[44] but the Prophet (ﷺ) was not satisfied with this demonstration; he gave further corroboration pertaining to the caravans that he had passed on his return to Makkah. He told them what had happened to the caravans, what he did with their belongings without being detected, and at what time they would arrive in Makkah. The polytheists looked out for the appearance of the caravans to verify his allegations. Although they were astonished at the exactness of the time that he predicted for the return of the caravans, and at the accuracy of all the occurrences that he had mentioned,[45] they still refused to admit his veracity, and even a number of those who had become Muslims apostatized.[46]

The reason for their rejection was the irrationality of such a journey, as they evaluated it according to their mental capacities, as is the custom of those who do not recognise that Allah is the Creator of the world and that He is the One Who can break its codes and do whatever He wills. If someone had said at that time that humans would travel to the moon, they would have ridiculed him or her, while this is a reality today and we can understand how it is possible.

'Imâd ad-Deen Khaleel noted an interesting point concerning the name of the animal used on the journey, al-Burâq. This name is derived from *barq*, which means flashes of lightning, matching the realm of light and electricity. Here, it was used at a time when no one knew anything about light and its speed or electrical energy and its output.[47]

This event is one of the greatest miracles demonstrated by the Prophet (ﷺ). The pagan Arabs did not deny only this marvel, but rather rejected everything that he produced by the will of Allah to persuade them. The Qur'an itself is the greatest miracle; indeed it is still a miracle today, for its contents as well as its wonderful and inimitable style, which the Arab disbelievers have always failed in their attempts to copy. Similarly, the disbelievers rejected the other miracles given to the Prophet (ﷺ), such as the division of the moon into two parts. They asked him for something extraordinary to prove his righteousness. He (ﷺ) directed them to look at the moon which was bisected, one part over the mountain and the other below it, and told them to be witnesses![48] They refused to accept even these very visible signs.

Still, there are a number of points and lessons to be noted in relation to the Prophet's night journey:

- Believing in it or denying it shows the belief in or the denial of Muhammad's prophecy.
- This event happened shortly after his journey to Ṭâ'if, prior to which he (ﷺ) lost his beloved wife, Khadeejah (رضي الله عنها) and his supportive uncle, Abu Ṭâlib. During the night journey, Allah the Almighty not only comforted him (ﷺ) but also recompensed him for his patience and his compassion for the people of Ṭâ'if, in addition to preparing him for the crucial stage that the Islamic religion was predestined to experience. The next stage required strong believers and the night journey proved an effective screening process, dividing the Muslim community from the doubters.[49]
- This miracle confirmed the exalted position of the Prophet (ﷺ) among all the Messengers of Allah, by elevating him to the highest level in heaven where none had been before. It also intimated that he (ﷺ) was the inheritor of all the preceding prophets, by the joining of Makkah and Jerusalem, and that he was superior to all of them, shown by his leading them in prayer. Therefore, it was expected that the followers of the previous prophets would imitate their prophets and line up behind the Prophet Muhammad (ﷺ), believe in him and support him.
- The importance of prayers in Islam is stressed because, unlike other obligations, the command to pray was received directly from Allah the Almighty while the Prophet (ﷺ) was in heaven. Furthermore, establishing the obligation to pray occurred in the heavens and this guides Muslims to ascend their souls to Allah five times a day[50] and to live spiritually according to the meanings of the verses of the Noble Qur'an, which descended from the heavens and which they recite during their prayers.

CHAPTER FIVE

The Dawn of Success

New strategy

The Prophet (ﷺ) continued his mission in the same manner that he had adopted prior to his visit to Ṭâ'if, but he changed his strategy in respect to contacting the Arab tribes outside of Makkah. Within the boundaries of Makkah, he (ﷺ) held meetings with visiting groups or individuals who came either on pilgrimages or for other business reasons. He communicated with many groups and major personalities to explain Islam, the concept of the Oneness of Allah, and the Qur'an. In order to clarify these matters, he used to recite verses from the Noble Qur'an to them.

Ibn Hishâm listed various tribes and groups to whom the Prophet (ﷺ) extended his message, but for the most part they did not show a favourable reaction towards Islam.[1] The most positive affirmation that he could achieve was offered by individuals like Suwayd ibn Ṣâmit and Iyâs ibn Mu'âdh,[2] who heard his words sympathetically but did not accept the full description of his mission.[3] Furthermore, a group from the tribe of Âmir ibn Ṣa'ṣa'ah disputed with him. If they supported him and he won authority in the land, they wanted a ruling role. The Prophet (ﷺ) refused to promise this, clarifying that it is the prerogative of Allah to bestow authority and power on whomever He wishes. So, they refused to support him.[4] Consequently, the Prophet (ﷺ) used to return empty-handed from most attempts to spread Islam.

The task which fell upon the Prophet (ﷺ) was arduous. This can be visualised by considering the general circumstances of the time. The Arab tribes were fanatically loyal and obdurate with regard to their traditions and creeds and thought that Islam would weaken their independence and self-importance. Nevertheless, the Prophet (ﷺ) continued his sacred mission without being hindered by the difficult experiences that he and his followers underwent, or the problems which resulted as they performed their sacrosanct duties.

It is worth mentioning that the Prophet (ﷺ) himself undertook the Muslim community's missionary activities. Without a doubt, his followers had significant roles but there is no certain or obvious information available to indicate that anyone regularly accompanied him as he performed this duty to call to Islam. During the early stages of preaching Islam, the obligation of this important task fell to him alone and no one shared in this responsibility.

The isolation of the Prophet (ﷺ) while he was performing his missionary rounds may be compared with that of some of the other prophets, such as Moosâ (عليه السلام). It also demonstrates a remarkable contrast between the two of them. Moosâ (عليه السلام) requested that Allah the Almighty support him by including his brother Hâroon (Aaron) (عليه السلام) as a supporting prophet. The Noble Qur'an described his request in the following verses:

﴿And appoint for me a helper from my family, Hâroon, my brother. Increase my strength with him, and let him share my task [of conveying Allah's Message] that we may glorify You much, and remember You much. Verily, You are ever All-Seeing of us [and our affairs]. [Allah] said: You are granted your request, Moosâ.﴿ *(Qur'an 20: 29-36)*

Several of the prophets were supported by other prophets among their followers. Ibrâheem (Abraham) had the assistance of his sons, Is-ḥâq (Isaac) and Ismâ'eel (Ishmael), and Looṭ (Lot). Ibrâheem's grandson Ya'qoob (Jacob) rejoiced in his prophet son, Dâwood (David), who was in turn supported by his son, Sulaymân (Solomon). In addition, 'Eesâ (Jesus) was preceded by his cousin, Yaḥyâ (John), who paved the way for him. Each prophet continued the message of the previous one, or in the case of 'Eesâ and Yaḥyâ, acted as an evangel for him.

In the case of Islam, Allah the Almighty chose to send the Prophet Muhammad (ﷺ) alone because he was to be the Seal of the Prophets, the final prophet who would gather the whole of humanity into a single unity under the teachings of a single religion. The previous prophets had been sent to their particular nations, while the Prophet Muhammad (ﷺ) was commissioned with calling the peoples of all nations, tribes and races to the path of Allah.[5] Thus, as the Seal of the Prophets, he (ﷺ) needed to be the sole authority in order to preserve humanity from the risk of becoming divided from attachment to different religious leaders. Consequently, the task of Prophet Muhammad (ﷺ) was more difficult than that of the other prophets, as the only assistance he received from the believers, especially in the beginning, was their confirmation of their belief in him and their bearing the tortures that were heaped upon them because of their faith.

Blazes of light in Yathrib

As the Prophet (ﷺ) was circuiting the Arab groups to explain Islam and show them to the way of Allah, he met six people from the Khazraj and Aws tribes[6] of Madinah, which was known at that time as the city of Yathrib. This event happened in the eleventh year of his prophethood, in 620 or 621 CE. Their meeting was at al-'Aqabah, a place close to Makkah where the pilgrims usually threw pebbles as a symbolic threat to Satan.

According to Ibn Hishâm, they had already heard about a new prophet from their Jewish neighbours. The information came through the continuous threats that were directed against them by their neighbours. These six individuals were looking to solve the internal hostility that raged between their two tribes, as well as frustrate the Jews' threats.[7] These factors combined with the message of Islam made them eager to become Muslims. After returning to Madinah, they propagated the Prophet's teachings among their citizens and invited them to embrace the new religion. Within a short period of time, Islam had penetrated into many of the homes there.[8]

The First 'Aqabah Allegiance

In the following year, Muslims from Madinah, ten from the Khazraj and two from their opponent tribe the Aws, made a pilgrimage to Makkah. At al-'Aqabah, they met the Prophet (ﷺ) and paid him homage.[9] This meeting was recognized in Islamic history as the First 'Aqabah Allegiance, as the Prophet (ﷺ) at that time said to them: «Pledge to me that you will not consider anything equal to Allah, nor steal, nor commit adultery, nor kill your children, nor utter slander, intentionally perpetrating a falsehood, nor disobey me in any kindness. If anyone of you fulfils (this covenant), his reward will be from Allah. But if anyone does any of these things, and is punished for it in this world, then the punishment will be a penance for him; and if anyone does one of these things but Allah covers it, then Allah will have authority over him, to punish or forgive him, as He wishes.»[10]

The delegation from Madinah pledged that they would comply with these instructions, directives which clearly reflect the fact that Islam is more than a mere confession of the Oneness of Allah and the prophecy of Muhammad (ﷺ). This pledge was the key to establishing a new society that was going to be ruled by Allah's law instead of the laws that had been created by the people and tainted by their desires to cater to the interests of those in power at the expense of the general public. The leaders of the Quraysh recognised the danger to their own self-serving interests if they were to accept Islam, and this is why they fought strongly against it, but the people from Madinah agreed to assume the duty of creating the new life.

Hence, the Prophet (ﷺ) had laid a foundation for erecting the promised Islamic society by ensuring that they now had a place where they could work to attain these objectives. He (ﷺ) delegated Muṣ‘ab ibn ‘Umayr (رضي الله عنه), one of his Companions, to teach them how to recite the Noble Qur'an, instruct them about Islam, and educate them about how to perform their religious duties. He (ﷺ) also entrusted Muṣ‘ab with leading the prayers, since the Prophet (ﷺ) recognised that each group, at that time, would dislike having their prayers led by someone from the opposing tribe.

Muṣ‘ab (رضي الله عنه) was about thirty-seven years old when the Prophet (ﷺ) selected him for this duty. He adhered to the teachings of the Prophet (ﷺ) and dealt gently with the community, calling them to Islam. In spite of the fact that many people from Madinah retained their heathen faith, Muṣ‘ab achieved great success by winning over two prominent individuals, Sa‘d ibn Mu‘âdh (رضي الله عنه) and Usayd ibn Ḥuḍayr (رضي الله عنه), whose conversion to

Islam resulted in the fast spread of the Islamic religion in Madinah.[11]

The Second 'Aqabah Allegiance

At the start of the next pilgrimage season, Muṣ'ab (ﷺ) returned to Makkah[12] and informed the Prophet (ﷺ) of how Islam was thriving in Madinah and the readiness of the majority of its inhabitants to accept hosting the other Muslims. Muṣ'ab was accompanied by seventy-five converts to Islam,[13] and they had travelled along with the pagans of Madinah on their pilgrimage. They arranged for a rendezvous with the Prophet (ﷺ) at the same place where their first group of Muslim converts had met him (ﷺ) during the previous pilgrimage season. This meeting was at midnight on the 12th of Dhul Ḥijjah,[14] corresponding to somewhere around the 29th of June 622 CE, and it was shrouded in secrecy. Ka'b ibn Mâlik (رضي الله عنه), a narrator of what happened that night, declared that they concealed the matter and, on the appointed night, appeared to sleep at their regular camp site. A third of the way into the night, they sneaked away and gathered in the valley at al-'Aqabah to wait for the Prophet (ﷺ).[15]

In fact, this secrecy meant that Islam at that early stage in Madinah remained confined to certain people, and the Muslims concealed their acceptance of the faith from their unbelieving kindred. This feature becomes most obvious in the story narrated by Ibn Hishâm that after they made their agreement with the Prophet (ﷺ), a devil, or Satan himself, shouted out louder than had ever been heard before to notify the Quraysh of the accord. In the morning, some people of the Quraysh visited the Madinan camp to verify the matter, but the pagans of Madinah denied it and the Muslims said nothing.[16] Surely, if the people of Madinah were aware that they had Muslims among them, they would have enquired from them about the truthfulness of the news. This situation shows that Islam had quickly permeated into the families in Madinah, but the general circumstances were not yet right for them to proclaim their faith openly.

The Prophet (ﷺ) arrived on time for the meeting. He was aware of its importance and of the grave danger they would be in if the pagans knew of it, so he did not wish for the gathering to last long. Ibn Katheer, quoting from al-Bayhaqi, narrated the event: «The Prophet (ﷺ) said: Let one of you speak and shorten his speech; heathens are spying on you and if they are cognisant of you, they will harm you. As'ad ibn Zurârah (a prominent Muslim of Madinah) told the Prophet (ﷺ): Muhammad, ask whatever you like from us, on behalf of your Lord and on behalf of yourself; and then inform us what our reward will be, from Allah and from you, if we comply with your demands. The Prophet (ﷺ) said: For my Lord, I ask you to worship Him and not to take anything into partnership with Him (in His divinity or in His worship). For myself and my Companions, I ask you to shelter us, champion us and defend us as you defend yourselves. If you do this, then Paradise will be granted to you.»

The Muslim believers of Madinah paid homage to the Prophet (ﷺ) on that basis.[17] The same core content of this agreement, which is known as the Second 'Aqabah Allegiance has been mentioned in other versions by various narrators.[18] The important detail relating to this event is that a man from the Aws tribe told the Prophet (ﷺ) that they were going to cut off their relations with their Jewish neighbours and he questioned whether the Prophet (ﷺ) might abandon them, even though they supported him, until he was victorious in achieving his goals. The Prophet (ﷺ) is reported to have said: «Your responsibility is mine; I belong to you and you belong to me, and I will fight those whom you wage war against and I will make peace with those with whom you are at peace.»[19]

This agreement provided a mutual reassurance for both sides and differed from the First 'Aqabah Allegiance in two respects. The first difference concerned the larger number of Muslims from Madinah promising allegiance to the Prophet (ﷺ). In the previous year, there had been twelve. Now, there were seventy-five. This contrast reflects the enthusiasm with which the Muslims had undertaken their roles in Madinah.

The second difference lied in the fact that the first allegiance had avoided any mention of physical protection or defence of each other. The second accord included a clear reference to protecting Islam, the Prophet (ﷺ), and his followers even if fighting was necessary for executing this protection.[20] It is worth mentioning that at this point Allah had not yet commanded the Muslims to fight or declare war for protecting the Muslims or spreading the religion; they had only been commanded to show patience during their adversities.

In the Second 'Aqabah Allegiance, the Prophet (ﷺ) openly announced the right of the believers to fight when necessary,[21] but he advised caution. He (ﷺ) asked the Muslims of Madinah to nominate twelve from among them to be assigned as their leaders. They chose nine people from the Khazraj tribe and three from the Aws.[22] It was clear to the new Muslims that their leaders were elected in a manner that differed from their usual tribal traditions. Here, they had a choice in proposing those who would assume the forthcoming responsibility. The Prophet (ﷺ) did not impose anyone upon them, although he had met with five of them the previous year. Thus, the Muslim converts of Madinah felt fully-integrated within the Islamic community, and they were content with regard to their leaders. This would allow them to successfully perform their duties as Muslims and adhere firmly to their agreement with the Prophet (ﷺ). Another notable point was that designating specific leaders for each tribe illustrated the necessity of acknowledging the ratio of those present; in this case, it was clear that the majority of Muslims in Madinah were from the Khazraj clans.[23]

Exodus to Madinah

The aforementioned allegiance laid the foundation for creating a secure place for the Muslims, after eleven years of strife and suffering for the sake of erecting the pillars of monotheism. The appointed twelve commanders held the responsibility for the Islamic issues in Madinah, including the preparation for receiving immigrant Muslims from the other parts of the Arabian Peninsula, particularly from Makkah. A number of families started preparing to host their coming Muslim brothers and sisters.[24]

The Prophet (ﷺ) advised his followers to emigrate to Madinah, telling them that Allah had arranged support for them there, and so they began their exodus to Madinah in groups.[25] There were now two contrasting situations: one in Madinah, where the Muslims found goodwill, altruism and a safe environment in which to worship Allah; and another in Makkah, where great anger arose at the new outlet that the Muslims had acquired.

The Quraysh recognised the strategic importance of the Muslims' escape to Madinah, and once again, felt that the Islamic mission was achieving great victory and success at their expense. Hence, they utilised their power and cunning to frustrate the Islamic scheme. They separated family members from each other; the family of Abu Salamah (رضي الله عنه) is an example of this. People belonging to Abu Salamah's wife's tribe watched him depart from Makkah with his wife and son. They then abducted his wife from him, which was followed by Abu Salamah's pagan family's abduction of the son from his mother. Consequently, each of them was kept segregated from the other for about a year.[26]

In other cases, they tried to deceive Muslims and kidnap them, as was the case for 'Ayyâsh ibn Rabee'ah al-Makhzoomi (رضي الله عنه). His two cousins, who were also his stepbrothers, came to Madinah and alleged that his mother swore not to sit in the shade unless she saw him. For the sake of his mother, he accompanied them, but on the way, they assailed him, bound him and brought him handcuffed to Makkah, encouraging their people to do the same with their own relatives. Eventually, they incarcerated him in a roofless room, not only to restrict his movement but also to make him suffer from the heat of the desert. 'Ayyâsh (رضي الله عنه) was imprisoned there until the Prophet (ﷺ), after his own emigration to Madinah, was able to send someone to release him.[27] In the case of Ṣuhayb (رضي الله عنه), they prevented him from leaving Makkah until he surrendered his wealth to them.[28]

These are just a few examples of the great suffering that Muslims experienced on account of their desire to emancipate themselves from the heathen system which oppressed them. They sacrificed everything in order to achieve their goal of preserving their faith. As the disbelieving powers wanted to suppress and eradicate them, they performed their emigrations as covertly as possible.

The Hijrah of the Prophet (ﷺ)

Despite using every means to muzzle the thunderous voice of Islam, the Quraysh failed to achieve their aims. Instead, all

Muslims, with the exception of a few individuals, gained their liberty from the confinement with which they were oppressed in Makkah. Nevertheless, three prominent people had still not left Makkah yet; these were Abu Bakr (ﷺ) and 'Ali (ﷺ) and the Prophet himself (ﷺ) who wanted to assure a good outcome for his followers and who was waiting for his Lord's order to leave.

The Quraysh wanted to devise a plan to prevent the Prophet (ﷺ) from joining his followers in their new province in order to abort his endeavour to establish a new religious life. They recognised that his success in this would be like laying the corner stone for their own destruction, so they held a meeting in Dâr an-Nadwah, the place where they used to discuss their affairs and make decisions. Representatives from every tribe attended the meeting, and after a long discussion, they decided to kill the Prophet (ﷺ) in a creative way that would prevent the Hâshim tribe from taking revenge and oblige them to agree to settle the affair upon the payment of blood money. The plan was to choose a noble, reliable and powerful youth from each tribe and supply each of them with a sharp sword with which to pierce the Prophet (ﷺ) simultaneously in order for his blood to be shed by all the families equally and then to coerce his tribe to accept wergild from them. Thus, they would be rid of the Prophet (ﷺ) and avoid any prospective war with the Prophet's family.[29]

Meanwhile, the Prophet (ﷺ) was obliged to adopt the required means in his conflict with the heathens. He (ﷺ) was continuing to oversee the emigration to Madinah with his cousin, 'Ali ibn Abi Ṭâlib (ﷺ), and his close friend, Abu Bakr (ﷺ) while awaiting the command of Allah on how to proceed. 'Ali (ﷺ) was designated to stay behind in Makkah for two reasons. The first was to wrap himself in the nightdress of the Prophet (ﷺ), when directed to do so, in order to make it appear that the Prophet himself (ﷺ) was lying in bed. The second was to hand over the consignments that had been entrusted to the Prophet (ﷺ) to their rightful owners after the Prophet (ﷺ) had left. Abu Bakr (رضي الله عنه) was preparing two riding camels since he had requested permission to emigrate, and the Prophet (ﷺ) told him to be patient in the hope that Allah might provide a companion for him. Abu Bakr (رضي الله عنه) envisaged that his travelling companion might be the Prophet himself. In addition, Abu Bakr had requested that 'Abdullâh ibn Arqaṭ or 'Urayqiṭ, who was a pagan, be their guide to Madinah at the proper time.[30]

Allah the Almighty disclosed the plan of the Quraysh to His Messenger (ﷺ) and granted him permission to emigrate. The Prophet (ﷺ) notified Abu Bakr (رضي الله عنه) about the permission that he had obtained and the arrangements that should be made for their journey.[31] Abu Bakr gave the riding camels to the prospective guide to feed and then bring along to a specific spot when he was sent for, probably after three days. He also asked his son 'Abdullâh (رضي الله عنه) to spy on the Quraysh during the daytime and report the news to them at night in their refuge, and he ordered his daughter Asmâ' (رضي الله عنها) to take responsibility for providing them with food at night. He further directed his servant, Âmir ibn Fuhayrah, to move his herds of cattle over their tracks,[32] in order to cover their footprints.

The conspirators lay in ambush at the home of the Prophet (ﷺ). The Prophet (ﷺ) took note of their presence, and then gave his green nightgown to his cousin 'Ali (رضي الله عنه) to wear, so that they would think that he was still in bed. While reciting verses from Soorat Yâ Seen,[33] he left his house. The plotters eyes were closed and the Prophet (ﷺ) placed some dirt on each one's head. They were not conscious of his departure nor did they realise the identity of the decoy who slumbered in the Prophet's bed until the next day dawned![34]

Aḥmad ibn Ḥanbal, a great savant of Hadith, narrated from Ibn 'Abbâs (رضي الله عنه), a cousin of the Prophet (ﷺ) and one of the most prominent Islamic scholars, that this happened on a Monday in the month of Rabee' I in the thirteenth year of the prophethood.[35] Ibn Katheer mentioned, from Ibn Is-ḥâq, that the Prophet (ﷺ) reached Madinah on Monday the 12th of Rabee' I. Hence, it remains unclear whether the Prophet's departure to Makkah or his arrival in Madinah was in Rabee' I. Also according to Ibn Katheer, the journey lasted for fifteen days. In any case, this event occurred in either September or October of 622 CE.

In addition to the fact that the Prophet (ﷺ) was granted complete success by Allah and directed by Allah to make sound choices, he demonstrated a skilful manoeuvre in remaining at home until the schemers had assembled at his gate. It was useful to have them all concentrating on one place, unable to consider other locations. Leaving them fixed in that one spot throughout the night provided sufficient time to escape easily and to carry out the second stage of the plan safely.

Rather than being ashamed of their collective defeat and of discovering dust on their heads, the pagan Quraysh did not comprehend Allah's support for His Messenger. This was an obvious miracle for them if they had been willing to understand it. Instead, they were far from reconsidering their enmity towards the Prophet (ﷺ). They offered a hundred camels as a prize to whoever captured or killed the Prophet (ﷺ) or Abu Bakr (رضي الله عنه).[36] People longed for this prize, and stormed throughout Makkah, hoping to catch one or both of them!

The Prophet (ﷺ) was aware that the Quraysh would be enraged when they discovered his absence, furthermore, that they would expect him to attempt to reach his Companions in Madinah, which is on the way to Syria in the north. Therefore, along with his

Companion Abu Bakr (ﷺ), he went in the opposite direction and hid in a cave known as ath-Thawr, which was on the way to Yemen in the south.

It was narrated that Abu Bakr (ﷺ) alternated between going in front of the Prophet (ﷺ) and falling behind him. When he was questioned about this, he replied that it was out of fear that the Prophet (ﷺ) might be attacked by his enemies from the front or back. Similarly, Abu Bakr (ﷺ) preceded him into the cave to search it, lest a predatory animal or snake might be there to endanger the Prophet (ﷺ).[37]

Still, once again, it was Allah the Almighty who protected His Prophet (ﷺ) from his enemies, and this occurred by His sending a spider to create a cobweb across the entrance to the cave, after the Prophet (ﷺ) and Abu Bakr (ﷺ) had gone inside of it.[38] It was also related that Allah the Almighty created a tree at the entrance to the little cavern, to whose branches the cobwebs were spread and in which two rock pigeons nested. Their pursuers lost track of their footprints at a distance of two hundred cubits from the grotto; then one of them advanced closer and heard the pigeons cooing. He did not continue since he thought that the pigeons would not be there if anyone was inside the cave, as he told his comrades. The Prophet (ﷺ) heard that comment and realised that Allah had defeated his enemies.[39] In a different narration traced to Abu Bakr, he (ﷺ) said to the Prophet (ﷺ), "If any one of them would look under his feet, he would see us."[40] Allah the Almighty revealed the situation in the following verse of the Noble Qur'an:

﴾If you help him [Muhammad] not [it does not matter], for Allah did indeed help him when the disbelievers drove him out, the second of the two; when they [Muhammad and Abu Bakr] were in the cave, he said to his companion [Abu Bakr]: Be not sad [or afraid]; surely, Allah is with us. Then Allah sent down His *sakeenah* [calmness, tranquillity, peace] upon him, and strengthened him with forces [of angels] which you saw not, and made the word of those who disbelieved the lowermost, while the Word of Allah became the uppermost; and Allah is All-Mighty, All-Wise.﴿ *(Qur'an 9: 40)*

'Abdullâh, the son of Abu Bakr (may Allah be pleased with them both), joined them at night, leaving them in the early morning to attend Quraysh assemblies in order to report everything back to the Prophet (ﷺ). He played the role of informer well, and when he notified the Prophet (ﷺ) that the eagerness of the Quraysh's search for him had diminished, the Prophet (ﷺ) decided to leave the cave and sent for the guide to come. Âmir ibn Fuhayrah, the servant of Abu Bakr, joined them too. The group, consisting of four people, set off for the coastal road,[41] which was furthest from the usual trail, for the purposes of exercising caution and disguise.

Surâqah ibn Mâlik, the leader of Midlij clan, received news that they had been seen and decided to get them alone in order to obtain the reward purely for himself. He narrated how he rode his horse, holding his spear, and set off for the coastal road, but he stumbled on the journey about four times, although he was insistent on apprehending them. According to him, the Prophet (ﷺ) was carefree, although Abu Bakr (رضي الله عنه) looked behind him many times. He approached so close to the travellers that he could hear the Prophet (ﷺ) reciting verses from the Noble Qur'an; then suddenly his horse's forelegs sunk in the sand up to the knees. No sooner had the horse freed its forelegs and straightened up than thick dust rose up like smoke. He realised that they were being protected by Allah and that he would not be able to catch them. He reported to the Prophet (ﷺ) about the Qurayshi plans against him, offered him some refreshments, and then asked him for an indemnity pledge! The Prophet (ﷺ) instructed Âmir ibn Fuhayrah to write one for him on a patch of leather and asked Surâqah to hide it,[42] which he did.[43]

A further extraordinary event occurred on the way to Madinah at the tent of a woman called Um Ma'bad. She used to follow the tribal custom of offering food and drink to passersby, but when the Prophet (ﷺ) and his companions arrived, she had nothing available to offer them and she apologised for that. The Prophet (ﷺ) glanced at her lean nanny goat and asked her permission to milk it. She told him that he was free to try but that he would probably find not even a drop in its udder. The Prophet (ﷺ) stroked it and mentioned the name of Allah, then rubbed its udder and mentioned the name of Allah, then called for a vessel and milked it until the container was full! He gave it to her to drink her fill, then he (ﷺ) milked it again and gave it to his companions. After their thirst was quenched, he drank some milk himself.[44] There are many narrations of this event, with minor differences; Ibn Katheer quoted them[45] and quoted from al-Bayhaqi his comment that all of them were the same story.[46]

As for 'Ali (رضي الله عنه), he stayed in Makkah for three days to return to the people their consignments which they had lodged with the Prophet (ﷺ). Once he had completed this duty, he left for Madinah and joined the Prophet (ﷺ) at Qubâ'.[47]

Arrival in Madinah

After about a two-week journey, the convoy of the Prophet (ﷺ) arrived at the suburbs of Madinah, in a district known as the quarter of the descendents of 'Amr ibn 'Awf, which is well-known now as Qubâ', where he stayed for a fortnight.[48] Ibn Hishâm mentioned that the Prophet (ﷺ) stayed with Kulthoom ibn Hidm, and he (ﷺ) either also stayed with Sa'd ibn Khaythamah or visited him often.[49]

This area was of particular importance for more than one reason. It was the first point at which the immigrants were welcomed before continuing towards Madinah. The Prophet (ﷺ) acknowledged its inhabitants' role by staying with them for a time. Another reason was its geographical position. It was a few miles from Madinah, towards Makkah. If the pagans of Makkah intended to come through, they would necessarily pass by there. So, by staying in the area and laying some stones to start the building of the first mosque there, the Prophet (ﷺ) may have been aiming to strengthen it morally against any anticipated invasion by the heathens. A third reason was that the Prophet (ﷺ), during his stay in Qubâ', planned how he was going to manage affairs in Madinah, not only between the Muslims, who belonged to a variety of tribes, but also between the Muslims as a community and other relevant people, such as the Jews and the disbelievers.

Prior to leaving this area, the Prophet (ﷺ) summoned the children of an-Najjâr who responded to him positively, girding themselves with their swords.[50] They were Muslims, and the maternal uncles of his grandfather, and a clear number of them had been conspicuous in the history of Islam since the allegiances of 'Aqabah in Makkah.[51] The procession, which probably consisted of five hundred Anṣâri[52] supporters,[53] escorted the Prophet (ﷺ) until the final point of his journey.[54] This scene displayed the power and position of the Prophet (ﷺ) not only to the Muslims in Madinah but also to its other sects, in order to prevent them from disrespecting him as a leader or the Muslims as a community. This sight, rather, introduced the Prophet (ﷺ) as the chief commander in the city, regardless of its inhabitants' denominational allegiances. Establishing his position, which seemed to be generally accepted, formed the main basis of the other steps that were taken subsequently for organising the issues of Madinah.

As for the Muslims, this picture reflected their deep joy at the Prophet's arrival. They were so happy that they flocked in mass to the roads and rooftops to welcome and greet him.[55] It was narrated that the leaders of the Anṣâr offered to host the Prophet (ﷺ). He (ﷺ) advised them not to stop his camel, as it was directed by Allah and would stop only as Allah instructed it. The camel carried on until it reached a site that was close to the house of Abu Ayyoob al-Anṣâri (رضي الله عنه) where it knelt down. The Prophet (ﷺ) dismounted from the camel and stayed with Abu Ayyoob al-Anṣâri until he finished the building of a new mosque and his domiciles.[56]

A number of lessons and points can be extracted from this journey and its accompanying events:

- ❖ Since guidelines and laws are established through the Prophet (ﷺ), the manner he uses in accomplishing matters becomes a religious obligation for all Muslims. In order to legislate caution and circumspection for Muslims while working out their affairs, he (ﷺ) chose to manage his emigration in the cautious manner outlined above.
- ❖ Despite the fact that the pagans refused to believe in the message of Islam and even accused the Prophet (ﷺ) of lying in this regard, they did not deem anyone else as honest and reliable. This is the reason that they entrusted him with their property instead of depositing it with others. Thus, when the Prophet (ﷺ) left Makkah, he gave 'Ali (رضي الله عنه) the job of returning all the property that had been consigned to him.
- ❖ During the Prophet's stay at the home of Abu Ayyoob al-

Anṣâri (ﷺ), this Companion served him (ﷺ) with nourishment and used to eat from the Prophet's hand (ﷺ) to gain a blessing from it.[57] This and similar occasions referred to by Bukhari, Muslim and others indicated that it was acceptable to seek blessings from the person of the Prophet (ﷺ). Therefore, Muhammad S. R. al-Booṭi and some other scholars also allowed the permissibility of seeking blessings from the relics of the Prophet (ﷺ).[58]

CHAPTER SIX

The Establishment of the State

Construction of the mosque

In different reports it is narrated that the Prophet (ﷺ) stayed less than a month or as long as seven months in the residence of Abu Ayyoob al-Anṣâri (رضي الله عنه).[1] During this time, he bought the plot of land on which his camel knelt down and built a community mosque and private rooms for his family.[2] He himself, along with his Companions, participated in constructing the mosque,[3] which was roofless apart from a veranda called the *ṣuffah*,[4] which was used as a guest house for those who came to Madinah and had no accommodation, or as a home for poor Muslim men. The buildings were very simple and the materials used for them were stones for the walls, palm branches stripped of their leaves for the roof and palm branches coated with clay and a mixture of sand and gravel for the flooring. The ceilings were just above head height, so that anyone could touch them. There was no knocker on the doors and visitors knocked on them with their hands to announce themselves.[5]

The Prophet (ﷺ) gave priority to the mosque, as this would be the place where Muslims gather not only to perform their prayers and other ceremonies, but also the location for teaching Islamic concepts and principles, receiving visitors and delegations to Madinah, promoting a communal social life and discussing all issues that were relevant to the Islamic society. So its establishment was crucial and a starting point for the creation of a systematic entity, a compact and settled Islamic society, as the Prophet (ﷺ) intended to establish.[6]

Fraternisation

Naturally, the immigration process resulted in increasing the population of Madinah, which became a safe haven not only for Muslims fleeing from Makkah, but also for Muslims from all over the Arabian Peninsula. Therefore, the new inhabitants of Madinah who had originally belonged to a variety of tribes and families consolidated into a single unity that had emerged from the Islamic faith rather than from tribal cultures. Having all the Muslims settle within one region allowed free practice of the religion and provided the opportunity to concentrate upon creating an ideal community ruled by the laws of Allah and embodying the Islamic teachings that attracted people to embrace Islam peacefully.

This rosy image was not devoid of social, economical and salutary inconveniences that accompanied the new life, however. The immigrants had left behind their wealth and families and they had different backgrounds of experience in comparison with that of the original inhabitants of Madinah. While the immigrant Muslims from Makkah had commercial experience, the people of Madinah were farmers and artisans.[7] It was difficult for the immigrants to succeed in the new town, since they lacked the experience required to fend for themselves there and lacked property or wealth to exercise their existing skills. In addition, the climate of Madinah did not suit many of the immigrant Muslims who, soon after they arrived, became sick with fever. 'Â'ishah

(ﷺ), the wife of the Prophet (ﷺ), narrated that her father, Abu Bakr (﵁), and Bilâl (﵁) were indisposed when they reached Madinah and used to repeat poetic verses that revealed their agony. She informed the Prophet (ﷺ) of this, and he prayed: «O Allah! Endear Madinah to us just like our love for Makkah or stronger, sanitise it, invoke Your blessing on its provisions for us and divert its fever towards al-Juḥfah.»[8]

As for the hosts, the Anṣâr or 'Helpers', they were disposed towards generosity, so they opened up their houses to the immigrants,[9] but the Prophet (ﷺ) wished to fully amalgamate them rather than be content with having them share supplies. He, therefore, commenced by linking each immigrant to one of the Anṣâr on the basis of fraternisation and declared this policy in the house of Anas ibn Mâlik (﵁).[10] Ibn Is-ḥâq mentioned the names of thirty four Muslims[11] who were associated in these brotherly relationships. This number included the Prophet (ﷺ) and his cousin 'Ali (﵁), who were tied with each other although they both were immigrants, as well as linking Ja'far ibn Abi Ṭâlib (﵁) as the brother of Mu'âdh ibn Jabal (﵁), despite the fact that Ja'far was in Abyssinia at that time.[12] Akram al-'Umari reported that the links had been made between ninety individuals, consisting of forty-five immigrants and forty-five Anṣâris.[13]

This fraternity held obligations for both sides that were even stronger than blood ties. Joining 'Abdur-Raḥmân ibn 'Awf (﵁) to Sa'd ibn ar-Rabee' al-Anṣâri (﵁) was an example of this. Sa'd offered to share his wealth equally with his new brother. Moreover, he asked him to choose one of his two wives and he would divorce her to enable his brother Muslim to marry her. 'Abdur-Raḥmân rejected this idea and asked his brother instead just to show him the way to the marketplace, where he started his commercial business.[14] During this early stage of life in Madinah, this brotherly association resulted in each part inheriting from the other, until the revelation of the following Qur'anic verse abrogated the provision:[15]

﴿And to everyone, We have appointed heirs of that [property] left by parents and relatives. To those also with whom you have made a pledge [of brotherhood], give them their due portion [by way of additional bequests, which can be up to a third of the estate]. Truly, Allah is Ever a Witness over all things.﴾ *(Qur'an 4: 33)*

Thus, the Muslim community was established on the grounds of a single faith. Fully endorsing fraternity and cooperation was a substantial way for strengthening and advancing it to achieve its objectives. Naturally, this sense of brotherhood involved affection and sympathy towards others in a general form, but when it united two individuals, and their families, each party felt responsibility for the other, and thus the whole community situation was inclined to be organised collectively. This principle of pairing the believers had been adopted in Makkah for supporting the new converts and confronting the pagans, and it gained an extra obligation in Madinah concerning inheritance. Even when its obligations had been abrogated, the sense of cooperation and assistance remained as it was, and the Prophet (ﷺ) carried on weaving it among his new followers.[16] The Noble Qur'an praised each group in the following verses:

﴿[And there is also a share in this war booty] for the poor emigrants, who were expelled from their property, seeking bounties from Allah and to please Him, and helping Allah [by helping His religion] and His Messenger [Muhammad]. Such are indeed the truthful. And [it is also for] those who, before them, had homes [in Madinah] and had adopted the Faith, who love those who emigrate to them, and have no jealousy in their breasts for that which they [the poor emigrants] have been given [from the booty], and give them [emigrants] preference over themselves even though they were in need of that [provision]. And whoever is saved from his own covetousness, it is they who will be the successful.》 *(Qur'an 59: 8-9)*

The constitution

Besides fraternisation as an internal factor for weaving the Islamic community, there remained need for further points to work as a ruling constitution, the articles to which all the inhabitants of Madinah would adhere. Thus, some general guidelines were issued. Part concerned the organisation of Muslim affairs and the other part related to the affairs of all of the inhabitants and their obligations towards the State, regardless of their religion.[17] Below are some of the articles contained in this important document:[18]

- [The believers] are one, and they are a distinguished nation.
- All believers in God should be against anyone who tries to outrage or tyrannise them, wants to extort [something] from them wrongfully, or [creates] aggression or wrong, or sows dissension among believers, so the whole [group of] faithful believers must be hand in hand in opposing such a person, even if he or she is a child of one of them.
- Believers must not ignore a needy person; [they must amicably help him or her] in paying ransom or blood money. [At the same time] a believer should not ally with a confederate of another believer without getting his or her permission.
- A believer should neither kill a believer in revenge for an infidel nor help a non-believer against a believer. If someone kills a believer arbitrarily, he or she will be killed unless the custodian of the victim is content with blood money. All the

believers must be against the killer, and they are compelled to adopt this position.

- ❖ Offering protection [to other people for the sake] of Allah is [authorised] equally for all [people in the community], and even the lowest person has the right of offering it. The believers, who are a part of the people, are patrons to each other and prevent and restrain each other.
- ❖ The peace of the believers is the same; a single believer should not make peace apart from a believer during the fight for the sake of Allah but [on the grounds] of rights and justice.
- ❖ A pagan has no right to offer protection to the wealth or people of Quraysh or to prevent a believer from doing so.
- ❖ Any Jew who follows us [and upholds the laws of the community] has the right of support and comfort.
- ❖ It will be an unlawful act of a believer who has faith in Allah and the Day of Resurrection to help or shelter anyone who commits a sin that requires punishment. May Allah's curse and anger befall any person who helps or shelters such a wrongdoer; no repentance or ransom will be accepted from him or her.[19]
- ❖ Any point of disagreement has to be referred to Allah and to Muhammad [to make a decision about it].

The first article concerns the definition of the growing community. It had been identified as a consolidated and distinguished nation.[20] Unlike those who complied with the tribal customs and believed in a variety of idols, its people conformed to the one dominating faith and to its Divine Orders. This submission did not necessarily mean that people were restricted in organising their lives. In the Muslim community, there was no class or social distinction among its members, who all equally obeyed the Islamic legislation as their ruling source and the general framework within which all Muslims operated. By depending on this notion, the Muslim community parted into smaller units that represented different families and shared the responsibility for the concerns of their members, such as blood money, ransom and poverty. This provided a sound pillar for merging each group into a sort of social solidarity that would help in reducing the tasks of the overall ruler.

Another element that the treaty highlighted was the equality of people in terms of offering protection to others. This was the right of every single Muslim and the protection he or she granted would have been considered as strong as that of any great person in the community. While this ostentatious characteristic was confined to the nobility in the tribal societies, opening it for every Muslim enhanced the element of equality. For, as people were equal in this major point, they were also equal in all other matters, regardless of their origin, gender, colour or wealth, which resulted eventually in creating a solid and sympathetic society.[21] Anyone joining the Islamic community would enjoy the same privileges.

There were two conditions for protecting equality from misuse. The first was that the infidels of Madinah were deprived of exercising this right over the individuals or wealth of the pagans of Quraysh. The proposed reason for this was that they might use it in such a manner that perhaps endangered the community as a whole. The second was that the Muslims were bound from retaliating against a Muslim in order to take vengeance for the sake of a disbeliever. This proviso was set up to support the idea that the Islamic religion should be the sole link between Muslims and must take precedence over any other kind of relationships. Besides that, security, in contrast to social activities, was a collective accountability, and every single Muslim was tied to the general policy of the State in whatever action he or she might take.[22]

Agreement with the Jews

The Prophet (ﷺ) entered into another pact with the Jews in Madinah. Some of its articles are as follows:[23]

- ❖ Jews are a nation [living] with the Muslims; each group has its own religion and supporters. As for wrongdoers and sinners, they destroy only themselves and their own households.
- ❖ None of them is allowed to leave Madinah without the permission of the Prophet Muhammad (ﷺ).
- ❖ Each group must give support to the other when entering into war, and they should exchange advice and offer assistance for the wronged party. They must bring help against those who break into Yathrib [later to be known as Madinah], and each group is invited to make peace with the allies of the other party, with the exception of those who fight the religion, and every group has to meet its share of the expenses.
- ❖ The area inside the boundaries of [Madinah] is inviolable for the people of this treaty. Any crime that might occur between the people of this pact, the result of which is feared to be detrimental, should be referred to Allah and the Prophet Muhammad (ﷺ).
- ❖ This pact [between us Muslims and the Jews] produces neither wrongs nor sins.
- ❖ Anyone who leaves [Madinah] is safe and so are those who stay there, except those who act unjustly or commit a sin. Allah, as well as Muhammad the Messenger of Allah (ﷺ), guarantee that for whoever fulfils [his or her obligations].

Al-Qâsim ibn Sallâm traced this treaty back to the time of the arrival of the Prophet (ﷺ) in Madinah.[24] That was before the demand of the *jizyah* poll tax[25] was required from the People of the

Book.[26] The Jews who had joined in an alliance with the Arab tribes in Madinah supported the agreement. As for the three great Jewish clans, Banu Qaynuqâ‘, Banu an-Naḍeer, and Banu Quraydhah, they allied with the Prophet (ﷺ) at a later date, but the text of their pacts was not recorded by the chroniclers, although they were thought to be similar to the aforementioned items.[27]

The treaty demonstrated that belonging to different religions was not a barrier to obtaining the rights of citizenship in Madinah. The Prophet (ﷺ) was inspired to recognize and share in the humanity of all people, disbelievers included, in tackling their questions fairly. By combining this vital tool with his clear discipline for administration, expressing equity when dealing with the internal security of Madinah and parity in dealing with the affairs of Madinah's inhabitants, including the Jews, was achievable. The Jewish residents had been strongly tied to the State and would have their needs and concerns addressed on a basis of mutual assistance. They would retain their right to resort to their own tribunals concerning their personal issues, although they were also allowed to present their cases before the Prophet (ﷺ). As for the general circumstances that affected the State as a whole, the Jews were to be equal with the other groups of citizens in yielding to the higher judicial power.[28]

Multi-religious society

In the period immediately following the Muslims' arrival in Madinah, the relationship between the Prophet (ﷺ) and the Jews was tolerable. He dealt with them respectfully as they followed a divinely-revealed religion, and he hoped that they would recognise the signs in their own Book about his prophethood in order to eventually accept his mission.

At the same time, the Jews planned to entice the Prophet (ﷺ) into acknowledging their manner of practicing religion.[29] They seemed captured by their own personal interests and were possibly led to unify their powers with those of the Muslims in order to ultimately realise their dream of ruling the Arabs. Indeed, as Ibn Hishâm mentioned, one reason that the people of Madinah had been more receptive to embracing Islam was that they heard from their Jewish neighbours something that stimulated them to investigate the Prophet (ﷺ) and adhere to his invitation:

> This is the time for an anticipated prophet to appear. We (Jews) will follow him and participate with him in killing you (pagans) in the same manner (as the) killing of the 'Âd and Iram (people, which completely destroyed them).[30]

So, while the Prophet (ﷺ) dealt with the Jews strategically and honestly, their response was tactical in nature. Once they realised their failure to obtain their aims and discovered that Islam is a religion open to all which differs completely from their isolated belief and that its following was growing among the people, they started planning to break their obligations to the Prophet (ﷺ) and destroy Islam in a variety of ways that will be discussed later.

This initial agreement by the two parties, however, was probably the first document in Arabic and Islamic history to establish the pillars for a State, set the population free from tribal concepts and promote the State as a united and integrated entity. The benefits of each group's contributions were shared equally in the society. Islam was the religion that guaranteed this achievement, promoted equality between individuals, and guided their relationships. Still, as a multi-religious society, all parties held equal responsibility for preserving the existence of the State and for preserving their own religious identities. In addition, the religious minorities had the right to tackle their personal issues within the framework of their religions. Hence, although the aim was to integrate them with the Islamic State, each had also preserved the elements of their own identity.

Securing the surrounding area

The aforementioned pacts played a great role in protecting Madinah internally and in bringing its inhabitants to a common objective of security and peace. Despite the dissimilarity between the factors that motivated the forming of the agreements, Madinah enjoyed the benefits of the treaties for some time. This situation allowed the Prophet (ﷺ) to begin securing the surrounding area. He (ﷺ) ordered his followers to take a census of the Muslims in Madinah so that he could assess his armed forces. The majority of the inhabitants were Muslims and the number liable for military service was fifteen hundred.[31] For that time, this was a remarkable figure and it made an equal impact on Muslims and non-Muslims.

The Muslims realised that they possessed significant power in this area, news of which spread. Still, the Prophet (ﷺ) prevented his followers from walking about alone at night through fear that they might be exposed to treachery.[32] Even he himself expected to become a target. His wife 'Â'ishah (رضي الله عنها) narrated: «The Prophet (ﷺ) once suffered insomnia and said: May a righteous man of my Companions guard me tonight. After a short time, we heard the clang of a sword. He asked: Who is that? [Sa'd (رضي الله عنه) said]: It is I, O Messenger of Allah; I came to guard you. Then the Prophet (ﷺ) slept.»[33]

This caution was before Allah revealed the noble verse:

﴾Allah will protect you [Muhammad] from mankind.﴿ *(Qur'an 5: 67)*

This verse offered the Prophet (ﷺ) some relief on two separate fronts. The first was in Madinah, as in addition to Jews and pagans, Madinah was also home to a group that is known in Islamic history as the 'hypocrites'. Their perilous effect upon Islamic society was disguised by the fact that they appeared to follow the teachings of Islam, while they subtly mocked the Prophet (ﷺ) and the Muslims and worked to thwart the Islamic mission. Allah the Almighty exposed them to His Messenger (ﷺ), and the Noble Qur'an warned of them and their aims in many verses. Nevertheless, the Prophet (ﷺ) took no negative action against them due to their outward Islamic appearance and out of fear of being criticised by his enemies for killing his 'followers'.[34] The maximum punishment he imposed on them was that, on one occasion, he commanded that a few of them be thrown out of his mosque.[35] Ibn Hishâm mentioned a number of the hypocrites by name, along with relevant information about their hypocrisy.[36]

The second front related to the Quraysh and the pagans of Makkah. They had failed to hinder the Prophet (ﷺ) and his followers from emigrating to Madinah, but their failure did not impede their endeavours to exterminate the Muslims. There is little information available concerning any specific danger from the Quraysh at this point in time; however, Abu Dâwood cited a narration about a communication between the strongmen of Quraysh and the famous hypocrite in Madinah, 'Abdullâh ibn Ubay, who might have ascended into a position of great authority in Madinah if the immigration had not occurred.

In this communication, the Quraysh blamed 'Abdullâh ibn Ubay and the people of Madinah for offering help to the Muslims and issued threats to attack and kill them and violate the females among them, if they did not declare war against the Muslims and throw them out of their territory. In response to this threat and probably as an outlet for his rage against the Prophet (ﷺ), whom 'Abdullâh believed had deprived him of sovereignty, he gathered together his supporters to implement the demands of the Quraysh. When the Prophet (ﷺ) became acquainted with these plans, he wisely defused it by reminding the prospective combatants that if they fought their own people, they would kill their own children and relatives. The Prophet's comments caused them to disperse.[37]

This event clearly reflected that the Quraysh were not willing to stop antagonizing the Prophet (ﷺ) and the Muslims. Following the immigration, the people of Makkah viewed Madinah as a hostile region. While the residents of Madinah used to visit Makkah freely, the people of Madinah now began seeking protection prior to entering Makkah.

Bukhari cited an occurrence concerning Sa'd ibn Mu'âdh (رضي الله عنه), who was one of the believers of Madinah, and Umayyah ibn Khalaf, who was one of the prominent pagans in Makkah. These two had been friends since before the rise of Islam and used to visit each other. Sa'd (رضي الله عنه) went to make *'umrah*, the minor pilgrimage, and asked his friend to allow him some quiet time to go around the Ka'bah in worship. When Abu Jahl, one of the strongmen in Makkah, found out about him, he exclaimed, "(Do) you circumambulate safely around the Sacred House while you sheltered (our) apostatising people and helped them! Had Umayyah not given you protection, you would not have returned intact!" Sa'd replied angrily, "Truly by Allah, if you prevent me from this, I will prevent you from what is more important to you than it, and that is your way through Madinah."[38] Sa'd was referring to the commercial passage to Syria, which was important for Makkan trade. Therefore, if there were a silent truce from the Qurayshi side, it was because of this strategic point.

The Prophet (ﷺ) was attentive to these happenings and to the possibility that the Quraysh might ally with the tribes around Madinah in order to attack the Islamic State. To show power, he (ﷺ) started sending out large troops just twelve months after his arrival in Madinah.[39] On certain expeditions he (ﷺ) led the troops himself. In the process, the Prophet (ﷺ) also established some non-aggression pacts with outlying tribes, such as occurred on marches to Waddân[40] and al-'Ushayrah,[41] to guarantee the security of the surrounding area and protect the people, at least from any prospective battle with the Quraysh. This was a crucial step prior to directing any attention towards affairs with the Quraysh. One of these peace agreements stated:

> In the name of Allah, Most Gracious, Most Merciful. This is a letter from Muhammad the Messenger of Allah to Bani Ḍamrah. Security is guaranteed to their properties and their lives. In addition, the Muslims will help them against those who oppose them unless they fight the religion of Allah, and they are also expected to respond to the Prophet (ﷺ) positively if he asks them for their help.[42]

Following this stage, the Prophet (ﷺ) sent at least five detachments to oppose the interests of Quraysh.[43] This targeting of Quraysh was due to two reasons. For one thing, Makkah was in an important location and was home to the Ka'bah, which provided it with a distinct social and religious position. Subduing the Quraysh was important for Muslims in order to return Allah's Sacred House to monotheistic control and spread the Islamic Mission. In addition, other Arabs were deferential to the Quraysh, so winning the struggle against them meant winning the struggle against the Arabs.

The second reason was that the Prophet (ﷺ) and his emigrant followers had left their properties behind for the sake of their religion, so the Quraysh were the cause of them losing their possessions. Thus, attacking the Quraysh's commercial caravans provided the opportunity to regain some of their lost property. However, in one of these operations, fighting began by Muslims that resulted in the killing and capture of many. The Prophet (ﷺ) condemned such actions, for he had not ordered his group to act in that way.[44]

CHAPTER SEVEN

The Struggle

The battle of Badr

The Quraysh had come to a clear recognition of the risk to its commercial activities, especially trade with Syria because that trade route led past the boundaries of Madinah. So, they increased the number of guards in their caravans and took extra precautions when they were within the scope of the Muslim dominion.

During Ramadan in the second year after Hijrah,[1] the Prophet (ﷺ) received information that a huge caravan, consisting of one thousand camels, was returning to Makah loaded with the entire funds of the Qurayshi merchants.[2] He (ﷺ) encouraged his followers to emerge and overtake the caravan so that Allah the Almighty might enable them to take it as booty.[3] Fighting was not anticipated in this movement, so less than three hundred and twenty Muslims joined in the expedition with light weapons.[4]

Abu Sufyân was in charge of the caravan and he was fully aware that the Muslims might attack it. Once he realised that his train was in danger, he sent someone to Makkah to warn its people of the problem and urge them to hurry to rescue their wealth.[5] Then, he changed direction and increased the speed of the caravan[6] in order to escape from the pursuing Muslims. As the caravan included property belonging to the majority of the people of Makkah, they all hurried to protect it, and a troop of around one thousand warriors set out for Madinah.

Abu Sufyân managed to escape with the caravan and asked the Qurayshi forces to withdraw. However, Abu Jahl decided to continue to Badr, an annual market for the Arabs, and remain there for three days to display their triumph and powerful army. This was not only to deter the Muslims but also to gain reverential awe from the other Arabs.[7]

The Prophet (ﷺ) consulted his Companions about the next step, since their venture had come to an unexpected end and there was some fear that the Qurayshi army might chose to march on Madinah. The Companions all offered their service and their lives for his support, upon which he directed his followers towards Badr, informing them of Allah's promise of winning either by capturing the booty or earning the rewards of a struggle fought for the cause of Allah against the polytheists.[8]

The Muslim troops reached the battlefield first. They organised pools for their water and built a headquarters for the Prophet (ﷺ) to oversee the battle. He (ﷺ) employed an unusual tactic in arraying his warriors in lines instead of adopting the attack and retreat method of fighting used by the Arabs.[9] This tactic enabled the Prophet (ﷺ) to control his troops and provide strong support for his army, by keeping the reserves for critical positions.[10] In addition, he directed his followers to avoid misusing their arrows and to release them only when the pagans were very close.[11] It was narrated that the Prophet (ﷺ) threw a fistful of pebbles at the pagans, a point which was referred to in the Noble Qur'an:

﴾You killed them not, but Allah killed them. And you [Muhammad] threw not when you threw, but Allah threw, that He might test the believers by a fair trial from Him. Verily, Allah is All-Hearing, All-Knowing.﴿ *(Qur'an 8: 17)*

The flare-up

On the seventeenth of Ramadan in the second year of Hijrah, around the 15th of March 624 CE, the Battle of Badr broke out between the two sides. Before and during this battle, the Prophet (ﷺ) continuously prayed to Allah, seeking His assistance. At the same time, he (ﷺ) utilised every beneficial strategy to assure a victory for his troops, thus teaching us about the necessity of taking the required actions in our affairs and then relying on Allah. In the Noble Qur'an and the Hadith, there are many indications that angelical aids operated in this decisive battle. The following examples are from the Qur'an:

﴾[Remember] when you sought help of your Lord and He answered you [saying]: I will help you with a thousand of the angels each behind the other [following one another] in succession. Allah made it only as glad tidings and that your hearts thereby might be at rest; and there is no victory except from Allah. Verily, Allah is All-Mighty, All-Wise.﴿ *(Qur'an 8: 9-10)*

﴾[Remember] when your Lord revealed to the angels: Verily, I am with you, so make those who have believed stand firm. I will cast terror into the hearts of those who have disbelieved, so strike them over the neck and smite off every fingertip of them.﴿ *(Qur'an 8: 12)*

Among the hadiths reported about this incident, Bukhari narrated an inquiry made by the angel Jibreel (ﷺ) to the Prophet (ﷺ) about the consideration of those who had fought in the Battle of Badr. The Prophet (ﷺ) commented that «they are the best Muslims», and Jibreel (ﷺ) said the same about the angels who presented at the battle, too.[12] Bukhari also reported that the

Prophet (ﷺ) said on the day of Badr: «This is Jibreel gripping his horse and putting on the apparatus of war.»[13]

Thus, Allah the Almighty supported his Prophet (ﷺ) and those who believed in his Message. This support actually underlies the great victory of the Prophet (ﷺ). The fighting lasted for one day only. Despite the facts that the Muslims did not come to the field intending to wage war, nor did they represent their actual power, nor had they been supplied with the full equipment necessary in such circumstances, and that the number of their soldiers was one third that of their enemy, they won a glorious victory. They killed seventy of the pagans, including some of their insolent leaders, and captured seventy, winning great booty from them with the loss of only fourteen lives on their own side.[14]

The pagans fled and the Muslims divided into three categories: one surrounded the Prophet (ﷺ) in order to guard him lest the pagans returned; the second pursued the pagans; and the third collected the booty.[15] The Prophet (ﷺ) sent glad tidings of the victory to Madinah, and along with his followers, stayed in Badr for three more days to bury the bodies[16] and give his soldiers the chance to rest.

Prisoners

The internees were treated in various ways. Two of them, who had been cruelly abusing the Muslims since the early stages in Makkah and who were anticipated to persist their fight against the Islamic religion, were killed;[17] their names were an-Niḍr ibn al-Ḥârith and 'Uqbah ibn Abi Mu'ayṭ. The rest were taken to Madinah, and the Prophet (ﷺ) conferred with his followers regarding their treatment. Abu Bakr (رضي الله عنه) preferred to release them in return for a ransom because of their domestic relations with the Muslims, but 'Umar ibn al-Khaṭṭâb (ﷺ) wanted to deter the enemies from aggression against Muslims and suggested that they be killed instead. The Prophet (ﷺ) inclined towards the view of Abu Bakr, which was admonished in the Noble Qur'an in the following verses:

﴾It is not for a prophet that he should have prisoners of war [and free them with ransom] until he had made a great slaughter [among his enemies] in the land. You desire the good of this world [and the money of ransom for freeing the captives], but Allah desires [for you the good of] the hereafter; and Allah is All-Mighty, All-Wise. Were it not a previous ordainment from Allah, a severe torment would have touched you for what you took. So enjoy what you have gotten of booty in war, lawful and good, and be afraid of Allah. Certainly, Allah is Oft-Forgiving, Most Merciful.﴿ *(Qur'an 8: 67-69)*

This criticism, though, occurred at the outset of Islam, when the Muslims had not yet achieved full authority in the land. 'Alâ' ad-Deen as-Samarqandi clarified how the leader of the Muslims has the choice of killing the warriors or enslaving them — except for the women and children who must not be killed but enslaved — and he had no right to give them their liberty.[18] However, in this case, the Prophet (ﷺ) either accepted a ransom for each of the captives or stipulated that they should teach the rules of writing to ten Anṣâri children.[19] As for the booty, it was distributed equally among the soldiers; nine of the Companions, who had not participated in the battle because the Prophet (ﷺ) had permitted them to remain in Madinah or elsewhere for some reason;[20] and the families of the casualties.[21]

News of the battle spread all over the Arabian Peninsula and evoked various reactions. The Quraysh decided to stop mourning for their casualties lest they cause the Muslims to rejoice at the misfortunes that they suffered, and they slowed down in ransoming their prisoners lest the Muslims heighten their demands.[22] At the same time, a famous man from Quraysh named Ṣafwân ibn Umayyah surreptitiously instigated 'Umayr ibn Wahb to take vengeance by killing the Prophet (ﷺ), provided that Ṣafwân took responsibility for his debts and children. The intended murderer sneaked into Madinah, and when he went to the mosque to find the Prophet (ﷺ) and execute his plan, the Prophet (ﷺ) asked him to approach him and explain the reason why he had come to Madinah. He fabricated a story, but the Prophet (ﷺ) informed him that he knew about his agreement with Ṣafwân. The matter so impressed the intended murderer and attested to the veracity of Muhammad's prophethood that it caused him to embrace Islam![23]

The Quraysh also ransomed back from the tribe of Liḥyân two Muslims that they held captive and beheaded them in order to avenge those killed in battle.[24] As for the Jews, they were disappointed at the Muslims' victory and vented their rage in various ways. They commented upon the event by saying that the Quraysh lacked experience in war. They also showed signs of breaking their pact with the Prophet (ﷺ).[25] At this point, the Prophet (ﷺ) gathered the Jewish tribes in the marketplace at Banu Qaynuqâ' and warned them that they would suffer the same fate as the Quraysh if they continued to ignore what their scriptures foretold about him, and he urged them to convert to Islam. Their answer to him was:

> You think us just like your people! Do not be deceived with winning the fight against people who have no knowledge (or experience) of war. If you fight against us you would realise that we are the men![26]

This attitude resulted, as we will see, in their eventual evacuation from Madinah. As far as the Muslims were concerned, the battle tested their true allegiance to Islam at the cost of their tribal and family relations. They encountered their fathers and brothers on the battlefield and did not hesitate to ignore their blood ties to fight them since they were opposing Islam. Based on this fact, the participants of this battle occupied a distinctive position throughout history,[27] in addition to the pride they felt at their triumph and their conviction of the support of Allah, which raised their morale.

Lessons of Badr

The Battle of Badr was a turning-point in the early history of Islam. From the events that transpired, many lessons can be learned:

❖ Despite the fact that the Muslims were motivated by having lost their property in Makkah and that they planned to replace it in some way by capturing the caravan, Allah the Almighty declared that their true success lay not in capturing the booty, but in fighting the battle which He had chosen for them. He diverted their attention from transient achievements, like material goods, towards the realisation that jihad, the struggle to make Islam supreme, was morally more important than simply capturing the caravan. This fact made a powerful impact on the souls of the Muslims and on the Qurayshi people and the other Arabs as well.

❖ The Prophet (ﷺ) consulted his followers about the war prior to deciding to engage in it, as well as consulting them about the handling of the prisoners. This consultation reflects the significance of utilising consultation in dealing with not only public and general issues but also personal matters.

- After seeking advice, the ruler is the one who makes the final decision concerning a war. Thus, even after conferring with advisors, especially in regard to jihad and securing a safe environment for Muslims to practice their faith, it is not obligatory for a leader to follow their advice. Their counsel plays an advisory role, and then the governing ruler must examine the different ideas and select the one that is closer, according to his understanding, to the religious approach represented in both the Noble Qur'an and the Prophet's Hadith.[28]
- This task of going to battle fell upon the Muslims during the month of Ramadan when Muslims are fasting. This shows that Ramadan should not be an occasion for slackness or laziness. Thus, fasting should not be an excuse for idleness.
- If it is determined that the Prophet (ﷺ) tackled the matter as a prophet, then the manner he adopted is binding to Muslims forever; however, if he dealt with the matter as an ordinary man or a ruler, separate from his prophethood, then adhering to his method of treating that particular point is not compulsory. Still, when the Prophet (ﷺ) made misjudged decisions as a man, he was usually corrected by Allah the Almighty in revelation in the Noble Qur'an.

Encounters

The glorious victory of the Muslims at Badr caused great concern among the groups situated near to the Qurayshi commercial caravan routes to Syria. They foresaw risks to their own interests if the trade route were blocked, risks that were similar to those which the Quraysh worried about. Trade was the Quraysh's main and perhaps only skill, and hence its lifeline. It was natural for such common fears to inspire efforts to destroy the Islamic control of the route.

The tribes of Sulaym and Ghaṭafân were examples of injured parties who planned to invade Madinah following the Battle of Badr.[29] They probably hoped to exploit the fact that the Muslims were still weary from battle in order to achieve their goals. The Prophet (ﷺ) was aware of such perils and kept a close eye on what was happening in that area. As soon as he became acquainted with the plan, he led some troops, no longer than seven days after his arrival back in Madinah, to a place known as al-Kudr,[30] which was situated on the eastern commercial route between Makkah and Syria. The crowds which had gathered to attack quickly disappeared, however, once they learned of the advance of the Muslims, and they left their camels behind, which were easily captured by the Muslims. The Prophet (ﷺ) remained in that area for three days and then returned to Madinah.[31]

Another foray occurred that was known as Dhi Amar. The Prophet (ﷺ) sent out a party to address the tribes in Najd who had gathered their troops to attack the Islamic region, but the enemy vanished prior to the Prophet's (ﷺ) arrival at their site.[32] The Prophet (ﷺ) led three hundred soldiers[33] until he reached a watering place called Dhi Amr in the direction of al-Furu'. There was no apparent reason for this military manoeuvre other than strengthening the siege on the trade route of the Quraysh, as this place was situated between Makkah and Syria. There was no fighting, the Muslims encountered no enemies, and they stayed there for more than a month before returning to Madinah.[34]

As for the Quraysh, they felt insulted and sought to regain their dignity by looking for an alternative trade route and by attacking Madinah. Abu Sufyân, who had been the overseer of the Qurayshi caravan and thus unable to participate in the Battle of Badr, swore not to take a bath until he had invaded Madinah. In order to keep this oath, he mustered two hundred combatants, camped in an area close to Madinah, and sent a squad of soldiers to a suburb known as al-'Urayḍ where they burned several palm trees and killed two peasants. As soon as the news reached the Prophet (ﷺ), he set off in pursuit of Abu Sufyân. The invading troops were successful in escaping at the cost of abandoning a huge amount of fine flour that they carried for their nourishment, and this was taken as booty.[35]

The Quraysh did find a new route for their trade that might release them from the grip of the Muslims. They decided that they would travel along the road to Iraq instead of directly to Syria. This plan proved successful, and they authorised Abu Sufyân to administer a caravan which was loaded with a great amount of silver. However, the Prophet (ﷺ) discovered the plan and directed a brigade led by Zayd ibn Ḥârithah to frustrate the policy and acquire the merchandise. In a place called al-Qaradah in the region of Najd, the Quraysh fled from Zayd and his soldiers and left behind their entire load, estimated to have been worth 100,000 dirhams,[36] which was then taken by the Muslims.[37]

These events occurred at the end of the second year of Hijrah and the beginning of the third, or sometime between March and December of 624 CE. The Quraysh failed utterly on both of their attempts to thwart the Muslims and lost many of their possessions and riches during this period following the Battle of Badr. Thus, they became even more resolved to gain vengeance for the defeat at Badr and recover dignity and significance amongst the Arabs.

CHAPTER EIGHT

Defence: The Battle of Uḥud

Qurayshi preparation

Following the Battle of Badr, the Quraysh reviewed the causes of their losses and began thinking of diving into a decisive campaign against the Muslims to put an end to their problems once and for all. To this cause, they resolved to dedicate the proceeds of their mercantile caravan that had escaped just before the Battle of Badr,[1] and they set out to fight. The battle which eventually ensued was called the Battle of Uḥud after the place where it occurred in the month of Shawwâl in the third year after Hijrah, or in March or April of 625 CE.

Although the Prophet (ﷺ) was aware that the Quraysh would try to attack, there is no sound evidence that he had knowledge of the details of their plans.[2] However, previous events supported the idea that an attack would come and likely happen sometime soon. The Quraysh gathered their forces and their allies in the tribes of Kinânah and Tihâmah to wage war against the Muslims. In order to keep their ardour kindled and to prevent them from absconding, they brought along their women to prod them on.[3] They amassed three thousand warriors, seven hundred of whom were armoured, and two hundred horses.[4]

Preparations of the Muslims

The Muslims discovered that the pagans had arrived and halted at Uḥud, a place near Madinah. Immediately, the Prophet (ﷺ) began discussing battle tactics with his Companions and gathering his army. He (ﷺ) inclined towards remaining inside Madinah and fortifying the city, so that they could make use of its lanes, which were unfamiliar to the enemy, for fighting and the housetops for hurling arrows and stones.[5] In addition, this would enable all of the inhabitants, including the women and children, to participate in the battle.[6]

The majority of Muslims who had not participated in the Battle of Badr, however, insisted on leaving Madinah to meet their enemies where they were encamped. This position was supported by the Anṣâr, in fulfilment of the treaty they made with the Prophet (ﷺ) in the Second 'Aqabah Allegiance since they felt that they would have been in breach of this treaty if they remained in Madinah. Most of the emigrants also deemed it their responsibility to defend Madinah from the outside to lessen the damage to the city. In addition, people felt that staying inside Madinah might allow the pagans to lay a prolonged siege, which was considered risky and could have other consequences.[7]

The Prophet (ﷺ) eventually adopted the view that the pagan army should be faced outside of the city, and he donned his armour in preparation of it, while his followers felt guilty for refusing his approach. To address the situation, they sent the Prophet's uncle Ḥamzah to tell him to do whatever he thought right, but he showed them the exigency of his resolve when he replied: «If a prophet puts on his armour, he should not take it off until he fights.»[8]

He (ﷺ) chose the night to lead his troops to the site where the Quraysh had camped and used a road that circumvented the invaders.[9] His forces were smaller than that of the Quraysh in terms of both number of warriors and armament. Of the thousand Muslims, only a hundred were armoured, and there were only two horses and a few women to nurse the troops.[10] The Prophet (ﷺ) inspected the soldiers and sent back the youths who were under fifteen years of age.[11] The number was further reduced when the hypocrite 'Abdullâh ibn Ubay betrayed the Muslims midway and withdrew with his supporters, who were a third of the army.[12] This action resulted in reducing the Muslim combatants to only seven hundred fighters, or four hundred according to certain reports.[13] The actions of the hypocrites nearly caused the army to lose two other groups, Banu Salimah and Banu Ḥârithah, but for the grace of Allah, they decided to remain and support the Muslims.[14] The Anṣâri companions asked the Prophet (ﷺ) to get help from their allies among the Jews, but he replied: «We do not need them.»[15]

In this battle, compared to the one at Badr, the Muslim troops were less than a quarter of the number of the pagan troops, and they had no time to rest before taking to the battlefield, while the opposing forces had been resting at that place for three days prior to the Prophet's (ﷺ) arrival.[16] The Prophet (ﷺ) marshalled his troops into lines, so that their backs were to the mountains, and ordered them not to start fighting until he gave the command to do so. He positioned fifty sharpshooting archers on a rear hill, bidding them not to leave it under any circumstances, whether the Muslims were victorious or defeated.

The combat

Intense warfare flared up between the two sides on Saturday morning, the 15th of Shawwâl 3 H. It resulted in fatalities on both sides, including Ḥamzah (رضي الله عنه), the uncle of the Prophet (ﷺ).[17]

After a short period, however, the Muslims gained a noticeable victory. The pagans fled from the battlefield, and it became easy for the Muslims to collect the booty. When the Muslim archers, who had been charged with defending their backs from the hill, witnessed the scene, they decided to descend from the hill, neglecting the directions of the Prophet (ﷺ), lest they be beaten to the spoils![18] In doing so, they committed a huge strategic mistake. The pagan leaders noticed the hill, now empty of them, and decided to detour around the Muslims to shock them by a sudden attack from behind.

The Muslims were completely surprised by the new assault and so confused that they even killed some of their own people by mistake.[19] The balance now tipped entirely in favour of the pagans who were in a good position to smite the Muslims.[20] Moreover, the pagans managed to reach the Prophet himself (ﷺ), and in their fight against him, they broke his tooth, split his lip and wounded his forehead and cheek.[21] They then shouted aloud that they had killed him, which had a further negative impact upon the Muslims. Some of the Muslim forces were so perplexed that they sought to gain protection from 'Abdullâh ibn Ubay[22] who had withdrawn from the troops midway; but a few Muslims, thought to be twelve, including some women,[23] either surrounded the Prophet (ﷺ) to guard him or sacrificed themselves in return for his life, and a few others defied death boldly and continued fighting against the pagans. They bravely opposed Quraysh, who failed to achieve a peremptory triumph and left the field without captives or spoils, realizing that they had failed to kill any prominent Muslim, particularly the Prophet (ﷺ). Their only achievement was a sense of the revenge they had exacted for the Battle of Badr.[24]

Even so, this battle, in some aspects, was considered as a debacle for the Muslims for several reasons. First, the Muslims had insisted on leaving Madinah to catch the enemy outside the city limits. This point is not deemed responsible for the defeat. Still, the Prophet (ﷺ) would have liked his warriors to entrench themselves inside of Madinah, but this was a very sensitive issue for them, and they failed to see that emotional motives should be put aside in decisive matters. The other reason was the marksmen's lack of obedience to the Prophet's instructions and the fact that they rushed onto the battlefield in order to get their share of the booty. Although this too was an emotional point, it also reflected an unheeded notion of the lesson of the previous battle, that at Badr, Allah the Almighty preferred for them to fight rather than capture the caravan. Thus, the temporary motive of material gain at Uḥud caused the sorrowful end of the struggle that resulted in the death[25] and mutilation[26] of seventy Muslims.

Abu Sufyân withdrew the Qurayshi army from the battlefield and shouted out for the Muslims to meet them in the coming year for their next battle to take place at Badr, an offer which was accepted by the Prophet (ﷺ).[27] Following the pagans' departure, the Prophet (ﷺ) directed his cousin 'Ali (رضي الله عنه) to follow them to find out whether they intended to proceed towards Madinah or return to Makkah so that he might tackle the situation accordingly. He found that they were heading for Makkah,[28] and that matter allowed the Muslims to bury their dead before they returned to Madinah.

Pursuing the Quraysh

On the day following the end of the battle, information reached the Prophet (ﷺ) that the Quraysh were reproaching each other for not exploiting Muslim weaknesses to gain a real victory over them. Despite the fact that the Muslims were wounded and wearied from warfare, the Prophet (ﷺ) prevented those who had not contributed to combat from pursuing pagan Quraysh.[29] He and his Companions who had participated in the battle chased the Qurayshi troops until they reached an area known as Ḥamrâ' al-Asad.[30] Aṭ-Ṭabari justified this action on the basis that the Prophet (ﷺ) intended to dismay his enemies and show them that the Muslim army was unaffected by their lack of substantial victory and still able to run after them.[31] The step was effective. While the pagans were considering a return to Madinah to uproot the Muslims, they received news that they were being followed, and they quickened their pace to escape from it.[32] In addition, the action informed other people, both inside and outside Madinah, of the Muslim's power, lest anyone try to profiteer from their setback in the battle.

Divine solace

After this battle, Allah the Almighty consoled the Prophet (ﷺ) and the Muslims in the following Qur'anic verses:

﴿Muhammad is no more than a Messenger, and indeed [many] Messengers have passed away before him. If he dies or is killed, will you then turn back on your heels [as disbelievers]? He who turns back on his heels, not the least harm will he do to Allah; and Allah will give reward to those who are grateful. No person can ever die except by Allah's leave and at an appointed term. Whoever desires a reward in [this] world, We shall give him of it; and whoever desires a reward in the hereafter, We shall give him of it; and We shall reward the grateful. And many a prophet [from among the prophets of Allah] fought [in Allah's cause] and along with them [fought] large bands of religious learned men; but they never lost heart for that which befell them in Allah's way, nor did they weaken nor degrade themselves; and Allah loves the ones who are patient [and steadfast]. And they said nothing but: Our

Lord! Forgive us our sins and our transgressions [in keeping our duties to You], establish our feet firmly, and give us victory over the disbelieving folk. So Allah gave them the reward of this world, and the excellent reward of the hereafter; and Allah loves those who do good. O you who believe! If you obey those who disbelieve, they will send you back on your heels, and you will turn back [from the Faith] as losers. Nay, Allah is your Patron [Lord and Protector], and He is the best of helpers. We shall cast terror into the hearts of those who disbelieve because they joined others in worship with Allah, for which He had sent no authority. Their abode will be the Fire and how evil is the abode of the wrongdoers [polytheists]. And Allah did indeed fulfil His promise to you when you were killing them [your enemy] with His permission, until [the moment] you lost your courage and fell to disputing about the order, and disobeyed after He showed you [of the booty] which you love. Among you are some that desire this world and some that desire the hereafter. Then He made you flee from them [your enemy], that He might test you; but surely, He forgave you, and Allah is Most Gracious to the believers. When you ran away without even casting a side glance at anyone, and the Messenger [Muhammad] was in the rear calling you back. There did Allah give you one distress after another by way of requital to teach you not to grieve for that which had escaped you, nor for that which had befallen you; and Allah is Well-Aware of all that you do. Then after the distress, He sent down security upon you. Slumber overtook a party of you, while another party was thinking about themselves [as how to save their own selves, ignoring the others and the Prophet] and thought wrongly of Allah — the thought of ignorance. They said: Have we any part in the affair? Say [O Muhammad]: Indeed the affair belongs wholly to Allah. They hide within themselves what they dare not reveal to you, saying: If we had anything to do with the affair, none of us would have been killed here. Say: Even if you had remained in your homes, those for whom death was decreed would certainly have gone forth to the place of their death, but that Allah might test what is in your breasts and purify that which was in your hearts [of sins]; and Allah is All-Knower of what is in [your] breasts. Those of you who turned back on the day the two hosts met [at the battle of Uḥud], it was Shayṭân [Satan] who caused them to backslide [and run away from the battlefield] because of some [sins] they had earned; but Allah, indeed, has forgiven them. Surely, Allah is Oft-Forgiving, Most Forbearing. O you who believe! Be not like those who disbelieve [like the hypocrites] and who say to their brethren when they travel through the earth or go out to fight: If they had stayed with us, they would not have died or been killed, so that Allah may make it a cause of regret in their hearts. It is Allah that gives life and causes death; and Allah is All-Seeing of what you do. If you are killed or die in the way of Allah, forgiveness and mercy from Allah are far better than all that they amass [of worldly wealth]; and whether you die or are killed, verily, unto Allah you shall be gathered. By the mercy of Allah, you dealt with them gently. Had you been severe and harsh-hearted, they would have broken away from about you; so pass over [their faults] and ask [Allah's] forgiveness for them; and consult them in the affairs. Then when you have taken a decision, put your trust in Allah. Certainly, Allah loves those who put their trust [in Him]. If Allah helps you, none can overcome you; and if He forsakes you, who is there after Him that can help you? And in Allah [alone] let believers put their trust.》 *(Qur'an 3: 144-160)*

Cause of defeat

The above verses pointed out that the core reason for the Muslim's defeat was their sins. If they look for victory, they should keep themselves from wrongdoing, and that is the secret of obtaining Allah's help. Disobeying the Prophet (ﷺ) is a great sin, but contradictory to the military mentality, these verses declare forgiveness for those who caused the defeat and instruct the Prophet (ﷺ) to seek Allah's mercy for them. They also remind the Prophet (ﷺ) to refer to consulting the Muslims and then depend on Allah. The Prophet (ﷺ) had fulfilled this in regard to the Battle of Uḥud; however, he (ﷺ) had also responded to the insistence of his followers and accepted their view even though it was opposed to his own inclination of what was best.

Lessons of Uḥud

A number of points came to light from these occurrences regarding the Battle of Uḥud:

- ❖ The Prophet (ﷺ) affirmed the need for a leader to consult advisors when he (ﷺ) discussed the whole situation with his Companions. Once the inclinations of the Companions were towards meeting their enemies outside of Madinah, the Prophet (ﷺ) put on his armour. He (ﷺ) showed determination when he refused to retreat and adopt his original position of defending Madinah from within. This unflinching stance was essential for steering the Muslims clear of any weakness or hesitation. Hence, upon facing the need to make a decision, consultation and then resolute steadfastness in implementing the chosen course of action are two of the main deduced teachings from these events.
- ❖ It is also important to overcome any sort of confusion, especially during crucial moments, in order to keep the means of success steady. While this lesson is drawn out from the withdrawal of 'Abdullâh ibn Ubay and his three hundred

supporters as they were advancing to the battlefield, another example of this is the sacrifice which the Muslims readily made for the sake of their religion.

- Seeking help from non-Muslims in battle is a matter of debate among scholars. Many of them disallow it, based on a saying of the Prophet (ﷺ): «We do not seek help from a polytheist.»[33]

  On the way to the Battle of Uḥud, the Prophet (ﷺ) declined the offer of a group of Jews to join them, even though the Muslims were short in number and the Jews were well-armed and ready to fight. One disbeliever offered to fight first and embrace Islam after the fight, but the Prophet (ﷺ) advised him to change his priorities: to become a Muslim, then to fight. The man responded positively to this idea, declared his conversion, fought, and was killed in the battle. The Prophet (ﷺ) said about him: «He gave little and was recompensed a lot.»[34]

  Imam Shâfi'ee, the great juristic scholar, said that if the leader has a good opinion of some disbelievers in respect to their honesty towards Muslims and there is a need to obtain their help, then it is permissible to seek it, but otherwise not.[35] The question also involves another factor and that is the motive for participating in a war. If a person's intention is to uphold the Religion for the sake of Allah, then if that person is slain, he or she would be considered a martyr.[36]

- It is necessary to avoid mistakes, sins and disobeying of commands in order to ensure victory. The Muslims were few in number compared to the pagans and were not in an ideal state of readiness for war, but even then, they achieved victory as long as they adhered to the instructions of the Prophet (ﷺ). Once some of them disengaged themselves from their duty and were distracted by material wealth, they prejudiced the outcome for all the Muslims. The following Qur'anic verse openly combined victory with obedience and defeat with insubordination:

﴿And Allah did indeed fulfil His promise to you when you were killing them [your enemy] with His permission, until [the moment] you lost your courage and fell to disputing about the order, and disobeyed after He showed you [of the booty] which you love. Among you are some that desire this world and some that desire the hereafter. Then He made you flee from them [your enemy], that He might test you; but surely, He forgave you, and Allah is Most Gracious to the believers.﴾ *(Qur'an 3: 152)*

Many Islamic leaders understood this lesson and used to advise their troops to be wary of all sins. Abu Bakr (رضي الله عنه), the first Islamic caliph, for example, warned the army dispatched to conquer Syria in the Battle of al-Yarmook not to commit sin, since this would be the cause of their defeat, not their small numbers.[37] Similarly, Sa'd ibn Abi Waqqâṣ (رضي الله عنه), the commander of the troops sent to conquer al-Madâ'in, the capital of the Persian Empire, commented that they would not be victorious unless their good deeds outweighed their misdeeds.[38] So, righteousness is the main factor in achieving victory rather than weapons and numbers. If this virtue is abandoned, then both sides will be similar in their sins, and consequently, the triumph will be granted to the side with the superior equipment.

❖ Even if a Muslim commits a great sin, this should not stop him or her from seeking the forgiveness of Allah, as He is the Most Compassionate, the Most Merciful. At Uḥud, Allah the Almighty clearly forgave the sins of the Muslims. So, while Muslims have to avoid committing sins, they must return to Allah immediately to renew their ties with Him whenever they falter.

- The Companions (may Allah be pleased with them) proved that they loved the Prophet (ﷺ) deeply. Their love was the main reason for sacrificing themselves for his sake. Muhammad S. R. al-Booṭi stated in this regard that Allah the Almighty has supplied human beings with intellect in order to reflect on and believe in what should be followed and with hearts to utilise them in loving what pleases Allah. So, if the heart is not occupied with loving Allah, His Messenger (ﷺ) and the pious Muslims, it will be full of loving fancies and forbidden things, and consequently belief without love will not stimulate sacrifice of the soul.[39]
- A martyr is interred in his or her grave without having the ritual washing and shrouding or the special prayer for funerals,[40] in order to manifest the high position of martyrs in Islamic culture.
- To demonstrate Islam's attention to knowledge and show the significance of achieving the rank of a knowledgeable person, the Prophet (ﷺ) gave precedence to interring those who were well-acquainted with the Qur'an over those whose knowledge was less.[41] If the action was thus with the slain, then it is even more worthy for the living to strive to be knowledgeable. Thus, through this act, the Prophet (ﷺ) wanted to persuade the Muslims to fill their lives with learning.
- Women have a role to play in war by performing medical, relief and welfare duties. Female Muslims contributed at the Battle of Uḥud as well as in other battles. During Uḥud, 'Â'ishah, Um Sulaym and Um Saleeṭ (may Allah be pleased with them) carried water and gave it to the wounded to drink,[42] while Fâṭimah (رضي الله عنها) bandaged her father, the Prophet (ﷺ).[43]

CHAPTER NINE

Ramifications of Uhud

Ar-Rajee'

Despite the fact that the Muslim army had pursued the Quraysh and chased them back to Makkah, the general consequences of the battle of Uḥud had stirred a few groups to plan attacks on Madinah. Banu Asad and Banu Hudhayl were among these groups and had gathered their fighters in two different places[1] to open two fronts against the Muslim forces so that they would be decimated and subjected to a straightforward defeat. As the pagan fighters did not appear to scrutinise the situation with care, they were very easily overcome at the hands of the two detachments that were sent to deal with them. They lost a noticeable amount of property and the commander of the Hudhayl group was killed.[2] This event took place sometime in Muḥarram 4 H, which corresponds to June 625 CE.

A month later, another incident occurred which seemed to be a sort of revenge for the previous event. People of the 'Aḍal and Qârah tribes, who had a strong relationship with the Hudhayl, came to the Prophet (ﷺ) pretending to be Muslims. They requested that the Prophet (ﷺ) allow a team of his Companions to accompany them in order to teach them the Noble Qur'an and develop their understanding of Islamic issues. The Prophet (ﷺ)

sent six of his selected followers with them for this purpose.[3] As soon as the group arrived at ar-Rajee', a place close to the Hudhayl region, the pretenders shouted out and called on the Hudhayl for help, who in no time surrounded them and pointed their sabres at them.

Bukhari mentioned that the Prophet (ﷺ) had allowed his Companions to go with them for the purpose of spying on them, as he suspected that their intentions were insincere, but the group was discovered by the Hudhayl and pursued by them.[4] So taking into account all of the narrations, the affair was one of war logic as well as betrayal. When barricaded, the Muslims refused to surrender, as they knew the Hudhayl would hand them over to the Quraysh. The Muslims refused this option and entered into battle, which resulted in the death of all of them but two, who were captured. One of the prisoners managed to escape and fight until he was murdered, but the other was sold to the Quraysh and killed in revenge for those slain in previous battles with the Muslims.[5]

The well of Ma'oonah

An incident similar to that of ar-Rajee' occurred with a large group of Companions, some say forty while others say seventy, who had been sent to Najd at the request of a Bedouin chieftain named Abu Barâ' 'Âmir ibn Mâlik, who had neither embraced Islam nor rejected it. The delegation was about a hundred miles from Madinah when they were encircled by two sections, Ri'l and Dhakwân, who belonged to the tribe of Banu Sulaym. Under these circumstances, the Muslim group was obliged to defend itself, even though their forces were unequal to those of their enemy. They showed extreme courage in fighting but they were all eventually killed, except for one who had been separated from the group when they were attacked; he brought the bad news back to the Prophet (ﷺ).[6]

Bukhari cites a narration that the Bedouin group had asked the Prophet (ﷺ) for help against their enemies. He (ﷺ) supported them with his followers, but they were treacherous towards their Muslim helpers.[7] This narration sounds closer to reality because the Prophet (ﷺ) was not accustomed to sending such a large number of envoys except as a contingent group for something tangible. This occurrence, however, which happened on the 10th of Ṣafar in the year 4 H, or around the 24th of July 625 CE, was known as the incident at the Ma'oonah well, and it caused the Prophet (ﷺ) to invoke Allah against the above two clans of that tribe for a whole month in his dawn prayers.[8]

The appointed battle at Badr

In Sha'bân during the 4th year after the Hijrah, according to Ibn Hishâm,[9] or the month of Dhul Qâ'dah, according to al-Wâqidi,[10] the Prophet (ﷺ) led fifteen hundred of his followers to meet Abu Sufyân and his forces at Badr, in conformity with the time that had been appointed for this meeting after the Battle of Uḥud. However, the Qurayshi troops left Makkah, moved for about twenty-five miles and then accepted Abu Sufyân's justification of the unfitness of that time for war due to drought and they retreated. The Prophet (ﷺ) and his forces stayed at the predetermined site for eight days, then left once it was certain that the Quraysh had withdrawn from the fight.[11] The Quraysh's breach of their appointment, likely influenced by fear of the possible consequences, helped the Muslims to restore their morale which had been affected at the battle of Uḥud.[12]

Raids and attacks

Other minor raids and attacks, which will not be covered in detail in this work, were occurring over this time period in the early history of Islam. Some of the manoeuvres were orchestrated by the Muslim forces as attempts to deal with threats to the Muslim community, provide proactive defence for Madinah, or propagate Islam among the tribes in the Arabian Peninsula. Other attacks were instigated by the disbelievers to take revenge for allies who had been killed by the Muslims in the earlier battles, to weaken or destroy the Muslims, or to assassinate the Prophet (ﷺ). Several of the planned raids, in the end, did not involve any fighting.

Banu al-Muṣṭalaq (al-Muraysi')

Word reached the Prophet (ﷺ) that the Banu al-Muṣṭalaq had mobilised their forces to attack Madinah.[13] Considering this, and the contribution of this tribe to the Battle of Uḥud against the Muslims,[14] the Prophet (ﷺ) took the initiative and gathered groups of his followers in a place that was known as al-Muraysi' and the two sides engaged in bitter conflict. The result was a great victory for the Muslims, whose enemies either became casualties or fugitives and left behind huge spoils, consisting of their women, children and wealth.[15]

Historians differ in their opinions of the date of this incursion. Bukhari stated that some considered it to be in the year 4 H, while others attributed it to the year 6 H,[16] but the historical critics have determined that it most likely happened in Sha'bân of 5 H, or December of 626 CE.[17]

Divisions

A few events arose from this battle, starting with a slight conflict between one of the immigrant Muslim youths and a man from the Anṣâr and a call by both on their respective factions for help. The hypocrites seized the opportunity and developed it into an internal clash between the two Islamic wings: the immigrants and their hosts, the Anṣâr. 'Abdullâh ibn Ubay tried to instigate his supporters to revolt against the Prophet (ﷺ) and said: "Indeed, by God, when we go back to Madinah, the mightiest one will eject the most servile from it."[18]

The Prophet (ﷺ) heard about what had happened, and he redirected his people to the Right Path. He (ﷺ) changed an old Arabic proverb from its narrow circle to reflect an Islamic concept. This proverb had been: "Help your brother, whether he commits injustice or he is wronged." He transformed the nature of this assistance and said to them: «Helping your brother is by preventing him if he commits injustice and giving him support if he is wronged.»[19]

He (ﷺ) advised the people to integrate themselves into a single unity, helping each other to promote justice and prevent inequity.

Although the Prophet (ﷺ) was sure of the positive effect of his teaching, 'Abdullâh ibn Ubay's comment had caused great flurry. 'Umar (رضي الله عنه), the respected Companion of the Prophet (ﷺ), suggested that 'Abdullâh ibn Ubay be sentenced to death sentence, but the Prophet (ﷺ) refused this idea, lest he be thought to be killing his followers. He (ﷺ) instead mobilized his forces to return towards Madinah, rather than resting for a time as usual after battle, and he (ﷺ) involved them in a continuous voyage for the next day and a half, just to occupy them from discussing the comments of 'Abdullâh ibn Ubay.[20] The following verse from the Noble Qur'an recorded this event:

﴾They [the hypocrites] say: If we return to Madinah, indeed the more honourable ['Abdullâh ibn Ubay ibn Salool, the chief of the hypocrites at Madinah] will expel from it the meaner [meaning Allah's Messenger]. But honour, power and glory belong to Allah, and to His Messenger [Muhammad] and to the believers, but the hypocrites know not.﴿ *(Qur'an 63: 8)*

'Abdullâh ibn Ubay's son, who was also named 'Abdullâh, contrary to his father, was a true believer. He went to the Prophet (ﷺ) once he thought that the Prophet (ﷺ) might order for his father to be killed, and he offered to perform this duty himself. The Prophet (ﷺ) tender-heartedly replied to him: «No, rather we will deal gently with him and return his companionship with good as long as he lasts with us (and still claims to be a Muslim).»[21]

The slander against 'Â'ishah

Another episode connected with this battle involved a false rumour that was spread against 'Â'ishah (رضي الله عنها), the wife of the Prophet (ﷺ). The hypocrites and some other simple Muslims had slandered her chastity when they saw her guided by a Companion behind the troops on their return from the battle. The rumour circulated among the people and touched on the personal affairs of the Prophet (ﷺ). It was an aspect of the hypocrites' propaganda levelled against the Prophet (ﷺ).[22]

This ordeal lasted for a month and only then were the verses in the Noble Qur'an revealed to acquit 'Â'ishah (رضي الله عنها) of the accusation and lay down the rules for tackling such matters of slander. The delay in the divine revelation during this month-long period implies two important points. The first is that the Prophet (ﷺ) remained limited by his human nature. The second is that inspiration was not a psychological feeling to emanate from himself or succumb to his will, otherwise the verses would have arrived much sooner.[23] The Qur'anic verses which clarified this matter are the following:

﴾Verily, those who brought forth the slander [against 'Â'ishah] are a group among you. Consider it not a bad thing for you. Nay, it is good for you. Unto every man among them will be paid that which he has earned of the sin, and as for him among them who had the greater share in it, his will be a great torment. Why then did not the believers, men and women, when they heard it [the slander] think good of their own people and say: This [charge] is an obvious lie? Why did they not produce four witnesses to prove it? Since they [the slanderers] have not produced witnesses, then with Allah, they are the liars. Had it not been for the grace of Allah and His mercy on you in this world and in the hereafter, a great torment would have touched you for that about which you spoke. When you were propagating it with your tongues, and uttering with your mouths that of which you had no knowledge, you counted it a little thing, while with Allah it was very great. And why did you not, when you heard it, say: It is not right for us to speak of this. Glorified are You [O Allah]! This is a great lie! Allah forbids you from it and warns you not to repeat the like of it forever, if you are believers; and Allah makes the *âyât* [proofs, evidences, verses, lessons, signs, and revelations] plain to you, and Allah is All-Knowing, All-Wise. Verily, those who like that [the crime of] illegal sexual intercourse should be propagated among those who believe, they will have a painful torment in this world and in the hereafter. Allah knows and you know not, and had it not been for the grace of Allah and His mercy on you and that Allah is full of kindness, Most Merciful [Allah would have hastened the punishment upon you].› *(Qur'an 24: 11-20)*

These verses clarify the fact that those who slander others without proof should be castigated. The Prophet (ﷺ) punished three people who had clearly been involved in the matter,[24] but 'Abdullâh ibn Ubay, who was the worst rumourmonger, managed to escape the penalty because he used to mould the gossip and relate it in such a way that he was not accused directly of creating the rumours that he used to circulate, while such punishment should only be issued against allegations which can clearly be proven true.[25]

Lessons

The experiences which affected the Prophet (ﷺ) and the Muslims at this time in history taught them the following lessons:

- ❖ It is necessary to pay great attention to watching the enemy, discovering the plans of adversaries and surprising them in demolishing the hopes for their evil intentions.
- ❖ The responsibility for preaching Islam or clarifying it rests with every Muslim. Nevertheless, if a group of the Muslims fulfils this obligation, that will be satisfactory and no sin will befall the rest of the community. If none of the Muslims fulfil this requirement, then all of the people will be called to account for the failure to implement this duty.
- ❖ The infidels showed their perfidious nature. Therefore, if they call Muslims to surrender in return for saving their lives, the Muslims have the option of refusing the offer and continuing to fight them until their last breaths. However, this position

does not prevent the Muslims from accepting the offer in the hope of escaping from them. In addition, Muslims should flee from the subjugation of disbelievers if they can do so, even if they are able to practice their religion while still in the hands of the infidels.[26]

- Muslims do not reciprocate perfidy with more of the same. After the battle at ar-Rajee‘, when Khubayb (رضي الله عنه) had been captured and sold to the Quraysh, he asked the homemaker, in whose house he was bound and held prisoner, to give him a razor to prepare himself for death. In the presence of her child, she gave him the razor and immediately realised the great mistake that she had made. She feared that the prisoner might take the opportunity kill her or her son and take his revenge in advance, but she was completely surprised by the prisoner's honesty and the safety he extended to them.[27]
- Extraordinary things might happen for pious people. That can be a sign of understanding that a person is on the Right Path and for others to take heed of it and consequently of the divine power which stands behind it. This lesson was taken from Khubayb (رضي الله عنه) also. The homemaker, in whose house he was held captive, mentioned that she saw him one day eating grapes during a season when there were no grapes at all.[28]

There is a similarity between astonishing occurrences and miracles in that the prophets are supported by extraordinary events; however, a difference between them lies in the fact that extraordinary events occur without the individual's will, while a miracle is usually a result of the challenges enunciated by rejecters of the prophecy.

CHAPTER TEN

Defence: The Battle of the Trench

Dates

This battle has been known as the Battle of the Trench (*al-Khandaq*) or the Battle of the Confederates (*al-Aḥzâb*). It occurred when a body of tribes attacked the Muslims in Madinah. According to Bukhari, the event took place in Shawwâl during 4 H, or March 626 CE. This is from a narration by Ibn 'Umar (رضي الله عنه) that the Prophet (ﷺ) had refused to allow him to participate in the battle of Uḥud due to the fact that he was under fifteen years of age, but he (ﷺ) did allow him to partake in the Trench battle since by then he was fifteen and fulfilled the condition.[1] Other biographers and historians identified Shawwâl during 5 H as the date of the conflict.[2] Ibn Katheer and Akram al-'Umari[3] denied that there was any inconsistency in the dates and explained that any discrepancies were due to the fact that some people of the time had dated the start of the Hijri calendar in Muḥarram of the second year after the Hijrah.

Jewish incitement

Some Jewish clans played a significant role in inciting this invasion. A band of Jews visited Makkah and met the leaders of

Quraysh to urge them to fight the Muslims in order to eradicate them, offering their full support to help complete this task. They may have been inspired by the Prophet's order (ﷺ) for group of them to be expelled from their places[4] because they had breached their agreement with the Muslims.

The Quraysh seemed to have been shaken in their faith due to the general disasters with which they and their fellow-pagans in the Arabian Peninsula had been afflicted in their struggles with the Muslims, who continually achieved success in their battles as well as in spreading their religion. Therefore, they asked the Jewish group, since the Jews claimed to have divine scripture, which of the two religions, idolatry or Islam, was better and more correct. The Jews affirmed the superiority of heathenism over Islam, which inspired the Quraysh to prepare for war. A verse of the Qur'an was revealed about this occasion:

﴿Have you not seen those [the Jews] who were given a portion of the scripture? They believe in *jibt* and *tâghoot* [or anything worshiped other than Allah] and say to the disbelievers that they are better guided as regards the Way than the believers [Muslims].﴾ *(Qur'an 4: 51)*

Then the Jews departed from Makkah and set off for Ghaṭafân and enticed them to go to war against the Muslims, too.[5] It has been reported that perhaps they offered the tribes half of the annual yield from Khaybar, a fertile Jewish oasis.[6] The Jewish delegation was successful in its task and mobilised ten thousand warriors from Quraysh, Ghaṭafân and their allies, who all set out for Madinah.[7]

Strategy of the Muslims

When the Prophet (ﷺ) learned of these machinations, he gathered his Companions to discuss the plan they would adopt to confront the invading troops. His follower Salmân al-Fârisi (رضي الله عنه) suggested digging a trench all around the open side of Madinah. This innovative notion pleased the Prophet (ﷺ) and his Companions,[8] for it was an unconventional combat technique in the Arabian Peninsula, and they hoped that it would prove helpful in protecting the city and defeating the invaders.

The Prophet (ﷺ) and his Companions enthusiastically began digging the trench as soon as they had perfected the final design for it. They utilised the geographical features of the city and its domestic distribution facilities in order to reduce the space needed and the time required to complete the job. Upon surveying the area, they observed that the eastern, western and southern sides of Madinah were blocked by high and contiguous houses, interlaced with palm trees, which made it difficult for animals and foot soldiers to pass through, while the southeast side was occupied by the Jews of Banu Quraydhah, who had been tied by a peace treaty with the Muslims. To benefit from all of these factors, the Prophet (ﷺ) decided to situate the Muslims where their backs would be protected by the mountain of Sala‘ and their sides protected by the existing fortifications. He, therefore, issued an order to excavate a wide trench along the northern side of Madinah, which was the only side open to the enemy.[9] The length of the project was five thousand ells,[10] its width was nine and its depth ranged from seven to ten ells. The Muslims were organised into groups and each was charged with digging forty ells.[11]

To encourage the Muslims to work hard and to set an example of a leader united with the populace, the Prophet (ﷺ)

worked with a group of them, digging and carrying away the earth.[12] He (ﷺ) was also the one to whom all of the groups resorted when they were tackling rocks that they were unable to remove or extract. By the grace of Allah, the Prophet (ﷺ) would strike even the hardest rocks and they would break into small pieces.[13]

The task was completed successfully within only six days,[14] despite the harsh circumstances. The weather was cold and there was a lack of food, with people spending a whole day without food at all, or existing on only a handful of spoiled barley.[15] At the same time, the hypocrites were well supplied, but they worked badly and inconsistently,[16] and although they were expected to report the matter to the invaders, they had no opportunity to leak out any information about this project at all. Then, to reassure his three thousand warriors that their families would not be endangered by their absence, the Prophet (ﷺ) ordered that the women and children should be gathered inside the most fortified areas.[17]

The siege

The invaders astoundingly observed the unfamiliar defensive techniques that had been taken up by the Muslims[18] and were compelled to alter their plans. Under these new circumstances, they had no choice other than laying siege to the city and trying to find ways to cross the trench.[19]

Meanwhile, the prominent Jew Ḥuyay ibn Akhṭab, who had already signed a peace agreement with the Prophet (ﷺ), made every effort to persuade Ka‘b ibn Asad, the chief of the Jewish tribe Banu Quraydhah, who also had made a peace agreement with the Muslims, to revoke their peace treaties. His efforts eventually bore fruit[20] and the Banu Quraydhah side of Madinah, which was formerly considered safe and secure, became a source of danger. The information of this breach reached the Prophet (ﷺ) and he quietly sent a band of his followers to verify it. The news proved true and was subtly reported to him, but he only commented: «Allah is the Greater, O Muslims! Have signals of glad tidings!»[21]

The news, however, soon spread rapidly and the plot severely affected the Muslims whose concern for their women and children increased dramatically, in addition to their worry about the possibility of being assailed from the Jewish hole at their backs. They formed patrols to tour Madinah in order to guard it from the Jews and to protect the trench from infiltrators.[22] Despite the fact that the Muslims had developed a deep trust in Allah, since they had witnessed during the digging of the trench many miraculous signs and the Prophet (ﷺ) had predicted that they would conquer many countries,[23] they now became utterly terrified. The Noble Qur'an reflects on the situation in the following verses:

﴾When they came upon you from above you and from below you, and when the eyes grew wild and the hearts reached to the throats, and you were harbouring doubts about Allah, there, the believers were tried and shaken with a mighty shaking.﴿ *(Qur'an 33: 10-11)*

At this critical time, the Prophet (ﷺ) and his Companions missed the obligatory aṣr prayer that afternoon. The Prophet (ﷺ) cursed the Jews saying: «May Allah fill up their houses and graves with fire as they diverted us from (performing) the middle prayer until the sun had set (and its proper time was over).»[24]

In order to undermine his enemies and diminish the grip of the blockade, the Prophet (ﷺ) considered making conciliation with the leaders of Ghaṭafân. This involved giving to the Ghaṭafân a third of the crop of Madinah in return for their withdrawal from the enemy coalition.[25] Prior to finalising the agreement, he consulted a number of his Companions from the Anṣâr (may Allah be pleased with them). They expressed their submission to this agreement if it were an order from Allah, but if it were not, they suggested that the Prophet (ﷺ) should not procced with it. They reasoned that the enemy was in a weaker position and did not dream of having anything at all from Madinah, so why should they give them something from it now, especially since Madinah had grown stronger since becoming a Muslim city.[26] Hence, the Companions were determined to confront their enemies. The Prophet (ﷺ) supplicated to Allah and asked Him to defeat and destroy the pagan-Jewish coalition.[27]

Despite the fact that the siege continued for about twenty-four days,[28] the trench proved successful protection, with a few exceptions. In one of these, the pagans offered ten or twelve thousand dinars or dirhams in exchange for the body of one of their fallen comrades. The Prophet (ﷺ) allowed them to have the body but refused to receive anything in return, stating that trading in corpses is not a practice of Muslims, or according to other narrations, that it was a malignant body and so its price would be malignant too.[29]

Pagan solidarity weakens

Two crucial events occurred and formed Allah's response to the prayer of His Messenger (ﷺ). The first was that Nu'aym ibn Mas'ood, a famous pagan who maintained good relations with each group of the pagan alliance and with the Jews, secretly converted to Islam. He asked the Prophet (ﷺ) about what he might do for the sake of Islam. The Prophet (ﷺ) directed him to fragment and cause dissent among as much of the confederacy as he could.

To create discord, Nu'aym started with the Jews of Banu Quraydhah. He highlighted his friendship with them, and then started throwing them his concerns about the current events. He focused on the contrast between them and the pagans, stressing the fact that the Jews were inhabitants of Madinah and had their property and families there, while the other confederates simply consisted of warriors. The pagans, therefore, would hunt down the Muslims if they had the opportunity, or alternatively, they would retreat, without subjecting their relatives to danger. If the pagans left the battlefield, the Jews would be obliged, with their limited powers, to encounter the Muslims, who would not overlook their revocation of the peace treaty at such a critical time. This image terrified the Jews, and Nu'aym ibn Mas'ood suggested that they should demand from both Quraysh and Ghaṭafân that a number of their nobles be placed in the Jews' hands as a pledge that they would continue to oppose the Muslims and not abandon their allies on the battlefield. The Jews were happy with this suggestion.

Nu'aym then went to meet the leaders of the pagans. He met the leaders of Makkah and reminded them of the cordiality that linked them as well as the fact that they shared in rejecting the Islamic Message, in order to give his advice credibility. Then he promised to inform them of the news from the Jewish side, provided that they would not disclose him as the source of the information. On this basis, he told them that the Jews were sorry that they had revoked their peace treaty with Muhammad (ﷺ). As compensation for breaching the treaty, they promised to bring the Prophet (ﷺ) members of the nobility from the Quraysh and Ghaṭafân in order for them to be killed, and then they would place themselves at the disposal of the Muslims to help them to eradicate the pagans, since as Jews they shared with the Muslims a divinely-revealed religion. Nu'aym warned them to be cautious of the trap.

Acting similarly, he also convinced the tribe of Ghaṭafân that the Jews would try to trap them.

On a Saturday evening, a delegation from the Quraysh and Ghaṭafân visited the district of Banu Quraydhah to explain the necessity of taking prompt action to reduce the cost of the war and to suggest beginning the fight the following day. The Jews rejected this proposal on the pretext that it was their Sabbath. They added that they would not fight Muhammad (ﷺ) unless they held a number of pagan notables as surety. This position corroborated with the news that Nu'aym had reported to them, and it shook the confidence of the pagans who refused to give the Jews any of their men as hostages. The Jews also believed that Nu'aym had been correct as soon as they received the pagans' rejection of their demands! Thus, Nu'aym ibn Mas'ood (رضي الله عنه) had succeeded in sowing distrust among the different tribes of the alliance, and the pagan troops began to disperse from Madinah.[30]

Despite the fact that this account was not reported in the Prophetic Hadith, it was widely circulated in the books concerning the biography of the Prophet (ﷺ) and it does not conflict with the rules of the legitimate policies of warfare.[31]

Divine reinforcement

The other crucial matter was the freezing weather which affected all sides of the conflict; however, the pagan side received the worst of it. A fierce storm ravaged them[32] so badly that their tents were destroyed, their fires extinguished, and their pots overturned. In addition to this terrible weather, the Jewish-heathen pact foundered and the siege proved hugely expensive while producing no actual results. For all these reasons, Abu Sufyân, the leader of the pagans of Makkah, decided to decamp and the people followed him.[33] The Prophet (ﷺ) said that Muslims had been helped by Allah's sending of a strong wind.[34] The Noble Qur'an described this scene and its conclusion in the following verses:

﴿O you who believe! Remember Allah's favour to you, when there came against you hosts, and We sent against them a wind and forces that you saw not [including troops of angels]. Allah is ever All-Seeing of what you do.﴾ *(Qur'an 33: 9)*

﴿And Allah drove back those who disbelieved in their rage; they gained no advantage [no victory, nor booty]. Allah sufficed for the believers in the fighting [by sending against the disbelievers a severe wind and troops of angels]; and Allah is ever All-Strong, All-Mighty.﴾ *(Qur'an 33: 25)*

The Prophet (ﷺ) was acquainted with the weakening of the alliance and sent Ḥudhayfah ibn al-Yamân (رضي الله عنه) to discover what was happening among them. The news of the enemy's departure was confirmed, and consequently, the Prophet (ﷺ) along with his warriors, returned to their homes in Madinah.[35] The Muslims were clearly the winners of this round, as the pagans had retreated with nothing, and the Prophet (ﷺ) declared to his Companions: «We will attack them from now on, and they will not (attack us).»[36]

Results and lessons

There are several points of benefit that emerge from this occurrence:

- The age of puberty for males in Islam is fifteen, and those who are still considered children should not be used in fighting wars.
- Islam forbids trading in corpses.

- Consultation is an essential principle of Islam. Each Muslim should abide by the productive decision made though the consultation of knowledgeable people for the welfare of the community, and this is applicable for all types of events and cases, as long as there are no Qur'anic verses or Prophetic teachings that conflict with the arrived-at decision.[37]
- Equality is a feature of Islam. This element was embodied by the Prophet (ﷺ) as he shared in his Companions' labour and hunger, even though he was their leader.
- The Prophet (ﷺ) was engaged in this event to such an extent that he missed the afternoon aṣr prayer. He (ﷺ) and His Companions were not able to perform it until after its correct time. This teaches Muslims of the necessity of making up any prayers that they have missed, for whatever reason, and of performing them consecutively before the next prayer is offered.

CHAPTER ELEVEN

Strategic Changes

Al-Ḥudaybiyah

The Battle of the Trench was a victory for the Muslims not only for their enemies' empty-handed withdrawal, but also for the influence it had on the power of the Muslim nation. This sense was noted in the Prophet's comment about the transformation of the Muslims' position from one of defence to one of offense. The first fruit of this victory was the chastisement of the Jews of Banu Quraydhah, which will be discussed later. The other major benefit was the Prophet's decision that it was time now to pay a ritual visit to the Ka'bah in Makkah. He declared his intention and asked his people to prepare themselves for this pilgrimage. Approximately fourteen hundred Muslims were ready to accompany him (ﷺ).

At the beginning of Dhul Qâ'dah 6 H, corresponding to mid-March 628 CE, they departed from Madinah for Makkah to perform their religious duty and exalt the Sacred House.[1] They openly proclaimed their peaceful intentions to all the people. Still, the Muslims anticipated some possible rejection or fighting and, therefore, went equipped for battle.[2] In the area that is known as Dhul-Ḥulayfah, which is about fifteen miles from Madinah, the Prophet (ﷺ) invoked the name of Allah upon his intention to perform 'umrah, the minor pilgrimage, and sent a scout, thought to be Bishr ibn Sufyân al-Ka'bi from the Khuzâ'ah,[3] to discover the effect of his intention upon the people of Makkah. The scout returned and informed the Prophet (ﷺ) that that Quraysh were preparing to confront him.

The Prophet (ﷺ) asked his Companions for advice. Abu Bakr (رضي الله عنه) told him, "You have left intending to visit the House peacefully, so go ahead with your purpose and if anyone rebuffs us from it we will fight him." The Prophet (ﷺ) replied: «Proceed in the Name of Allah.»[4]

To avoid clashing with the Quraysh, he inquired about a guide who could show the Muslims another route that would not lead them close to the pagans. Thus, they were guided along a difficult route until they reached the al-Ḥudaybiyah area, close to Makkah, where the camel of the Prophet (ﷺ) knelt down. The Islamic camp was in close proximity to a poor well, but the Prophet (ﷺ) spat into it and told the Muslims to leave it for a while before supplying themselves and their animals with its water. They followed his directions and then found that the water was plenty to fulfil their needs until they left that place.[5]

Waiting outside Makkah

The Prophet (ﷺ) took the kneeling down of his camel as a sign to abandon any notion of fighting anyone who prevented them from conducting their sacred visit. For this reason, he said: «I will agree with whatever the Quraysh offer me today as long as it complies with glorifying the rites of Allah.»[6]

The Quraysh sent out scouts to discover the aim of the Prophet (ﷺ), and they concluded that his purpose was peaceful in nature.[7] Notwithstanding this, the Quraysh formed groups to surround the Muslims in order to capture some of them, but on the contrary, they fell into the hand of the Muslims, and the Prophet (ﷺ) subsequently released them.[8] Although the Quraysh were nervous and tense, the Prophet (ﷺ) promoted a sense of peace. He (ﷺ) selected 'Uthmân ibn 'Affân (رضي الله عنه) to take a message to the leaders of the Quraysh concerning the reason for his presence there.

'Uthmân (رضي الله عنه) delivered the message and was given permission by the idolaters to worship around the Sacred House, but 'Uthmân refused to precede the Prophet (ﷺ) in performing the rites of pilgrimage. Still, the time he spent in Makkah was so much longer than expected that a rumour spread among the Muslims that he had been killed.[9] Fearing that this might be true propelled the Prophet (ﷺ) to decide not to leave before fighting Quraysh to avenge this affront. Seeing that the Muslims had left Madinah for the purpose of worship, not fighting, the Prophet (ﷺ) asked them, under these new circumstances, to pledge to fight with him and not flee from the battlefield until they had victory or death.[10] This homage was known as Bay'ah ar-Riḍwân, or the Homage of Gratification, which means that Allah the Almighty had bestowed His pleasure upon those who paid homage to the Prophet (ﷺ) at this critical time. The following Qur'anic verse recorded this occurrence:

﴿Indeed, Allah was pleased with the believers when they gave the pledge to you [Muhammad] under the tree. He knew what was in their hearts, and He sent down calmness and tranquillity upon them, and He rewarded them with a near victory.﴾ *(Qur'an 48: 18)*

The Muslims deserved Allah's pleasure for they proved their loyalty to the Prophet (ﷺ) and to their religion by making their pledge without hesitation. The situation calmed down as soon as the falseness of the news of 'Uthmân's death was clarified.

The peace treaty

The Quraysh delegated Suhayl ibn 'Amr to negotiate an agreement with the Prophet (ﷺ) that the Muslims would refrain from entering Makkah that year to perform religious rites. The reason for this was ascribed to their fear that the other Arab tribes would think that the Muslims had entered Makkah forcibly,[11] and the Prophet (ﷺ) agreed to the disadvantages of having the Arabs believe this.

When they commenced writing the treaty, Suhayl refused to begin it with the Islamic phrase 'In the name of Allah, the Most Gracious, the Most Merciful' and suggested that they should write 'By Your Name, O God', which would be recognized and acceptable to both the Muslims and the non-Muslims. He also rejected the use of the formal Islamic name of the Prophet (ﷺ), 'Muhammad the Messenger of Allah', and suggested that merely his name should be stated. Although the Muslims found it difficult to accept these objections, the Prophet (ﷺ) acceded to them and he himself erased the phrase 'the Messenger of Allah' from the document, after its writer, 'Ali (رضي الله عنه), refused to do so. The agreement was eventually concluded with the following articles:

- There would be peace between the Muslims and the Quraysh for ten years, during which the people would be safe and would not attack each other.
- Muhammad must return to the Quraysh any of their men who had gone to him to embrace Islam without the permission of his custodian or patron, but if anyone from the Muslim side went to the Quraysh to apostatise from Islam, the Quraysh would not send him back.
- Whosoever wants to ally with Muhammad or with Quraysh has the right to choose freely.

- The Muslims had to return to Madinah that year, and they could come back to worship in Makkah the following year. They would be allowed to stay then for only three days, on condition that they did not carry any arms except for their swords which would remain sheathed.
- Both sides should fulfil the covenant sincerely and genuinely.[12]

Sadness and jubilation

It was hard for the Muslims to agree with the Prophet (ﷺ) in accepting these points, and they strongly debated with him about approving such stipulations, which they considered oppressive.[13] Their sorrow led them to refuse to disengage themselves from the state of ritual consecration, despite the fact that he had ordered them three times to do so. The Prophet (ﷺ) called in on his wife Um Salamah (رضي الله عنها), who was travelling with him, and told her about the people's disobedience of his order. She advised him to go out and disengage himself, without speaking to any of thcm so that, once they saw him doing this, they would immediately copy him. When the Muslims saw the Prophet (ﷺ) sacrificing the animals that accompanied him on his ritual visit and shaving his head, they all hurried to free themselves and started shaving one another, as dejectedly as if they were slaying each other![14]

The outward appearance of the conditions of the treaty initially made the Muslims consider it oppressive, but they later realised how wrong they were. The case was similar for the pagans, who reckoned that they had achieved a moral victory, since they had prevented the Muslims from entering Makkah at that time. They felt that they had obtained the consent of the Prophet (ﷺ) to return to them any people whom they did not authorise to become Muslims, without agreeing to treat in a similar manner those Muslims who abandoned Madinah. Nevertheless, the Prophet (ﷺ) was divinely guided to make the correct decision when he agreed to the treaty. Time and events proved that his anticipations were accurate.

New people of Quraysh who converted to Islam disliked having to live in Makkah with the pagans and did not wish to approach the Prophet (ﷺ) by emigrating to Madinah, although some of them did that and the Prophet (ﷺ) returned them, in conformity with the agreement.[15] So, instead of going to Madinah, they congregated along the seashore and made raids upon Qurayshi commercial caravans to Syria. The pagans of Makkah were consequently obliged to appeal to the Prophet (ﷺ) to revoke that part of the treaty and allow all of the Muslims to join the Islamic State in Madinah![16]

On another front, the peacefulness created a proper environment for the Muslims to dedicate their efforts to preaching Islam freely, both inside and outside the Arabian Peninsula. The Prophet (ﷺ) communicated with the kings and the rulers of his time, explaining the Revelation and inviting them to believe in his Message and warning them of the sins they would bear on behalf of their nations if they rejected his call.[17] In general, there was limited compliance with his invitation.[18]

Still, the number of Muslims increased greatly during the following two years, compared with the numbers calculated from the beginning of the rise of Islam up to that point. There were only fourteen hundred Muslims with the Prophet (ﷺ) at al-Ḥudaybiyah, while just two years later, this number had increased to ten thousand Muslims, who accompanied him when he travelled to Makkah.[19] The contrast between these two figures shows a clear sign of how far the Islamic mission had developed, following the pact that had been disquieting to the Muslims at the time but which showed, however, the perceptive insight of the Prophet (ﷺ).

In reality, the consequences of the treaty were distinguished and that is why the Noble Qur'an uses the phrase 'manifest victory' to describe what would result from this treaty:

﴾Verily, We have given you [O Muhammad] a manifest victory.﴿ *(Qur'an 48: 1)*[20]

Performing the postponed 'Umrah

A year after the signing of the treaty, the Prophet (ﷺ) called the people who had been prevented from performing their 'umrah to prepare themselves to perform the minor pilgrimage now in Dhul Qâ'dah 7 H, or March 629 CE. It was also called the 'Requital Pilgrimage' since the Prophet (ﷺ) had been prevented from performing it in the same month of the previous year.[21]

Despite the fact that this visit had been agreed upon in the peace treaty, the Prophet (ﷺ) was cautious and made allowances for a possible betrayal by the Quraysh. So, while he adhered to the clauses of the pact and instructed his followers to keep their swords sheathed, he left a party of soldiers under the leadership of Muhammad ibn Maslamah encamped a short distance from Makkah. The soldiers were accompanied by one hundred horses and carried cold steel and spears[22] to defend the pilgrims if they encountered any unexpected treachery. The Quraysh were alarmed when they learned of this development and promptly sent one of their members to assess the situation. The Prophet (ﷺ) reaffirmed his fidelity to the treaty and his decision not to take arms into Makkah but to keep them close by as a precautionary step.[23]

The Quraysh had also spread rumours that the Muslims were depressed, weary [24] and weakened by the fevers of Madinah.[25] The Prophet (ﷺ) tackled this matter in two ways. He (ﷺ) surrounded himself with followers, who carried their sheathed swords, lest the pagans be tempted to harm him.[26] He (ﷺ) also directed his followers to show themselves strong and fortitudinous[27] when moving around the Sacred House. Hence, they were instructed to walk briskly during their first three circuits around the Ka'bah.[28]

The Muslims entered Makkah and exclaimed aloud the grandeur and Oneness of Allah. The image of over two thousand Muslims [29] repeating this, wearing uniform clothing and running in some of their revolutions around the Sacred House and their trips between Ṣafâ and Marwah Mountains, deeply affected the Quraysh, who watched from a short distance.[30] On their own territory, while they were still pagans, the Oneness of Allah was openly and freely pronounced. This infuriated the pagans, particularly their nobles, who in envy and fury, moved away from the sight.[31]

Lessons

This occurrence was a turning point in the Islamic movement. Its results granted recognition to the Islamic State and allowed the Prophet (ﷺ) and the Muslims to advance the Islamic mission even further. In addition to this strategic attainment, the details of this event taught several lessons by example, as follows:

- Peace is a primary feature of Islam, while war is exceptional and will be resorted to only when there is no other way of performing religious duties freely. The fact that the Prophet

(ﷺ) concluded an agreement with the unbelievers reflects the permissibility of Muslims to have an armistice with their enemies. This can be for a maximum of ten years, depending on the literal understanding of the Prophet's agreement, or for more than ten years if the Muslim commander observes that the Islamic interests lie in concluding such an armistice for a longer period.[32]

- ❖ The Prophet (ﷺ) consented to begin the treaty with the words 'O God by Your Name', instead of the usual Islamic phrase, and accepted that his name could be stated without the phrase 'the Messenger of Allah'. Therefore, Muslims have the authorisation to compromise in such matters for the sake of bringing a reasonable covenant to fruition, if they protect the fixed pillars and principles of the religion.

- ❖ Deliberation, as has been illustrated more than once in this book, is one of the most significant and obligatory aspects of Islam,[33] to which Allah the Almighty as well as the Prophet (ﷺ) drew people's attention. To promote its theoretical importance into a practical system, the Prophet (ﷺ) used to apply it not just when tackling issues concerning the Islamic State, even the smallest matters, but also in his own personal matters. Except in this occurrence, after consultation with his followers, he still decided to engage in a treaty with the Quraysh, against the wishes of his followers, as long as the Quraysh presented him with an offer that would help the Muslims to glorify the religious rites established upon them by Allah.

By combining the cases when the Prophet (ﷺ) followed the advice of his advisors and the case here where he rejected it, we notice that the measure of consulting other people in Islam is an advisory rather than a binding formula. The leader discusses the issues with his consultative board and then chooses the appropriate action, or extracts from the whole discussion the position that best harmonises with the common good, providing that this is in line with the principles of the Noble Qur'an and the teachings of the Prophet (ﷺ).[34] In this event, the decision of the Prophet (ﷺ) was conditional upon allowing the Muslims to glorify Allah through the rituals He prescribed, something which is at the core of the Islamic mission. So, he (ﷺ) was enlightened by his prophecy and better comprehended particular points than his followers, whose stances were emotional and less astute. The Muslims very soon discovered that the treaty contracted by the Prophet (ﷺ) was an essential key to their future success.

❖ Muslims are allowed to perform obligatory prayers individually or at home in case something, such as rain, prevents them from attending the collective performance of their duty.[35]

❖ It is allowed to seek blessings from whatever belongs to the Prophet (ﷺ). It was mentioned by 'Urwah ibn Mas'ood, the delegate of the Quraysh, that he noticed Muslims hurrying to take blessing from contact with things that the Prophet (ﷺ) had intimately touched, such as remnants of his saliva, the water he used in ablution and so on, and to moisten and rub their bodies with them.[36]

❖ It is acceptable for a leader to have a guard standing beside him when he is sitting with his enemies, even if just to show the dignity and strength of the Muslims. A statement of the same Qurayshi delegate[37] reveals this point.

❖ Attributing all happenings to the will of Allah is something inevitable but ascribing any of them to a creator other than Him will lead to excluding a person from the circle of belief. This sense is entirely clear from a statement made by the Prophet (ﷺ) after a rainy night in al-Ḥudaybiyah. The Prophet (ﷺ) reported that Allah the Almighty said: «The one who said they were showered with rain by the favour and the grace of Allah is a believer in Me, but the one who said they were showered by such and such a star is an unbeliever in Me and has faith in that star.»[38]

❖ A person who intends to perform a major or minor pilgrimage but encounters strained circumstances and is unable to complete the rites is to sacrifice a sheep and then shave or cut his hair, or shorten it slightly, as in the case of women. This disengages the person from the state of being a pilgrim and its restrictions. Some of the scholars also said that this compensation clears the pilgrim of the necessity to complete the un-performed rites at a later time, if this is a voluntary pilgrimage; but many Ḥanafi scholars are inclined to consider it obligatory to return and complete the rites, when possible, on the basis that all the Companions (may Allah be pleased with them) returned the following year to perform the minor pilgrimage, with the exception of those who had died in the meantime.[39]

CHAPTER TWELVE

Jewish Relations with the Islamic State

Background

The immigration to Madinah triggered direct contact between the Muslims and the Jews, who had resided there for a long time.[1] As noted earlier, the Prophet (ﷺ) struck an agreement with them as soon as he entered the region. The treaty admitted right of inhabitancy to the Jews in the first Islamic State of Madinah, with their full religious rights.

From the Arabic sources, one can easily infer that the Muslim historiographers adopted the opinion that the Jews were far from serious in agreeing to this pact and were persuaded to do so for their own temporal reasons. This is why the relationships between the two parties, the Muslims and the Jews, were marked by sensitivity in spite of their various social and commercial links.

Ibn Hishâm referred to two prominent Jews, Ḥuyay ibn Akhṭab and his brother Abu Yâsir, who visited the Prophet (ﷺ) when he was in Qubâ' soon after he first arrived in Madinah[2] to examine him and compare his personal features with the information that they already possessed about a long-awaited prophet. Quoting Ṣafiyah (رضي الله عنها), the daughter of Huyay ibn Akhṭab who later became a wife of the Prophet (ﷺ), Ibn Is-ḥâq related how the two personages had recognised clearly the exact concurrence of the Prophet's features (ﷺ) with the Jewish scriptures. Nevertheless, instead of believing in him, they decided to ignite animosity against him.[3] Despite the fact that the chain of narrators is not continuous from Ibn Is-ḥâq to Ṣafiyyah, which weakens the account, it matches other accounts that focus on the Jewish enmity towards the Muslims after they entered Madinah.[4]

Based on this attitude, Ibn Hishâm mentioned that the Jewish rabbis constantly questioned the Prophet (ﷺ) and tried to vex him and confuse him, but the revelations in the Noble Qur'an answered their questions and uncovered their subterfuges.[5]

Contempt from the Jews

A few Jews truly believed in the new prophecy and declared their conversion to Islam,[6] but others did so falsely.[7] The Prophet (ﷺ) is reported to have said: «If (only) ten of the Jews had (true) faith in me, then (all of) the Jews would believe in me.»[8]

However, despite the prolonged disputes with him concerning many issues, including the proof of his coming in their scripture, the Jews refused to admit his prophethood and resisted him relentlessly. Moreover, they tried to unnerve the Muslims by mocking them and doing anything that might enrage them. The following are a few examples of their behaviour:

- They tried to harm Muslims by isolating them from their social councils and whispering to each other in presence of the Muslims, making certain Muslims think that they had heard some information about the death or injury of their own absent relatives. The case was hurtful and unnerving for them, until their relatives returned home.[9]

- They distorting the way of greeting among the Muslims; so instead of saying '*Assalâmu 'alaykum*' (meaning 'Peace be upon you'), they said: '*Assâmu 'alaykum*' which meant 'Death to you!' The Prophet (ﷺ) therefore directed his Companions to respond briefly to their 'greetings' by saying, 'And to you!'[10]
- Allah the Almighty had directed His Messenger (ﷺ) to react to the Jews' prejudice with patience. The Prophet (ﷺ) adhered to these instructions, but a Jewish poet, named Ka'b ibn al-Ashraf, insisted on demonstrating his deep hatred of the Muslims and seeking their destruction. He tried to realise his endeavours politically, by cursing the Prophet (ﷺ) and persuading the Quraysh to invade the Islamic State in Madinah, and socially, by composing love poems about Muslim females,[11] which he was aware was disgraceful according to both Arabic and Islamic customs. His overstepping the limitations of decorum, as well as the agreement between the two peoples, resulted in the Prophet's (ﷺ) order to a few of his followers to eliminate him.[12] Abu Dâwood referred to this event as the main factor leading to the signing of the peace agreement between the Prophet (ﷺ) and the Jews.[13]
- They provoked the Muslims by claiming that they only won the battle against Quraysh at Badr because of the Quraysh's inexperience in fighting. They threatened the Prophet (ﷺ) and warned him that they were the truly courageous and expert men of battle, if he were to think of fighting them.[14]
- They infuriated the Prophet (ﷺ) and the Muslims by swearing at Allah the Almighty, His angels and the prophets, although they were supposed to believe in Allah, the sole Creator of the world, since they were people supposedly following the previous prophets and scriptures. Still, they impudently asked

the Prophet (ﷺ): Who created God?![15] Allah sent down verses to answer such an impertinent question:

﴾Say [O Muhammad]: He is Allah, the One, the *Samad* [the Self-Sufficient Master, Whom all creatures need, but Who is in need of nothing]. He begets not, nor was He begotten; and there is none co-equal or comparable unto Him.﴿ *(Qur'an 112: 1-4)*

Then they asked him about Allah's features, and a further verse was revealed to answer that question,[16] which was not asked for the sake of discovering the truth but for the sake of mockery and confusing the minds of the Muslims. As for the angels, they announced their enmity of Jibreel (ﷺ) and pretended that they would believe in the Prophet (ﷺ) if another angel was revealing the Noble Qur'an to him![17] In addition, they not only rejected the prophethood of Muhammad (ﷺ),[18] they also refused to believe in Jesus (ﷺ) and his followers.[19]

❖ They formed an alliance with the hypocrites of Madinah and worked with them in order to raze the foundations of the Muslim community,[20] despite the fact that they were supposed to observe their alliance with the Muslims. This was a serious breach of the agreement to which they were bound. Moreover, a group of them had sided with the pagans against the Muslims in the Battle of the Trench while their peace treaty with the Prophet (ﷺ) was still active and required them to support the Muslims against outside aggressions.

Consequences

The above actions, together with many other occurrences, left their effects upon the Muslim-Jewish relationship and led to individual and communal clashes, including the case of Ka'b ibn al-Ashraf that was dealt with in secret to avoid creating more problems and to clarify that resorting to such treatment was restricted to dire necessity.[21] The executors of the punishment, however, sought permission from the Prophet (ﷺ) to pretend disbelief in Islam in order to trap the target, which he (ﷺ) duly granted.[22] Thus, Islamic jurists educed the possibility of abandoning specific duties at particular times of dire need, if pious scholars determined that it was important to do so.[23] The group deceived Ka'b to perform their task, and from the Islamic legislation viewpoint, misleading the enemy is something permissible.

Ka'b was a confederate who had publicly accepted the leadership of the Prophet (ﷺ) in Madinah. Therefore, his deviation from his obligations would naturally lead to his punishment in proportion to his offence. So, as an individual, he was subjected to the sanction while his tribe was not, and the Prophet (ﷺ) renewed the peace treaty with them.[24]

The case of Abu Râfi' 'Abdullâh ibn Abil-Ḥuqayq was conducted in a similar manner. He was assassinated for continually harming the Prophet (ﷺ) and aiding enemies against him.[25]

Banu Qaynuqâ'

Eventually, the Prophet (ﷺ) was obliged to take rigorous steps against the tribes of the Jews, when they became treacherous in respect to their alliances with him. In Shawwâl of 2 H, or March or April 624 CE, the Muslims gathered their soldiers to oppose Banu Qaynuqâ'.[26] The incentive for this operation was the public antagonism of Muslims by Banu Qaynuqâ', particularly after the Muslim victory at Badr. Banu Qaynuqâ' threatened the Prophet

(ﷺ) and spread corruption in Madinah,[27] so it was time to control the situation and put an end to their disturbance. The Prophet (ﷺ) was inclined to solve the problem peacefully and, therefore, warned them that they might suffer a similar fate to the Quraysh, but they belligerently replied that the Quraysh were inexperienced fighters, while they were skilled men of the sword.[28]

Consequently, the Prophet (ﷺ) decided to solve the problem by force, as his opponents suggested. The Muslims held them besieged for fifteen days until they yielded to the verdict of the Prophet (ﷺ).[29] Then, they handed over their property to the Prophet (ﷺ).[30] He ordered them to be bound, intending to sentence them to death for treason.[31] They were seven hundred warriors, but 'Abdullâh ibn Ubay, who had previously been their ally, persisted in asking the Prophet (ﷺ) to forgive them, and eventually they were released and expelled from Madinah with their families.[32]

The Prophet (ﷺ) complied with this request, even though he was acquainted with the hypocrisy of the intercessor. The main reason for this was his merciful nature, his desire to save 'Abdullâh ibn Ubay from hypocrisy and to show his followers that any individual is dealt with as a Muslim as long he or she claims to be a Muslim and exhibits an exterior appearance that is Islamic.[33]

Teachings

The following two points arise from the aforementioned events:

- ❖ Patience takes priority when dealing with the aggression of disbelievers to deep-root this trait in the souls of Muslims and preserve open methods of communications for attracting non-believers to Islam. This patience, however, is not infinite. If it fails to preserve the dignity of the Muslims, then alternative measures should eventually be taken so that the enemies of the Muslims may understand that their patience is not a sign of their weakness.

❖ Islam deals with the outward appearance of the people in respect to considering them Muslims or non-Muslims. Only Allah the Almighty truly knows what is in the hearts and interiors, and He (ﷻ) will judge them according to their real intentions.

Banu an-Naḍeer

Banu an-Naḍeer was another Jewish tribe that faced banishment from Madinah. The chroniclers assign different dates to this event. Some of them attribute it to the beginning of the 3rd year after Hijrah, sometime in August or September 624 CE,[34] while others placed it a year later in 4 H.[35] The Jews of this tribe were punished because they had attempted to kill the Prophet (ﷺ).

There were different narrations about the plot. One variation involved a Jewish proposal that the Prophet (ﷺ), accompanied by thirty of his followers, should meet with thirty of their rabbis midway between the territories of both and that they would believe in him if the rabbis accepted his Message. When they approached the meeting place, the Jews suggested that each side should reduce its number to three, and then supplied their representatives with daggers with which to murder the Prophet (ﷺ). One of their women informed her Muslim brother, who immediately reported the conspiracy. The Prophet (ﷺ), naturally, drew up his battalions and lay siege on them. They eventually accepted their expulsion, on condition that they could take whatever their camels could carry, leaving their weapons behind.[36]

Abu Dâwood, the famous scholar of Hadith, offered other relevant narrations. In one, he mentioned the suggestion that thirty people from each side should meet, but he said that the Prophet (ﷺ) examined the matter and instead beleaguered their region with his battalions and invited them to come agrec to a covenant. Their refusal to attend provoked a battle against them, which ended in their expulsion from the area, allowing them to carry off all of their belongings, even the doors and wood of their homes.[37] The more detailed version of events that clearly included a reference to the Jewish intention to kill the Prophet (ﷺ) seems to be closest to reality, particularly since its chain of narration is composed by reliable narrators.[38]

Another plot to kill the Prophet (ﷺ) by Banu an-Nadeer was narrated by Ibn Is-ḥâq, one of the most famous biographers of the Prophet (ﷺ). He mentioned that the Prophet (ﷺ) asked this tribe of Jews to contribute to the blood money of two men who had been killed mistakenly by some Muslims, as sharing in this responsibility was part of the agreement they had made with each other. They pretended to assent to this request, but while he (ﷺ) was leaning on a wall in their quarter of Madinah, they decided to kill him by throwing a rock on him from above. As the angel Jibreel (عليه السلام) alerted him to this plot, he (ﷺ) rushed home to prepare his warriors to take retaliation against them.[39]

These two plots may relate to the same action according to two different accounts or may refer to two separate attempts. Whatever the case, this treachery violated the treaty that had been made with the Prophet (ﷺ). In addition, this Jewish tribe had infringed on their agreement with him previously when their leader, Sallâm ibn Mishkam, informed Abu Sufyân of the situation of the Muslims at the time he attacked Madinah following the Battle of Badr.[40]

After only six days of siege, during which the Prophet (ﷺ) ordered the burning and cutting down of some of their palm trees,[41] they yielded to his decision. They demolished their houses to take all useful material from them, and a group of them went to Khaybar, while others headed for Syria[42]. The Noble Qur'an recorded this event in the following verses:

﴾All that is in the heavens and all that is on the earth glorifies Allah, and He is the All-Mighty, the All-Wise. It is He Who drove out the disbelievers among the people of the Scripture [meaning the Jews of the tribe of Banu an-Naḍeer] from their homes at the first gathering. You did not think that they would get out, and they thought that their fortresses would defend them from Allah! But Allah's [punishment] reached them from a place from where they did not expected it, and He cast terror into their hearts so that they destroyed their own dwellings with their own hands and the hands of the believers. Then take admonition, O you with eyes [to see]! Had it not been that Allah had decreed exile for them, He would certainly have punished them in this world; and in the hereafter theirs shall be the torment of the Fire. That is because they opposed Allah and His Messenger [Muhammad]; and whoever opposes Allah, then verily, Allah is Severe in punishment. What you [Muslims] cut down of the palm trees [of the enemy], or you left standing on their stems, it was by leave of Allah, and in order that He might disgrace the *fâsiqoon* [the rebellious, the disobedient to Allah]. And what Allah gave as booty to His Messenger from them — for this you made no expedition with either cavalry or camelry; but Allah gives power to His Messengers over whomever He wills, and Allah is Able to do all things.﴿ *(Qur'an 59: 1-6)*

Banu Quraydhah

The invasion against this tribe occurred after the Battle of Trench in the year 4 or 5 H, or 625-626 CE. In the previously-given description of this battle, reference was made to the breach that this tribe committed by taking sides with the heathen Arabian alliance in opposition to the Muslims. This was a major sign of their disregard for their covenants with the Muslims and a clear proof of the danger they posed to the inhabitants of Madinah.

After the Battle of the Trench, the angel Jibreel (عليه السلام) directed the Prophet (ﷺ) to continue towards Banu Quraydhah.[43] He (ﷺ) persuaded his followers to push along, saying: «No one should pray the afternoon prayer except in the (region) of Banu Quraydhah.»[44]

He led the campaign, which according to Ibn Sa'd, consisted of three thousand warriors and thirty-six horses,[45] and blockaded them for twenty-five days.[46]

The Jews had no choice but to consult some of their previous allies about what steps should be taken. They summoned Abu Lubâbah ibn 'Abdul-Mundhir (رضي الله عنه) and asked him if they should submit to the decision of the Prophet (ﷺ). He said yes, but wiped his hand across his neck, revealing that death would be the result. He soon felt guilty about his revelation and decided to bind himself to a column of the mosque of Madinah until Allah the Almighty forgave him.[47]

As the blockage was intense, the Jews proclaimed that they would accept the outcome that their former ally Sa'd ibn Mu'âdh (رضي الله عنه), the leader of the Aws tribe in Madinah, decided for them. They begged Sa'd to consider his previous alliance with them and be merciful towards them. The Jews were hoping to solve the problem in a way similar to that of the problem with Banu

Qaynuqâ'; and 'Abdullâh ibn Ubay, a hypocrite and the leader of the other tribe of Madinah, the Khazraj, agreed and tried to obtain the approval of the Prophet (ﷺ) to simply expel that tribe of Jews. However, Sa'd was furious about the Jews' disloyalty during the siege of Madinah, which could have led to the destruction of the Muslims in Madinah. He recommended that the Jewish warriors should be put to death, their women and children enslaved and their wealth confiscated. The Jews had made Sa'd's decision binding upon them, and it was followed only after it had been approved by the Prophet (ﷺ).[48]

Khaybar

Khaybar, a complex of forts occupied by a mixture of Jews and pagan Arabs, was located approximately one hundred miles to the north of Madinah. The area was flourishing economically and considered an impregnable fortress in military terms.

In the wake of the expulsion of the Jews of Banu an-Naḍeer from Madinah, a large portion of them had chosen to settle in Khaybar and increased the Jewish population in that region.[49] The expelled included three prominent men, Sallâm ibn Abil-Ḥuqayq, Kinânah ibn ar-Rabee' ibn Abil-Ḥuqayq, and Huyay ibn Akhṭab. According to Ibn Is-ḥâq, they entered Khaybar in a swashbuckling and boastful way that had never been witnessed before and were accompanied by tambourines and stringed instruments.[50] They appeared to be aiming to show the Jews of Khaybar their strength despite the catastrophe of their expulsion. The full submission of the inhabitants of Khaybar to these leaders upon their arrival[51] testifies to their success in this regard.

This marked the beginning of a new policy of Khaybar towards the Prophet (ﷺ) and the Muslims. In addition to the hatred that the Jewish leaders had stirred up against the Muslims, they planned to get vengeance for their eviction. They also played a significant role in urging their associates of Banu Quraydhah to break their peace treaty with the Prophet (ﷺ) during the Battle of the Trench.[52]

The Prophet (ﷺ) started considering Khaybar as a dangerous area since it had become a centre for the rancorous Jews. In addition, so many different enemies distributed throughout the surrounding area hindered the preaching of Islam outside the Arabian Peninsula. Meanwhile, the peace treaty that he had concluded with Quraysh had allowed him to devote his endeavours to dealing with other foes. Khaybar was of significant importance, as it was situated on the route to Syria and had an alliance with the Ghaṭafân, a large and powerful pagan tribe and one of the major confederates involved in the Battle of the Trench. Therefore, tackling the problem of Khaybar would be a masterstroke for weakening those who were hostile to Islam and a crucial step towards enabling Islam to spread out towards Syria without fearing unexpected events.

Movement and conquest

The Muslims marched towards Khaybar enthusiastically and mentioned Allah loudly, but the Prophet (ﷺ) advised them to lower their voices as the One whom they called on was with them.[53] The route that they had chosen for the march was so elaborately planned that the people of Khaybar were surprised by the sudden appearance of the Muslim troops around them.[54] The Prophet (ﷺ) had effectively isolated Khaybar from Syria as well as its alliance with the Ghaṭafân.[55]

In view of the sudden change in their situation, the Jews entrenched themselves inside their strongholds. Their allies from the Ghaṭafân hastened to aid them but soon abandoned their efforts, fearing that if they left their region empty of warriors, it would become an easy target for the Muslims.[56] Thus, the Jews were left to fight alone. Although they owned the equipment necessary for defence, most of their forts fell easily into the hands of the Muslims.[57] There was resistance in a few of their besieged citadels, but at most that lasted only two weeks.[58]

The Prophet (ﷺ) handled the subdued Jews in Khaybar according to their attitudes. While some of them faced the death of their warriors and the enslavement of their women and children,[59] others were expelled,[60] and yet others were left to cultivate the land in return for half the harvest, on condition that the Muslims reserved the right to expel them, if circumstances changed.[61] The Prophet (ﷺ) divided the spoils of Khaybar into thirty-six shares; he shared half of it among his followers and devoted the other half to the general needs of the Muslims.[62] Ṣafiyyah (رضي الله عنها), the daughter of Ḥuyay ibn Akhṭab, was allotted to the Prophet (ﷺ), and he liberated her so that he could take her as his wife.[63]

Controlling Khaybar and putting the Jews in check was a significant victory for the Muslims as it put an end to their conflict with the Jews in the Arabian Peninsula. News of the defeat of Khaybar unnerved the Jews of Fadak,[64] who hastened to offer the Prophet (ﷺ) their wealth in return for sparing their lives, an offer which he (ﷺ) accepted.[65] Thus, Fadak was a pure prize for the Muslims, as it fell into their hands without any military expedition.[66] This was efficacious in impressing the pagan disbelievers and shook their confidence in their own power since the outcome of these military manoeuvres was in complete contrast to their expectations.[67]

Juristic issues

The Islamic ruling on some juristic issues transpired from the events of the triumph over Khaybar and Fadak. They can be summarised as follows:

- The Prophet (ﷺ) prohibited the practice of temporary (*mut'ah*) marriage.[68]
- He (ﷺ) had commissioned one of his followers with bringing the dates from Khaybar, and this person had exchanged the fruit with that of another quality. The Prophet (ﷺ) directed the Muslims not to exchange things of the same kind, as this involves a kind of interest or usury, but rather to sell the thing which is least preferred and then use the profits to buy what is desired.[69]
- It is permissible for Muslims to sharecrop with non-Muslims.
- Priority is for inviting people to Islam over other matters. Before invading Khaybar, the Prophet (ﷺ) instructed his cousin 'Ali (رضي الله عنه) to go to the Jews and invite them to Islam and to explain what their duties would be if they responded positively. Furthermore, he notified 'Ali of the utmost reward that is gained from Allah when someone becomes the cause of converting others to the Islamic faith.[70] The scholars have understood from this that it would be possible, without prior notice, to invade those who had been already acquainted with the Islamic mission and had recognized the reality of Islam, if they still refused to embrace it.[71] If the Jews had become Muslims, then they would have continued to live in Khaybar in much the same way as they had been living there before.

CHAPTER THIRTEEN

In the Direction of Syria

Background

Following the peace agreement between the Muslims and the Quraysh, the Prophet (ﷺ) devoted his efforts to spreading the Mission outside the region in which he had previously focused. To fulfil the task of conveying the Islamic Message to the whole world, he (ﷺ) sent messages to the leaders of the surrounding regimes and the great powers of the day. Responses to this communication varied. One of the leaders, Shuraḥbeel ibn 'Amr al-Ghassâni, who was Heraclius' representative ruler in Buṣrâ, showed his enmity towards the Muslims. Neglecting the custom of receiving foreign delegations, he killed the Muslim envoy.[1] The ruler of Damascus, al-Ḥârith ibn Abi Shamr al-Ghassâni, rudely received the Muslim delegate and threatened to attack Madinah.[2]

Such responses formed a reasonable cause for considering this part of the world, which was relatively close to Madinah, as antagonistic towards the Muslims. This further led to the necessity of defending the Muslims from these enemies who might be planning to destroy the new religion at any time. In spite of the fact that there were similar negative attitudes from the rulers of other empires in other directions, the Prophet (ﷺ) decided to deal with Syria first. Several reasons make this an important and strategic next step. This could help the Muslims to avoid clashing with a large number of enemies simultaneously. In addition, because the tribes who resided along the route to Syria had submitted to the Muslims, the route was relatively safer than the main roads to Iraq, for example, which were still fraught with dangers from the pagans.

The Battle of Mu'tah

In Jumada I in the eighth year after the Hijrah, or August-September of 629 CE, the Prophet (ﷺ), with full awareness of great risk, assigned Zayd ibn Ḥârithah (رضي الله عنه) to take three thousand warriors and depart for Syria, which was ruled by governors who were subordinate to Heraclius. Contradictory to his other detachments, he designated two substitute leaders to take responsibility for commanding the military forces, consecutively, should something happen to Zayd.[3]

Having arrived at Ma'ân, the Muslim army received word that Heraclius had drafted one hundred thousand fighters to challenge them, in addition to a similar number who had joined him from numerous Arabian tribes.[4] The Muslim leaders thought of apprising the Prophet (ﷺ) of the fact that they were outnumbered by the enemy so that he might provide them with more troops or give further instructions in light of this information. One of the substitute leaders, 'Abdullâh ibn Rawâḥah (رضي الله عنه), urged the people not to hesitate, and drew their intention to the fact that they actually relied on their faith rather than their numbers when fighting their enemies. Furthermore, their ultimate goals were victory or martyrdom, and they had to plunge themselves into the war in order to achieve either. The warriors accepted this conclusion and continued their journey until they reached

Mu'tah.[5] There the Muslim army was overwhelmed. Despite the fact that the Muslims fought courageously, the war resulted in the deaths of the three Muslim commanders successively.[6]

Tactics and withdrawal

Khâlid ibn al-Waleed (ﷺ), who was a relatively new Muslim and one of their most skilful fighters, assumed command of the Muslim forces. He exchanged the positions of the right and the left wings of the army and ordered part of the army to advance from behind in order to delude the enemy into thinking that new troops were assisting the Muslims.[7] He was successful in his plan, frightened the enemy, and achieved a great victory.[8] According to Ibn Hishâm, only twelve Muslims were lost.[9]

Prior to receiving communication from the battlefield from a news carrier, the Prophet (ﷺ) described the whole scene in detail to his followers in Madinah. He announced the deaths of the three leaders, Khâlid's assumption of the command and described the triumph as a success granted by Allah.[10]

The word 'success' drove Ibn Hishâm to interpret it as a withdrawal that was implemented by Khâlid.[11] A number of the Prophetic biographers also adopted this idea.[12] If this battle had been lost by the Muslims, then the retreating troops would have been followed by their enemy, which did not happen. Neither side gained any booty from this conflict, whereas a thorough defeat of the enemy would have resulted in spoils. Furthermore, the enemy outnumbered the Muslims in this battle by over sixty times, and even then they had fallen back and been afflicted by a huge loss of their warriors, on top of failing to exterminate the Muslim troops. Khâlid ibn al-Waleed (ﷺ) preferred to be satisfied with that extent of victory.

This outcome, therefore, granted the Muslims with an impression that they had won in the fighting. At the same time, some Arabian tribes considered it a defeat for them and tried to attack the Muslims, thinking that the conflict had weakened them. The Quḍâ'ah, a tribe supportive of Heraclius, was an example of this and massed its fighters in order to attack Madinah. The Prophet (ﷺ) sent three hundred soldiers, led by 'Amr ibn al-'Âṣ (رضي الله عنه), to thwart their intentions. It was not long until they were reinforced with a further two hundred, including Abu Bakr (رضي الله عنه) and 'Umar (رضي الله عنه) in an invasion known as Dhât as-Salâsil. The Muslim army penetrated into Quḍâ'ah territory and forced them to disperse.[13]

Inferences and lessons

Several points were learned from these events, such as the following:

❖ Allah the Almighty grants victory to those who hold the true faith. His victory will not be achieved by great numbers of warriors or developed equipment. The Noble Qur'an revealed this fact, and the Battle of Mu'tah was a living example of this Qur'anic verse:

﴿How often a small group overcame a mighty host by Allah's leave; and Allah is with those who are patient.﴾ *(Qur'an 2: 249)*

❖ It is permissible to install leaders in a chain of command such that if one leader is incapacitated, the next one steps up to lead the forces. In addition, people have the right to choose a leader for themselves if the one in charge of their affairs is absent or killed, or if the ruler recommends this to them, instead of choosing leaders for them in advance.[14]

- Ja'far (ﷺ), who was one of the leaders, slaughtered his horse prior to plunging into the battle. He did so either to show that he would not desert the battlefield or to prevent his enemies from benefiting from it if he were killed. His action attracted no criticism, and therefore, scholars have inferred the permissibility of slaughtering one's mount in order for it not to be utilised by one's enemy.[15]
- The Prophet (ﷺ) informed his Companions (may Allah be pleased with them) about the fate of each of his appointed leaders and about Khâlid (ﷺ), who assumed leadership following the consultation of the warriors and based on his achievements on the battlefield.[16] This information came immediately after the happenings and was a miraculous sign for the Prophet (ﷺ) and his followers.
- It is possible to put highly-regarded individuals of distinction under the leadership of someone else, who is lower in position, provided that this leader has the characteristics and the merits for leading the activity.[17] This point can be taken from the fact that Abu Bakr (ﷺ) and 'Umar (ﷺ), who would be the first and second Islamic caliphs, fought under the command of 'Amr ibn al-'Âṣ.

CHAPTER FOURTEEN

The Conquest of Makkah

Breach of the Peace Treaty

Not only had the Quḍâ'ah misinterpreted the consequences of the battle of Mu'tah, the Quraysh also had fallen into the same trap by supporting their ally, the people of Bakr, against the tribe of Khuzâ'ah, which was in alliance with the Muslims. The Quraysh probably thought that the Muslims were at their weakest point after the battle of Mu'tah, and therefore, paid no attention to the peace treaty between themselves and the Muslims. When the tribe of Bakr invaded the Khuzâ'ah, the Quraysh participated in the invasion with armament and warriors, concealing their identities under the darkness of night. The people of Khuzâ'ah sought refuge at the Ka'bah to prevent the attackers from killing them out of respect for the sanctity of the place, but the leader of the attackers refused the request to save their lives, and he uttered something rude about the Sacred House and its Lord.[1]

Consequences

This event clearly broke the agreement of al-Ḥudaybiyah, which was supposed to ensure peace for ten years. It was also an insult to the Sacred House. The Prophet (ﷺ) learned about what happened and decided to help his allies.[2] Groups of the Quraysh discerned the consequences of breaking the peace treaty and clearly realised that the Muslims would stand up for their confederates. Thus, they sent Abu Sufyân to Madinah in order to renew the treaty and extend its effectiveness.

The Prophet (ﷺ) was inspired with news of this and informed his followers about it prior to Abu Sufyân's arrival in Madinah.[3] He (ﷺ) had time to ponder the matter and determine his position, and when Abu Sufyân came to present him with the Qurayshi viewpoint, he offered nothing in response. Abu Sufyân tried then to conciliate with some of the prominent Companions, namely Abu Bakr, 'Umar and 'Ali (may Allah be pleased with them), but again failed and was obliged to return to Makkah empty-handed.[4]

The Prophet (ﷺ) had already asked his wives to prepare the necessary equipment for him to go to battle, and soon he declared his destination and prayed to Allah to blind the Quraysh so that the Muslims could surprise them in their own territory.[5] The situation was clearly indicating an anticipated clash between the Muslims and Quraysh, and the people could easily conjecture his target, even if he concealed his intention at first.

The Muslims of Madinah, along with those who lived in the surrounding areas, were summoned to participate in the proposed march. Ten thousand fighters assembled[6] and left Madinah on the 10th of Ramadan 8 H,[7] or the 2nd of January 630 CE. The Muslims were allowed to withhold from fasting during their trip, but most of them continued to observe the state of fasting until they were closer to their destination and had reached a place known as Qadeed, approximately 50 miles from Makkah.[8] Several people of the Quraysh left Makkah and came to the Prophet (ﷺ) to declare their conversion to Islam.[9] In other accounts it was reported the Quraysh were unaware of the movement of the Muslim troops until they reached Mar adh-Dhahrân, about ten miles from Makkah.[10]

Entering Makkah

Three of the major personages of the Quraysh, including Abu Sufyân, tried to probe for news that might help in discovering what the Muslims were intending to do.[11] At the same time, al-'Abbâs ibn 'Abdul-Muṭṭalib (رضي الله عنه), an uncle of the Prophet (ﷺ), rode the Prophet's mule and left the Muslim camp in order to give advance warning to the Quraysh, so that they could emerge and submit their obedience safely, prior to Makkah being taken by force.[12] There is no evidence that he had been given permission to undertake this mission. Unexpectedly, al-'Abbâs met Abu Sufyân and led him to the Prophet (ﷺ), or as narrated by Bukhari, Abu Sufyân was captured by some of the Muslim guards and taken to the Prophet (ﷺ).[13]

The Prophet (ﷺ) announced to him that safety would be granted to anyone in Makkah who avoided fighting, stayed at home with the doors closed or entered the Sacred House. Out of respect for Abu Sufyân's rank, the Prophet (ﷺ), showing deep political insight, told him that anyone who chose to enter his house would also be safe.[14] As part of his tactics for taking Makkah without great bloodshed, the Prophet (ﷺ) had intended to shake Abu Sufyân internally and weaken his resistance and the Qurayshi resistance through him by directing al-'Abbâs to position him in such a way that would allow him to discern the power of Islam and its forces. Everything went according to plan. Abu Sufyân returned to Makkah and exhorted the people not to resist the Muslims.[15]

The Muslim forces entered Makkah from two directions and the Prophet (ﷺ) continued carrying his arms and wearing the dress of a soldier, visibly not changing his condition into the dress and state of a pilgrim. The Islamic procession met little opposition and few individuals were killed on either side.[16] The Prophet (ﷺ) had already issued instructions to his soldiers to restrict their fighting to those who insisted on an armed struggle. He (ﷺ) offered safety to everyone else, except a handful of individuals who were guilty of serious crimes.[17]

Submission to Islam

After the submission of Makkah to the Islamic State, the populace of the Arabian Peninsula, and many of their leaders, pledged their allegiance to the Prophet (ﷺ). Prior to the conquest of Makkah, they had embarked upon observing the struggle between him and his kindred among the Quraysh, increasingly believing that if Muhammad (ﷺ) were receiving true prophecy, he would be victorious. Once this victory disclosed the credibility of the Prophet (ﷺ), they set out to accept Islam and join the Islamic State.[18]

However, as Makkah had come under Islamic control, the formulation of the homage that was pronounced by the new Muslims was slightly changed compared with that of those who had given it before the conquest of Makkah. The new formula did not involve a reference to immigration but was restricted to accepting Islam, believing in the prophecy of Muhammad (ﷺ) and jihad, the struggle to make Islam supreme on the face of the earth.[19] As Makkah, the religious centre of the Arabs, had now become a Muslim city, the believers could worship their Lord in safety whenever they wished.[20]

Attitude of the Prophet (ﷺ)

Three important points were notable about this event. First, the Prophet (ﷺ), in contrast to ordinary conquerors, showed no conceit or haughtiness when entering Makkah, but instead was full of humility and gratitude for Allah's grace.[21] Secondly, he (ﷺ) preferred not to take vengeance against the inhabitants of Makkah, who had harshly oppressed him and his followers and who had not been satisfied with merely expelling him from that territory eight years previously, but had also opposed him vigorously and planned to destroy his mission. At this turning point, he (ﷺ) showed great mercy and issued a general amnesty to the people of Makkah.[22] Lastly, he was entirely faithful to the people of Madinah who had supported him. Therefore, contrary to their expectation that he would remain in his homeland of Makkah once it rallied around him, he declared that he would return to live in Madinah until his death.[23]

Sanctification of Makkah

The Prophet (ﷺ) and his troops remained in Makkah for nineteen days,[24] until everything had settled down. He removed three hundred sixty idols that had been scattered around the Ka'bah[25] and illustrations of Prophet Ibrâheem (عليه السلام) and his son Ismâ'eel (عليه السلام) which were used with arrows to seek luck or make decisions. He commented that the people were well acquainted with the fact that Ibrâheem and Ismâ'eel had never done that.[26] He was not satisfied with removing the heathen symbols but also rejected most of the pre-Islamic traditions, apart from the custodianship of the Ka'bah and supplying the pilgrims with water.[27] He declared the sanctity of Makkah and the inviolability of shedding blood or cutting plants there. Whosever sought to profane it under pretence of fighting for the Prophet (ﷺ) should be warned that had been allowed only to the Prophet (ﷺ) for a short time on the day of the conquest, after which the sanctity reverted to how it had been previously.[28]

In addition, he reminded the new converts about the prohibition of alcoholic drinks.[29] Breaking this divine command would result in a severe punishment, just as he showed no leniency towards a woman who stole during the conquest of Makkah. Her family had begged his adopted grandson, Usâmah ibn Zayd (رضي الله عنه), to intercede for her so that the Prophet (ﷺ) might forgive her. As he was establishing the divine laws of Islam on earth, he refused to accept the intercession and delivered a speech in which he mentioned that the previous generations had been destroyed because they executed punishments against weak people when they committed crimes and yet allowed the nobility to get away without punishment. To confirm the equality of all, he swore that if his own beloved daughter Fâṭimah (رضي الله عنها) were to steal, he would cut off her hand according to divine law.[30]

Islamic rulings from the conquest

This occasion inspired the scholars to deduce many Islamic verdicts. The most important points in this regard are summarised as follows:

- ❖ A visitor to Makah is permitted to enter it without being in the state of ritual consecration, if major or minor pilgrimage is not his or her intention.
- ❖ Some scholars ruled that the shortening of prayers during a journey lasts only for nineteen days. In this regard, Ibn 'Abbâs

(رضي الله عنه) declared that he abridged his prayers for only this period, and in cases where he stayed for longer than this, he would start after that amount of time to perform his prayers according to their regular, complete form.[31]

❖ During his advance on Makkah, the Prophet (ﷺ) fasted for many days before using the concession to break one's fast while travelling. Observing that, while travelling, the Prophet (ﷺ) sometimes fasted and sometimes did not, Ibn 'Abbâs granted the people the option either to keep their fast or to break it while travelling.[32]

❖ Makkah is a place of sanctity, and as a result, it has not been dealt with in the same way as other conquered places in respect to its lands and the imposition of taxes. This is why some of the scholars were of the opinion that it was prohibited for the lands of Makkah to be sold or its houses to be rented out. Nevertheless, other scholars took a different view, inclining towards the belief in the permissibility of selling the land and renting out the houses.[33]

Considering the sanctity of Makkah, as well as the directions of the Prophet (ﷺ) about abstaining from fighting there, and the relevant texts about fighting unbelievers and oppressors and punishing criminals, the scholars said that unbelievers are not allowed to enter Makkah.[34] So, if they intend to do so, they should be fought either prior to their entrance or when they have been caught inside of its boundaries. As for oppressive people and criminals, the best approach is to apprehend them and take them out from the sanctity of Makkah where they can be chastised.[35]

❖ On the day when Makkah was conquered, the Prophet (ﷺ) rode on his she-camel while reciting *Sooal-Fatḥ*[36] with beautiful intonation.[37] This hadith shows the acceptability of modulation when reciting the verses of the Noble Qur'an, if this does not impact on the soundness of the recitation or result in altering the proper articulations.[38]

❖ The Prophet (ﷺ) refused to enter the Ka'bah until the drawings and statues had been removed from it. Relying on this position, as well as other hadiths, the scholars concluded the prohibition of carving and images of living beings, though some of them allowed certain exceptions in the case of toys.[39]

❖ Pledges of homage were given to the Prophet (ﷺ) individually by both men and women. The hadiths about this matter show that he (ﷺ) shook hands with men as a part of this process, while he was satisfied with women's verbal allegiance. Joining both genders in this procedure reflects the equality of the two in holding the responsibility for adopting the religion and constructing the new life accordingly. Hence, women have to comprehend Islam and know how to manage their affairs, exactly as men do. If they neglect this duty, then they and their society will be liable to fall prey to the wiliness of their enemies.

This process of pledges also reveals that it is unacceptable in Islam for men and women to shake hands or touch one another unless there is a genuine need for it, like receiving medical treatment.[40] This prohibition of physical contact does not apply between men and women who are so closely related that a marriage between them would be incestuous.

CHAPTER FIFTEEN

The Invasion of Ḥunayn

Weakening of the heathen banner

Makkah had been the main centre for the heathenistic practices of the Arabs, and its collapse had convulsed the status of idolatry in the Arabian Peninsula. Some of the other Arab tribes felt that they might be the next target of the Muslims, particularly the Thaqeef tribe, from whom the Prophet (ﷺ) years earlier had sought assistance and been rudely evicted, and the Hawâzin. Prior to conquering Makkah, these two tribes heard that the Muslim army had departed from Madinah and wondered if the Prophet (ﷺ) would attack them, and so they prepared to oppose him.[1] At this stage, they were unacquainted with the clear aim of the Islamic troops that left Madinah, and thus they felt awe at the possibility of being the target of the invasion.

After the conquest of Makkah, the Hawâzin, a mighty tribe in the Ṭa'if area, wanted to protect their idolatrous practises. Perhaps they also thought that since Makkah was a region of the Quraysh of which the Prophet (ﷺ) himself was a part, its situation, from the tribal viewpoint, had merely undergone a change of leadership. As the Hawâzin were a separate tribe, its people were afraid of losing their independence if they became subordinate to the Prophet (ﷺ). Hence, the two great tribes, Hawâzin and

Thaqeef, were stimulated by different motives, but they shared an interest in levelling their powers against the Muslims to crush them before matters escalated.[2]

Plan of resistance

Mâlik ibn 'Awf an-Naḍri, then aged thirty, was the dynamic force behind this alliance, which was joined by many additional tribes, and he was installed as leader of the united troops.[3] He decided that all the families, children, slaves, and animals should escort the warriors until the last minute to encourage them to fight, as well as allow the troops to protect their families and belongings. Moreover, he urged his combatants to break their scabbards as soon as they encountered the Muslims, to terrify their opponents, and then assail them compactly in order to eradicate them.[4]

They arrived at the valley of Ḥunayn[5] and took the best places in preparation of ambushing the Muslims. It has been narrated that Mâlik ibn 'Awf arranged his troops in an impressive manner. He lined up his cavalrymen in the front row, followed by the infantry, next the women, then the sheep and goats, and then the camels,[6] to use their height to make the Muslims believe that his forces were greater than they actually were. It was thought that his army was at least twenty thousand in number.[7] This figure, however, seems to include the non-combatants who participated in the procession. As-Sindi, in his annotations on the hadiths of Bukhari, mentioned that there were four thousand fighters,[8] which sounds more acceptable.

The Prophet (ﷺ) was informed about this concentration, and he deputised 'Abdullâh ibn Abi Ḥadrad al-Aslami (رضي الله عنه) to penetrate the masses, explore their power and gather intelligence on them. The Prophet (ﷺ) decided to direct his followers to fight against the heathen alliance. The Muslim troops consisted of ten thousand warriors or, according to Ibn Katheer, twelve thousand who had participated in the conquering of Makkah, and a further two thousand new converts from Makkah.[9] To support his fighters, the Prophet (ﷺ) asked Ṣafwân ibn Umayyah, who was still a polytheist at that time, to lend him weapons and armour. Ṣafwân asked if this was an order of confiscation, but the Prophet (ﷺ) replied that it would be a guaranteed loan until they were returned. Ṣafwân agreed to this and lent him one hundred suits of armour with their related weapons.[10]

Muslim advance

On the 5th or 6th of Shawwâl in 8 H, corresponding to the 27th or 28th of January 630 CE, the Prophet (ﷺ) marched with his troops towards Ḥunayn. Someone commented that the Muslims would win because of their huge number. Many narrators attributed this comment to an unknown person, but some of them weakly attributed it to the Prophet (ﷺ) himself[11] or to Abu Bakr aṣ-Ṣiddeeq (رضي الله عنه).[12] As-Sindi pointed out that this comment displeased the Prophet (ﷺ),[13] although it reflected the fact that the Muslim troops vastly outnumbered the heathen alliance.

When the Muslim forces were descending the slopes of the valley of Ḥunayn, intending to pass it during the half-light of dawn, they were surprised by their enemies swooping in from all directions. The Muslims retreated without heed for one another.[14] Only a small number of people stood by the Prophet (ﷺ). Some of them were members of his family, like 'Ali ibn Abi Ṭâlib, Rabi'ah and his brother Abu Sufyân, the children of al-Ḥârith ibn 'Abdul-Muṭṭalib, al-Faḍl ibn al-'Abbâs, Ayman ibn 'Ubayd, and the

Prophet's adopted grandson Usâmah ibn Zayd. There were also a few immigrants, like Abu Bakr and 'Umar (may Allah be pleased with them all).[15] The Prophet (ﷺ) burst into the conflict exclaiming:

> I am really the Prophet — it's no fib!
> I am the son of 'Abdul-Muṭṭalib![16]

At the same time, he asked his uncle al-'Abbâs to call back the Anṣâr, his supporters from Madinah who had paid him allegiance prior to the immigration. Once they heard this call, they responded by saying, "Here we are at your service!" They started returning, despite the huge tumult that accompanied the whole situation. In some cases, they dismounted and left their riding animals behind them, if their mounts hindered them from returning to the Prophet (ﷺ).

Approximately a hundred people assembled with the Prophet (ﷺ) and entered into a violent battle. He (ﷺ) dismounted from his mule and joined his Companions in the severe fighting until the heathen alliance had been clearly vanquished and withdrew from the battlefield, leaving behind thousands of their people and belongings to be captured by the Muslims.[17]

Reasons for victory

It would be unfair to ascribe the confusion and the failure at the beginning of this battle to the new converts who fought[18] since they were only two thousand out of twelve thousand warriors. Their lack of a deep belief was just one factor in this confusion, but the main reason for the initial chaos was the inaccuracy of the information they had received about their enemy. The Muslims were surprised to find their enemy occupying every part of the field.

In addition, the sense of reliance upon their own power rather than Allah's help, as exhibited by the comment that the Muslims would not be defeated as long as they had so many fighters, was an invisible cause. The Muslims had been guided by the Qur'an and the teachings of the Prophet (ﷺ) to prepare the equipment vital for any military operation without forgetting that their hearts should be tied only to Allah the Almighty, not to their arms. The fact that many Muslims failed to prioritise this latter principle resulted in their first defeat, but correct belief was soon reactivated in the souls of around a hundred of them, who returned to endure with the Prophet (ﷺ) and share in attaining a peremptory victory. This was a lesson to the Muslims, who were like others in their desires and presentiments, to equip themselves with the requisite items for their proposed manoeuvres but not to forget that tangible triumph is always granted by Allah. The Noble Qur'an mentioned this point clearly in the following verses:

﴾Truly, Allah has given you victory on many battlefields, and on the day of Ḥunayn when you rejoiced at your great number, but it availed you naught and the earth, vast as it is, was straitened for you, then you turned back in flight. Then Allah sent down His *sakeenah* [calmness, tranquillity and reassurance] on the Messenger [Muhammad] and on the believers, and sent down forces [of angels] which you saw not, and punished the disbelievers. Such is the recompense of disbelievers. Then after that Allah will accept the repentance of whom He wills; and Allah is Oft-Forgiving, Most Merciful.﴿ *(Qur'an 9: 25-27)*

Routing the pagans

The defeated group dispersed to Awṭas and Nakhlah, and their main forces, including their young leader, Mâlik ibn 'Awf, headed towards Ṭâ'if.[19] The Prophet (ﷺ) worked to prevent them from rallying their forces and sent groups of his fighters to pursue and destroy them.[20] He (ﷺ) directed his followers to watch over the booty in a place known as al-Ji'rânah. The loot consisted of six thousand women and children,[21] four thousand ounces of silver, twenty four thousand camels, and over forty thousand ewes, in addition to an unknown number of horses, cows and donkeys.[22] Despite the possibility that the above figures may have become exaggerated, they clearly reflect the resounding victory won by the Muslims and the huge loss suffered by the heathen alliance, as paganism was dealt a deathblow.

The siege of Ṭâ'if

Meanwhile, the Prophet (ﷺ) himself led the remaining Muslims and laid siege to Ṭâ'if, a province that he had visited alone a few years previously, seeking aid from its leaders in preaching his mission. Although we have no actual information about their psychological position during this period, we may suppose that the people of Ṭâ'if were feeling deep remorse for disappointing him, as they lost the glory that they would have won had they supported him at that critical time. They had opposed him because they espoused idolatry but also to preserve their standing amongst the Arabs, which they deemed would be imperilled by following him.

In resisting the Muslims, the people of Ṭâ'if benefited from its geography: it had mountains, as well as strong fences and defensive forts. The only way to enter or exit from it was through the gates, which were firmly bolted. The expectation of a prolonged blockade led the people of Ṭâ'if to store a great deal of food and armament.[23]

The Muslim troops were encamped close to its walls, so they were within arrow range and that resulted in some fatalities. As they were unable to break into the forts since the Prophet (ﷺ) refused to forfeit his warriors futilely, he decided to move them out of arrow range and beleaguer Ṭâ'if from a slight distance.[24] This condition persisted for about twenty days, during which new weapons were used. It was narrated that the Prophet (ﷺ) was the first to pelt Ṭâ'if using mangonels, or catapults.[25] In addition, a few Muslims advanced with a testudo, or tank-like structure, to approach the wall and pierce it or burn it, but molten hot iron was thrown upon them obliging them to leave the tank so that they were open targets of arrows, which killed some of them. Due to this, the Prophet (ﷺ) ordered his followers to chop down their vinyards so that the beleaguered people of Ṭâ'if[26] would become demoralised. Twenty-three slaves of Ṭâ'if went to the Prophet (ﷺ) to profess their belief in Islam, and he liberated them, refusing to reinstate them to their former owners even if they became Muslim.[27]

Breaking into Ṭâ'if did not seem possible, so the Prophet (ﷺ) spoke to some of his Companions about lifting the siege,[28] seeming inclined to take this step. A number of his followers found it hard to withdraw without having conquered it, but eventually they agreed with his plans.[29] This decision was motivated by the fact that continuing the siege might place the Muslim troops in a weak position militarily and the fact that the Prophet (ﷺ) had supplicated to Allah to guide the Thaqeef tribe to embrace Islam.[30] Ṭâ'if, the homeland of Thaqeef, was surrounded by tribes that had become Muslim or surrendered to the Prophet (ﷺ), and there was anticipation that it would eventually declare its acceptance of the new religion, too.

Booty and the Anṣâr

The Prophet (ﷺ) returned to al-Ji'rânah, where the booty was stored. He stayed there for almost two weeks without distributing it, hoping to return it to the Hawâzin, if they arrived and paid him homage.[31] When it became clear that they were unlikely to return, he began to divide the booty amongst his warriors, focusing on the new converts from the Quraysh and excluding the Anṣâr, his supporters from Madinah.[32] The Anṣâr appeared unhappy about that and voiced their disappointment.

The Prophet (ﷺ) summoned them alone to a meeting and asked their opinions. Their leaders did not dodge the situation but explained that some of their young men had said, "May Allah forgive the Prophet (ﷺ) for he is giving to the Quraysh and leaves us while our swords drip from blood."[33] The Prophet (ﷺ) justified his division of the booty, saying that he had done this in order to give the hearts of the new converts a stronger attachment to Islam and the other Muslims. Moreover, the Anṣâr were the real winners, because they would return with him, whereas the other people would return to their homes with only camels and cattle. In addition, the Prophet (ﷺ) boasted of his love for them, saying: «Had there been no migration, I would have been one of the Anṣâr; and if the people go in one direction, I will surely take the way of the Anṣâr. May Allah have mercy on the Anṣâr, their children, and their grandchildren.»[34]

This was sufficient to return the situation to normal.

Acceptance of Islam

Following the distribution of the loot, deputations of the Hawâzin came to the Prophet (ﷺ), converted to Islam and pledged loyalty to him.[35] They requested that their riches and captured people should to be restored to them, but this came too late. Although the Prophet (ﷺ) had waited for them to come for many days, they came after everything had been shared out. Nonetheless, he asked them to opt for their riches or captives, and they chose the latter. He harangued his followers in this regard, saying: «Your brothers have come to us turning to Allah in repentance and I wish to restore to them their captured people. Whoever is willing to relinquish (his portion) willingly or alternatively be compensated as soon as Allah gives us more booty, let him do it.»

The people announced that they would relinquish the captives without expecting any payment for it. For further confirmation, he (ﷺ) asked them to state their views freely to their senior officers so that he could learn if there were any objections to this. Individually, they passed on their consent to the Prophet (ﷺ) via their officers and then all of the captives were released.[36] This prudent conduct stabilised the victors who abandoned their achievements and paved the way for the new Muslims of Hawâzin to integrate with the Islamic society. The Prophet (ﷺ) was not satisfied with merely fulfilling his promise but also designated the ex-opponent commander, Mâlik ibn 'Awas the chief of the Muslims of Hawâzin.[37]

The minor pilgrimage

The Prophet (ﷺ) was now free to return to Makkah in a state of worship to praise and thank his Lord. He (ﷺ) intended to make a minor pilgrimage to Makkah from al-Ji'rânah. Completing this, he appointed 'Attab ibn Aseed (رضي الله عنه) as governor of Makkah and designated Mu'âdh ibn Jabal (رضي الله عنه) to educate the people about

Islam and teach them the Noble Qur'an. Then, he returned to Madinah.[38]

Lessons

There are many teachings that can be extracted from these invasions:

❖ Living or being in a non-Muslim State is not an excuse for not reprimanding a guilty person. The Prophet (ﷺ) chastened an intoxicated person when he was in Ḥunayn.[39]

❖ The possibility of seeking help from non-Muslims or relying on their assistance during a battle is illustrated by the Prophet (ﷺ) as he borrowed armour and weapons from Ṣafwân ibn Umayyah. In accordance with other teachings of Islam, the scholars have put two conditions on such help and reliance: a feeling of confidence that the disbeliever will keep his or her word and not harm the Muslims in return, and avoidance of allowing the disbelievers to prevail in battle or put an end to it at the expense of Islamic predominance.[40]

❖ Killing children, women and the hirelings and slaves who assist in a war is illegal.[41] However, Muslims must oppose them if they start fighting, kill them if they refuse to stop fighting and leave them if they flee.[42]

❖ The property left by an unbeliever who is killed in battle belongs to the Muslim soldiers who killed the person.[43]

❖ It is permissible for the leaders of the community to distribute donations to new converts in order to make things easier for the converts and create a stronger relationship between them and the rest of the Islamic community.

- It is permissible to spy on the enemy to discover their plans and proposed military tactics.
- Women can participate in the battles in positions to support the soldiers by feeding them and nursing them and so on, and in cases where an enemy attacks an Islamic territory, all of its inhabitants, including the women, should fight the enemy. Women's participation in the actual fighting is bound by necessity, and they should continue to follow Islamic dictates while doing so, such as wearing appropriate Islamic dress. However, if their participation is not truly needed or causes them to do what is prohibited, then their going out is forbidden.[44]
- Jihad does not mean holding a grudge against disbelievers; rather it is a sort of warning so that people may escape from punishment in the hereafter. Jihad is the struggle for implementing Allah's religion on earth. This is why the Prophet (ﷺ) prayed for Allah to guide the Thaqeef tribe to the Right Way when he lifted the siege that he had laid upon them.[45]

CHAPTER SIXTEEN

The Battle of Tabook

Background

Towards the end of Dhul Ḥijjah 8 H, corresponding to April 630 CE, the Prophet (ﷺ) returned to Madinah[1] after his minor pilgrimage that followed the events of Ḥunayn. He (ﷺ) felt that his warriors needed to rest after completing several crucial military operations within a six month period, including the battle of Mu'tah, the conquest of Makkah, the invasion at Ḥunayn and the siege of Ṭâ'if.

The menace of idolatry was obviously waning in the Arabian Peninsula now that many of its tribes had embraced Islam. Correspondingly, the disbelievers no longer had the ability to create serious difficulties for the Muslims. Hence, there was scope for Islam to move in the direction of the neighbouring territories with the aim of spreading the faith, so that it might be embraced or alternatively result in peaceful agreements that would enable the Muslims to go even further afield.

Once again, the Prophet (ﷺ) looked towards Syria, since the land in that direction was under the control of Rome and many of its inhabitants were Christians. The gap between them and the Muslims was less than the gap with the pagans and made it more likely that they would accept Islam. Ibn Katheer also narrates that two verses from the Noble Qur'an lay behind this idea:

﴾O you who believe! Verily, the polytheists are impure. So let them not come near al-Masjid al-Ḥarâm [the sacred sanctuary at Makkah] after this year; and if you fear poverty, Allah will enrich you if He wills, out of His bounty. Surely, Allah is All-Knowing, All-Wise. Fight against those who believe not in Allah, nor in the Last Day, nor forbid that which has been forbidden by Allah and His Messenger and those who acknowledge not the religion of truth [Islam] among the people of the Scripture, until they pay the *jizyah* [poll tax] with willing submission, and feel themselves subdued.﴿ *(Qur'an 9: 28-29)*

According to Ibn Katheer, preventing the disbelievers from approaching Makkah had caused the Quraysh to fear that they would be deprived of the benefits of visitors to the Sacred House, since they depended on these revenues as Makkah was not suitable land to support farming.[2] Whether the people accepted Islam or not, Allah told them not to fear; He would provide for them. Both Muslims and non-Muslims would continue to be a source of income, either through what they spent during their pilgrimages in Makkah if they became Muslims, or via paying the poll tax if they preferred to maintain their own religion. Despite observing an economic benefit from this, it does not mean that was the true reason for their plans, which was the desire for spreading Islam itself, nor does it mean this is the reason for the poll tax. However, we may infer from this one of the external incentives that caused Heraclius to mobilise his troops to invade Madinah.[3]

Recommencement towards Syria

Unlike his previous military expeditions, the Prophet (ﷺ) plainly declared the destination of their next target and instructed his followers to prepare themselves to attack the Byzantine empire of Rome, pre-empting them before they could collect their forces and attempt an invasion of the Muslim lands. The season when the decision was taken was sultry and a time of drought. It was the month of Rajab in the year 9 H, or in October and November of 630 CE. Therefore, the long journey, the time constraint and the large forces of the enemy were the reasons for revealing the proposed location, so that people might gird themselves fully for action.[4] Although the Muslims were not looking forward to challenging the powerful Roman forces, they fully complied with this plan.[5]

The Prophet (ﷺ) stimulated his Companions to participate in the invasion and partake in its cost. True Muslims strove to outdo one another in making their contributions and donated as much as they could. 'Uthmân ibn 'Affân (رضي الله عنه) led in his charitable donations in response to the Prophet's saying (ﷺ) that paradise would be secured for the people who equipped the troops.[6] Ibn Isḥâq narrated that 'Uthmân's outlay was huge and no one else could have afforded as much as he did.[7]

At the same time, the hypocrites worked to frustrate the Muslims and dissuade them from affiliating with the proposed battle. They spread gossip about the difficulties that would beset them on their journey because of the hot season. They used to gather in a house that was owned by Suwaylim the Jew in order to thwart the Prophet's preparations. When the Prophet (ﷺ) became aware of this collusion, he acted resolutely and sent a few of his Companions to set fire to the house.[8] Other hypocrites planned to flee from their obligations by asking the Prophet (ﷺ) to excuse them from participating in the expedition.[9] 'Abdullâh ibn Ubay, the most famous hypocrite, recruited fellow doubters and camped separately from the troops led by the Prophet (ﷺ). As soon as the true Muslims started to advance, he lagged behind with his dissembling soldiers.[10] He was repeating the actions he had performed at Uḥud to shake the Muslims' resolve and divert them from the proposed task.

The Prophet (ﷺ) left Madinah with over thirty thousand Muslim fighters[11] and headed for Tabook, a distance of 778 miles away.[12] The majority of these fighters were true believers, but there were also a few doubters among them.[13] As for those who did not attend the campaign, they were mainly hypocrites but also those who could not meet the requirements for battle and a further three individuals who failed to show an intention to participate in it.[14] The Prophet (ﷺ) directed two of his respected followers to remain in Madinah: Muhammad ibn Maslamah al-Anṣâri (رضي الله عنه), who was in charge of governing the State on behalf of the Prophet (ﷺ), and 'Ali ibn Abi Ṭâlib (رضي الله عنه), who was commissioned with taking care of his own family and that of the Prophet (ﷺ).[15]

However, the hypocrites seized this opportunity to vilify 'Ali, who was the Prophet's cousin and his son-in-law, by assuming that he had been left behind because the Prophet (ﷺ) could not tolerate him! 'Ali was disturbed by this rumour and hastened to catch up with the Prophet (ﷺ) when he was three miles from Madinah in order to report this rumour and demand the truth. The Prophet (ﷺ) accused the hypocrites of lying and asked 'Ali (رضي الله عنه): «Aren't you satisfied to be in my consideration similar to Hâroon's (Aaron) position in the view of Moosâ (Moses)? Except that there will not be any prophet after me.»

This remark, cited by Bukhari, informed 'Ali of the high position that he occupied in the heart of the Prophet (ﷺ) and he returned calmly to Madinah to fulfil his duties.[16]

Suffering and divine assistance

Under very difficult circumstances, the Muslim troops advanced towards Tabook, a two-week journey away. Some narrations reflect the hardship they endured as well as the miraculous nature of the Prophet (ﷺ) that deepened the belief in the souls of the Muslims and helped them to bear their arduous tasks. Besides lack of money and mounts, Ibn Katheer narrated that groups of two or three soldiers took turns riding on a single camel that, in some cases, they were obliged to slaughter in order to drink the water that it stored. They asked the Prophet (ﷺ) to pray for them so that Allah the Almighty might supply them with water, and as soon as he started his prayer, the heavens clouded over and rain poured down on their camp.[17]

A similar event is described by Ibn Katheer, but it involved nourishment. The Companions expressed their worry to the Prophet (ﷺ) about the insufficiency of their mounts if they slaughtered them for the purpose of nutrition. They suggested bringing him their provisions in order to ask Allah to invoke His blessing on them. He agreed to their suggestion and they began to throw before him handfuls of corn, dates or pieces of bread. This resulted in a relatively small pile, but through his prayer, it was increased so much that they were able to eat their fill and fill all of the vessels that they had brought with them in the camp, and there were still some leftovers.[18]

Meanwhile, several of those who had lagged behind in Madinah now came to regret not joining in the military expedition and hastened to catch up with it. The notable point in this connection is that the Prophet (ﷺ) used to say, when he was informed that a rider had been observed, «Let him be so-and-so», mentioning the name of one of the absentees. Once the rider's identity was established, it would be discovered that he was the one whom the Prophet (ﷺ) had wished it to be.[19] This information actually indicated two important points arising from his prophethood. First, despite the huge number of the warriors, he was acutely aware of the presence or absence of any one of them. Secondly, his ability to identify the riders from a great distance was not only a marvel but was also a clear sign of his discernment of the personalities of his followers and, consequently, his capacity to utilise their peculiarities in ruling the growing Islamic state.

The ruins of Thamood

On their way towards Tabook, the Muslim army passed al-Ḥijr, the former homeland of the Thamood people who had rejected the message of their Prophet Sâliḥ (عليه السلام) and had been punished by Allah.[20] The soldiers looked around the terrain, drew water from its wells, kneaded their dough, and filled their pots with meat in preparation for cooking. The Prophet (ﷺ) directed them to empty out their pots and feed the dough to their animals. Instead of using such defiled water, he led them to the well that was used by the miraculous camel of Prophet Sâliḥ (عليه السلام).[21] In this regard, he advised his followers not to enter the regions of people who had destroyed themselves unless they entered there weeping, lest the same scourge strike them.[22]

Peace treaties

When the Prophet's troops reached their intended destination, they found no massing of their enemies. Either the Roman forces had dispersed because of the Muslim advancement or they had been unsuccessful in mustering up an army to fight the Muslims. Instead of a battle, the rulers of the surrounding area began appearing and pledging homage to the Prophet (ﷺ). Yooḥanna ibn Ru'bah, the ruler of Aylah, in addition to the people of Jarbâ' and Adruḥ, came to him and agreed to pay him remuneration in return for their safety.[23] Ibn Hishâm quoted the letter of security that was given to Yooḥanna:

> In the Name of Allah, the Most Gracious, the Most Merciful. This is a safety (guarantee) from Allah and from the Prophet Muhammad, the Messenger of Allah, to Yooḥanna ibn Ru'bah and the people of Aylah and their ships and caravans. They, as well as those who are with them from among the people of Syria, Yemen, and the people of the sea, have been guaranteed the security and protection of Allah and of the Prophet Muhammad. If any of them creates a problem, his/her wealth will not save him/her and taking it (the wealth) will be acceptable. They should not be prevented from water that they come to nor from a passage through which they want to go, either by land or sea.[24]

A few rulers, like Ukaydir ibn 'Abdul-Malik, the king of Doomah, did not hurry to make a peace agreement with the Prophet (ﷺ), but binding the entire area with agreements of security was crucial for the Muslims. Therefore, the Prophet (ﷺ) sent out a group of warriors, led by Khâlid ibn al-Waleed (رضي الله عنه), to fetch Ukaydir for this purpose. To enable Khâlid to recognise the king and complete this task successfully, the Prophet (ﷺ) gave him a description of exactly what Ukaydir would be doing when he found him. These details were so accurate that Khâlid was able to capture the king and take him to the Prophet (ﷺ). The king agreed to pay the Muslims a poll tax, and then he was released.[25]

Moral victory

Despite the fact that the general situation was difficult throughout the troops' advancement and no booty was gained since there was no battle, the trip to Tabook was a moral victory for Islam. Through this expedition, the Muslims were able to examine themselves closely to discover their truthfulness in their belief. Those who had hesitated but had a genuine intention towards Islam had the opportunity to refresh their spirits, either just after the departure of the troops for Tabook or following their return. This moral power, which was the basis of Islamic victory throughout history, was associated with practical strength.

Psychologically, they broke the barrier of their own fears about marching for hundreds of miles into the heart of their enemies' territory. On top of this, they managed to bind with the people of that region through peace agreements, which transferred their loyalty from Rome to the Islamic State. In addition, the great numbers and strength of the Muslim army terrified its enemies about the growing weight of Islam in the Arabian Peninsula.

Incidents on the return

When the Prophet (ﷺ) was fully satisfied with the situation and the outcome of the operation, he led his troops back to Madinah.[26] On the way, there was some flowing water, and he instructed his followers not to use it if they reached it prior to him, until he had also arrived. A few of the hypocrites arrived at the trickle of water, neglected his instructions, and this resulted in its depletion. The Prophet (ﷺ) chastised them for their disobedience, then placed his hand underneath the trickle and prayed, seeking blessings from Allah. The water gushed out and the people took their fill of it. He commented that those who lived longer would eventually witness the valley as a most fertile spot.[27]

Another matter occurred during his return to Madinah that pertained to a mosque that would be known as 'aḍ-Ḍirâr', or the Mosque of Harm. The Prophet (ﷺ) had been asked to pray in that new mosque by a few people pretending to be seeking his benediction of it, but as he (ﷺ) was about to set off for Tabook, he could not spare the time to visit it. On his return, he learned of the true motives of those who had built it. The hypocrites had constructed it seemingly for religious purposes, but in reality, planned to use it as a centre for their assemblies and for waging war against the Muslims. Therefore, the Prophet (ﷺ) delegated two of his Companions to go and burn it down, and this resulted in the dispersion of its supporters.[28] The following verses are relevant to this incident:

﴾And as for those who put up a mosque by way of harm and disbelief and to disunite the believers and as an outpost for those who warred against Allah and His Messenger aforetime, they will indeed swear that their intention is nothing but good. Allah bears witness that they are certainly liars. Never stand therein. Verily, the Masjid whose foundation was laid from the first day on piety is more worthy that you stand therein [to pray].﴿

(Qur'an 9: 107-108)

Rewards and excuses

While approaching Madinah, the Prophet (ﷺ) informed his Companions that some of those who had remained in Madinah had shared with them in all their tasks, despite not being physically present among them. This declaration meant that those people enjoyed the same level of rewards on the basis that true and sincere reasons had kept them from participating in the march.[29] These non-participants, however, were not the hypocrites, who apologised for their truancy. Despite the fact that the Prophet (ﷺ) disapproved of their excuses, he sent the hypocrites away and left their conditions to Almighty Allah.[30] It was decided that three Companions who offered no excuses and refused to fabricate any lies to the Prophet (ﷺ) should be isolated until Allah had judged them. They were boycotted for about fifty days, during which time they were completely humbled until life had become so straightened for them that they could bear it no more, and only then did the noble verses come down to the Prophet (ﷺ), granting them the forgiveness of Allah:

﴾Allah has forgiven the Prophet, the Muhâjiroon and the Anṣâr who followed him [Muhammad] in the time of distress [Tabook expedition], after the hearts of a party of them had nearly deviated [from the Right Path], but He accepted their repentance. Certainly, He is unto them full of kindness, Most Merciful. And [He did forgive also] the three who did not join [the Tabook expedition and whose case was deferred by the Prophet for Allah's decision] until for them the earth, vast as it is, was straitened and their own selves were straitened to them, and they perceived that there is no fleeing from Allah, and no refuge but with Him. Then He forgave them, so that they might beg for His pardon [and repent unto Him]. Verily, Allah is the One Who forgives and accepts repentance, Most Merciful. O you who believe! Be afraid of Allah, and be with those who are true [in words and deeds].﴿

(Qur'an 9: 117-119)[31]

Juristic matters

The Noble Qur'an described this invasion in detail and set forth the distinguishing criterion for true Muslims. This criterion was based on their readiness to fight for the sake of Islam, with both their wealth and their lives. The following verses clearly illustrate this:

﴾March forth, whether you are light [being healthy, young and wealthy] or heavy [being ill, old and poor], and strive hard with your wealth and your lives in the cause of Allah. This is better for you, if you but knew. Had it been a near gain [booty in front of them] and an easy journey, they would have followed you, but the distance [on the Tabook expedition] was long for them; and they would swear by Allah: if we only could, we would certainly have come forth with you. They destroy their own selves, and Allah knows that they are liars. May Allah forgive you [O Muhammad]. Why did you grant them leave [for remaining behind; you should have persisted in your order for them to proceed on jihad], until those who told the truth were seen by you in a clear light, and you had known the liars? Those who believe in Allah and the Last Day would not ask your leave to be exempted from fighting with their properties and their lives; and Allah is the All-Knower of the pious believers. It is only those who believe not in Allah and the Last Day and whose hearts are in doubt that ask your leave [to be exempted from jihad]. So in their doubts they waver, and if they had intended to march out, they would have made some preparation for it.﴿ *(Qur'an 9: 41-46)*

The willingness to spend one's life and wealth in the cause of Allah is a crucial measure that defines real believers and gives them success in the hereafter. This is why the Prophet (ﷺ) declared that paradise will be secure for those who gave their wealth to equip the Muslim troops heading for Tabook. 'Uthmân ibn 'Affân (رضي الله عنه) provided money and mounts far more than any other individual,[32] so the Prophet (ﷺ) repeated the following phrase twice: «Nothing will harm 'Uthmân from now on.»[33]

So, while true Muslims strive with their selves and their riches to help and support Islam, disbelievers devote their efforts to creating havoc for it. The hypocrites are most treacherous; for they cover their true intentions with a fake mantle of Islam and work on destroying it from the inside. The people who built the Mosque of Harm (aḍ-Ḍirâr), which was outwardly for worship but secretly for intriguing against Islam, are an example of this. Dealing harshly with such a group rather than treating them with mercy is essential for maintaining the solidity of the Islamic society.

As for juristic issues, several points can be drawn from this expedition. The most important lessons that may be noted are as follows:

- Training soldiers strictly is necessary to enable them to bear the difficulties of defending their State.
- Islam did not compel Jews and Christians to abandon their original religions, but complying with the norms of the Islamic society in which they lived was essential for harmony. If they decided not to embrace Islam, they had agree to a State poll tax for adult males, and they all had to avoid engaging in certain practices which conflict with Islamic values, such as drinking wine openly. In return, they were granted safety, protection and exemption from military service.
- Passing through ancient archaeological sites ought to be for the purpose of learning and asking Allah to protect oneself and other believers from a similar disastrous end. It should not be for enjoyment or distraction, particularly if the remains belong to penalised nations.[34]
- Breaking off company with an individual for more than three days is legitimate if it is motivated by a religious factor. This

sense was taken from the experience of Ka'b ibn Mâlik (رضي الله عنه) and his two colleagues, who, as mentioned earlier, were kept away from other Muslims for about fifty days. This event also suggests the possibility of not responding to the greetings of those who have been disassociated for a religious reason.[35]

❖ It is permissible for someone who is lower in religious position to lead the prayers when someone who is higher is present. This possibility was understood from the Prophet's (ﷺ) absence one day during the Tabook expedition, when he went to perform his ritual ablution and was delayed for some reason which caused His Companion, 'Abdur-Raḥmân ibn 'Awf (ﷺ), to lead the dawn prayer instead of him. When the Prophet (ﷺ) returned, 'Abdur-Raḥmân tried to vacate his position as the imam of the prayer, but the Prophet (ﷺ) signalled to him to continue and he (ﷺ) joined in the prayer with the rest.[36]

CHAPTER SEVENTEEN

Religious and Social Victories

Thaqeef

Following his return from Tabooto Madinah in Ramadan in the year 9 H, near the end of 630 CE, the Prophet (ﷺ) entertained dignitaries from numerous tribes who had come in order to surrender to the Islamic State or embrace the Islamic religion.

Thaqeef, which participated in the battle of Ḥunayn against the Muslims and had been subsequently besieged for a while in their homeland of Ṭâ'if, sent one of these delegations. Complying with thc Prophet's prediction, the people of Ṭâ'if discerned their inability to enter into a war against the whole adjoining area and had decided to convert to Islam. This realization led them delegate six individuals, representing all Ṭâ'if families,[1] to visit the Prophet (ﷺ) with the hope of implementing a conditional pact.

Their desire was to retain their idol that was known as al-Lât for three years and excuse themselves from the obligation to pray. However, the Prophet (ﷺ) explained the monotheism of Islam and rejected their first demand. They tried to shorten the period progressively until they asked him to leave the idol for just a month, but he still refused. Eventually, they were compelled to agree to his position and requested him to exonerate them from demolishing it themselves, a condition to which he did agree. To carry out this function, he assigned al-Mugheerah ibn Shu'bah (رضي الله عنه) and Abu Sufyân ibn Ḥarb (رضي الله عنه), the former leader of the pagans of Quraysh[2] who also had links with the people there. As for the prayer, he merely remarked on the futility of a religion without prayer, so they reluctantly agreed to its performance.[3]

Their further demands concerning being ruled by their natives and being set free from the obligation to participate in jihad were accepted by the Prophet (ﷺ).[4] He designated their youngest individual, 'Uthmân ibn Abil-Âs, to run their affairs due to his interest in learning the Qur'an and understanding the religion.[5] Abu Dâwood, one of the most famous scholars of Hadith, narrated that Thaqeef stipulated that it would neither pay alms nor partake in jihad.[6] It seems that the Prophet (ﷺ) accepted this condition and commented that they would be philanthropists voluntarily and wage jihad when they became real Muslims in their hearts.[7]

Other delegations

Other deputations like that of the tribes Banu Tameem,[8] 'Abdul-Qays in Bahrain,[9] Zubayd,[10] the delegates of the kings of Ḥimyar in Yemen,[11] Banu Asad, Banu Fizârah, Banu Murrah[12] and Banu Ḥaneefah[13] came to the Prophet (ﷺ) and declared their submission to Islam. The number of delegations was so great that the 9th year after Hijrah was called the Year of Delegations.[14] Regarding Banu Ḥaneefah, the deputation involved Musaylimah ibn Ḥabeeb, who later on alleged that he himself was also a prophet and was dubbed al-Kadhdhâb, or 'The Liar', for doing so. He tried to become the Prophet's governor to assume the role of the Prophet (ﷺ) after him, but the Prophet (ﷺ) refused to grant him even the leaf of a palm tree.[15]

Some delegations came seeking peace with the Muslims but were not ready to convert to Islam. A group of people were commissioned by the Christian inhabitants of Najrân to meet the Prophet (ﷺ) in response to the call that he sent them to convert to Islam. Despite the fact that they thought Muhammad (ﷺ) might be a prophet, they debated with him about several points and finalised their debate by concluding an agreement according to which they had to pay annual tax in return for keeping their belongings and churches.[16]

The Prophet's manners

Engagement with many delegates did not stop the Prophet (ﷺ) from preaching the message with which he was charged or from the prophetic manner that he used to adopt in tackling matters, even those with his enemies. In this connection, there were two distinguished examples. The first concerned the deputing of Abu Moosâ al-Ash'ari (رضي الله عنه) and Mu'âdh ibn Jabal (رضي الله عنه) to Yemen[17] on one occasion, as well as 'Ali ibn Abi Ṭâlib (رضي الله عنه) and Khâlid ibn al-Waleed (رضي الله عنه) to other parts of the same region at another time.[18]

His counsel to Mu'âdh (رضي الله عنه) realistically reflected his insight and belief in gradual progress in calling others to espouse the divine Message. It represented a vital teaching about the way his followers should go about attracting others to seek equity in Islam instead of preaching it blindly. The Prophet (ﷺ) advised Mu'âdh to be satisfied in the first stage with calling the people to believe in the Oneness of Allah and his prophethood. This is the momentous foundation of the true religion. It is the basis of belief that justifies and smoothes the progress of bearing the other teachings of Islam.

Then, when Mu'âdh (رضي) found the people agreeing to accept this statement, he could inform them about the five prayers each day that Allah (سبحانه) had commanded. If they obeyed that, then he could move forward to enlighten them about the alms that Allah had imposed to be taken from the wealthy and distributed to the poor. Additionally, the Prophet (ﷺ) emphasised two crucial matters. First was the necessity to avoid taking the peoples' most valuable possessions as their alms, and second was to shun injustice, since no screen stands between the invocation made by a wronged individual and Allah.[19] Regarding the manner of preaching Islam, the Prophet (ﷺ) laid down a further guideline that involved facilitating things for the people and bringing glad tidings to them.[20]

The second important example of the Prophet's method of dealing with people concerned the death of the greatest hypocrite in Madinah, 'Abdullâh ibn Ubay ibn Salool. Despite the fact that he had extremely antagonised the Prophet (ﷺ) and spared no effort in letting him and the Muslims down when they were in most need of support, the Prophet (ﷺ) dealt with him while he was dying and after his death in a very merciful way. Instead of seeking revenge or leaving him to his deserved fate, he visited the hypocrite and reminded him with numerous pieces of advice not to line up with the enemies of Islam.[21] When he died, the Prophet (ﷺ) sent his clothes to shroud him and agreed to perform a funeral prayer over his body in spite of the protest of 'Umar (رضي).[22] Ibn Katheer narrated that 'Abdullâh ibn Ubay himself requested these actions of the Prophet (ﷺ). Moreover, he mentioned that the Prophet (ﷺ) came to the grave of 'Abdullâh ibn Ubay and asked the people to exhume his corpse. He positioned him on his thighs, anointed his body with his saliva and dressed him in his shirt.[23] Whatever the case may be, the Prophet (ﷺ) liked to reveal his wish of saving

'Abdullâh ibn Ubay from hell in spite of Ibn Ubay's clear collusions against Islam. He inclined to tackle the case in that manner because of 'Abdullâh ibn Ubay's outward adherence to Islam and because Allah had not yet prohibited him from standing at the graves of hypocrites.

According to Abu Shuhbah, this treatment was also aimed either to attract 'Abdullâh ibn Ubay's supporters to abandon hypocrisy and truly join the Islamic religion, or alternatively, for the sake of 'Abdullâh ibn 'Abdullâh ibn Ubay (ﷺ), the son of the hypocrite, who was a genuine follower of the Prophet (ﷺ).[24] In any case, the wave of hypocrisy in Madinah waned after the death of 'Abdullâh ibn Ubay. Those who had followed him in hypocrisy endeavoured to emerge from this circle. Only a few people persisted in their crooked stance and the Prophet (ﷺ) named all of these individuals surreptitiously to his Companion Ḥudhayfah ibn al-Yamân (ﷺ).[25]

Pilgrimage

Visiting Makkah to perform pilgrimage was appealing to the Prophet (ﷺ), but a form of pilgrimage was still executed by the pagans, who despite being reduced in number, continued to preserve customs that Islam rejected. The Prophet (ﷺ) was of the opinion that it was time to cleanse the rites of pilgrimage of its pre-Islamic customs. To accomplish this objective, he appointed Abu Bakr (ﷺ) to lead the Muslim pilgrims in Dhul Qâ'dah of 9 H, February of 631 CE, and he (ﷺ) told Abu Bakr to notify all the people in Makkah that the pagans would not be allowed to undertake pilgrimages to Makkah after that year and nude worshippers would be prohibited from circling round the Ka'bah.[26]

Just after Abu Bakr (رضي الله عنه) left Madinah, forty verses were revealed to the Prophet (ﷺ), verses that declared the manner with which the pagans should be dealt. The following are a few of them:

❨Freedom from [all] obligations [is declared] from Allah and His Messenger to those of the polytheists [pagans, idolaters, and disbelievers in the Oneness of Allah] with whom you made a treaty. So travel freely [you pagans] for four months [as you will] throughout the land, but know that you cannot escape [from the punishment of] Allah; and Allah will disgrace the disbelievers. And a declaration from Allah and His Messenger to mankind on the greatest day [the day of 'Arafah during the pilgrimage, on the 10th of Dhul Ḥijjah, the 12th month of the Islamic calendar] that Allah is free from [all] obligations to the polytheists and so is His Messenger. So if you [pagans] repent, it is better for you, but if you turn away, then know that you cannot escape [from the punishment of] Allah. And give tidings [O Muhammad] of a painful torment to those who disbelieve; except those of the disbelievers with whom you have a treaty, and who have not subsequently failed you in aught, nor have supported anyone against you. So fulfil their treaty to them until the end of their term. Surely, Allah loves the *muttaqoon* [the pious believers of Islamic Monotheism who fear Allah much and abstain from all kinds of sins and evil deeds which He has forbidden and love Allah much and perform all kinds of good deeds which He has ordained].❩ *(Qur'an 9: 1-4)*

The Prophet (ﷺ) entrusted his cousin 'Ali (رضي الله عنه) to convey these instructions to the people gathering in the pilgrimage area. 'Ali's message supported the task with which Abu Bakr (رضي الله عنه) had been commissioned; in addition, it dealt with two further issues. The first was that no disbeliever could be admitted to paradise unless he or she believed in the Oneness of Allah. The second was that any agreement concluded with the Prophet (ﷺ) would remain effective until its expiry date, but it would not be extended. Disbelievers were given four months' notice to warn their parties about the new policy, as they would not be granted the same covenant or security afterwards.[27] The messages were delivered and the verses recited, and from this time no idolaters or disbelievers have been allowed to visit Makkah for the purpose of pilgrimage or circumambulation of the Sacred House.[28] It was a great sign that heathenism had been vanquished from the Arabian Peninsula.

The Farewell Pilgrimage (*Ḥijjat al-Wadâ'*)

The Prophet (ﷺ) himself performed the hajj pilgrimage in the year 10 H, corresponding to March 632 CE. It became known as 'the Farewell Pilgrimage' because it was the last time that he was in Makkah. It was also called 'the Islamic Pilgrimage' because it was the only time he (ﷺ) discharged this duty since migrating to Madinah, despite the fact that he had done it many times both before and during his prophethood while he still resided in Makkah.[29] In addition, it was also known as a bulletin hajj, or hajj of instruction, for the Prophet (ﷺ) clarified the rituals and instructions of the hajj pilgrimage through his words and deeds during the hajj.[30]

According to Ibn al-Qayyim, the Qur'anic verse concerning the obligation of pilgrimage was revealed in the tenth year of the Islamic calendar,[31] and that was why the Prophet (ﷺ) only once visited Makkah for the purpose of hajj. However, this view is questionable because Abu Bakr (رضي الله عنه) was sent, as was noted, in 9 H to lead the Muslim hajj pilgrimage and he was followed by 'Ali (رضي الله عنه) to convey the message about hajj and treaties.

Farewell speech

Besides illustrating all the rituals concerning pilgrimage in order that they could be copied by the Muslims, the Prophet (ﷺ) delivered a speech elucidating substantial affairs that shape the religious, social and economical relationships of the Muslims with each other. As a matter of fact, he (ﷺ) did not raise new issues, but rather reminded his followers of certain points, referring to their significance lest he not be with them the next year, as he declared.[32] The axes of his admonition were as follows:

1. Social Relations — He (ﷺ) powerfully shed light on the inviolability of the Muslims' blood, wealth and honour, and with ardour he outlawed profaning them until doomsday.[33] In this regard, he openly prohibited usury and affirmed the right to have one's capital returned, and advised his confidents to return the consignments, with which they had been entrusted, to their owners. Similarly, he prohibited avenging blood from wrongs committed during the pre-Islamic period. To reinforce the impact of these two verdicts, he abolished the claims of his own close relatives for blood revenge and interest on loans.[34]

   Safety of lives and wealth is a vital element in weaving ties among the Muslims that are based on fraternity. To keep the Muslim social construction solid, he banned Muslims from the property of their Muslim brothers and sisters unless it was offered willingly.[35] This does not suggest that it is possible to accept usury under the pretext of a gift, as usury was strictly forbidden. The Arabic context of the Prophet's speech clearly includes the sense of preventing extortion. These instructions, however, appertained to the social affairs of the Islamic society as they interlocked with the economical interests.

2. Conjugal Home — The Prophet (ﷺ) explained the mutual rights of married couples. Wives must not allow into their homes those whom their husbands dislike, and wives ought to avoid perpetrating any atrocity. If they commit sin, then their husbands are allowed to refuse to share their beds until they give up their outrages; but if this treatment is not efficacious, then they may chastise them, but not severely.

   As for husbands, they must provide reasonable financial support for their wives and are recommended to deal with them tender-heartedly, since they married them of Allah's volition, and keep them in trust because the wives are dependent on their husbands. The Prophet (ﷺ) prompted the Muslims to ponder his words and comprehend his advice in this connection.[36]

3. Religious Affairs — Although the Prophet (ﷺ) was sure about Satan's despair of being followed in paganism in the Arabian Peninsula, he warned his followers of sins that they belittle. In this regard, he focused on personal interests that can incite a person to temporarily change, or 'bend', the rules. The matter which he highlighted was the postponing of a sacred month by which disbelievers are led astray, for they make it lawful one year and forbid it another year in order to adjust the number of months forbidden by Allah; however, by doing so, they make lawful what Allah has forbidden and vice versa.[37] This is an example of alteration that Satan can exploit and use to alienate Muslims from the Right Path. Hence the Prophet (ﷺ) instructed his followers to stick to both the Noble Qur'an and his Sunnah (practice and tradition) in order to remain on the virtuous way.[38]

To acquit himself of any possible charge of not revealing Allah's full message to them, he addressed a question to his followers to discover whether they confessed to his conveying of the message. They fervently replied in the affirmative; and the Prophet (ﷺ) requested Allah to be his witness.[39] This particular mention reveals clearly the task that falls to every Muslim in transferring the religious teachings and preaching Islam in view of the fact that the core of the Islamic Mission is to guide people to know Allah the Almighty and to apply His laws, both individually and communally.

Religious knowledge

Several teachings can be extracted from the Prophet's (ﷺ) pilgrimage and speeches; the following are just a few examples:

- The Prophet (ﷺ) illustrated that the hajj may be performed in one of three ways.[40] He also touched the Black Stone[41] and kissed it[42] and sometimes he just waved towards it.[43] He allowed the pilgrims to shave, slaughter their animals, and circumambulate the Sacred House without the necessity of performing them in sequence.[44] Through this, the Prophet (ﷺ) again showed that there is some flexibility when it comes to the rites of worship in Islam. Thus, differences are acceptable as long as they are in accord with one of the ways in which the Prophet (ﷺ) taught the Muslims to worship. The scope is wide then for his followers to choose the easiest option which fits their circumstances.
- The Prophet (ﷺ) walked briskly during the first three rounds around the Ka'bah and walked normally on the remaining four rounds, when he performed both the 'umrah and the hajj.[45] This suggests that Muslims should strive to have physical strength and stamina in addition to strength of faith and

personality, and that it is good for the Muslims to appear strong-bodied.

- A menstruating woman performs all the ceremonies of pilgrimage except for moving around the Ka'bah until she is clean from her menstruation.[46] She is also allowed to leave Makkah without doing a final circumambulation of the Sacred House, if she has fulfilled the compulsory circling of the hajj (the *Ṭawâf al-Ifâḍah*).[47] This is another example of how Islam takes a moderate stance towards women in that they are not declared untouchable during their times of menstruation nor are they prohibited from supplication to Allah during these times. It also shows that they are given some leniency during menstruation so that their pilgrimage can be just as acceptable as the pilgrimage of males.
- Prayers of four units are shortened to prayers of two units during the pilgrimage time spent in Minâ.[48] Pilgrims should not fast on the 9th of Dhul Ḥijjah, which is the day when they assemble on Mount 'Arafât,[49] and the frail can leave Muzdalifah at night to throw pebbles at the symbol of Satan in Minâ.[50] Here, the Prophet (ﷺ) showed that Muslims should accept the concessions that Allah gives them in His mercy, such as the shortening of prayers while travelling and ease during the hajj rite for those who are weak, and not submit themselves to unwarranted difficulties.
- The Prophet (ﷺ) continually repeated the *talbiyah* (saying 'O my Lord! I am at Your service') until he threw the pebbles on the 10th of Dhul Ḥijjah.[51] This shows that the Prophet (ﷺ) was most humble and submitted himself fully to Allah (ﷻ), and thus, he (ﷺ) is the ultimate example for Muslims to follow.

Return to Madinah

After fulfilling the pilgrimage and showing Muslims all the details which they need to observe when performing this duty, the Prophet (ﷺ) returned to Madinah where he stayed for a short while, two or three months, and continued calling the people to Islam. He dispatched envoys to a number of rulers to invite them and their people to embrace Islam. To deal with the arrogance of the Roman Byzantines against the Muslims, he (ﷺ) prepared troops to invade al-Balqâ' and ad-Dâroom of Palestine.

He (ﷺ) authorised Usâmah ibn Zayd (رضي الله عنه), the son of his adopted son, Zayd ibn Ḥârithah (رضي الله عنه) who was killed at Mu'tah, to lead the army, which included even the older and experienced pioneer Muslims.[52] Usâmah was very young, probably around eighteen or twenty, and installing him in this position reflected the Prophet's appreciation of the new generation and its potential.[53] The hypocrites used this occasion to try to cause havoc by saying that the Prophet (ﷺ) had positioned great Companions under the command of a young person whose father was only a slave! The Prophet (ﷺ) realised the intents of the hypocrites, so despite his illness, which will be described shortly, he came out of his house and delivered a speech in which he explained Usâmah's merit for the position.[54]

The army gathered and encamped about a league away from Madinah. There it stalled waiting for what might happen next, due to the illness of the Prophet (ﷺ).[55] As soon as they learned that the Prophet's condition was seriously worse, they returned to Madinah. Usâmah went to visit him, but as the Prophet (ﷺ) was temporarily unable even to speak, he (ﷺ) raised his hand towards heaven and then placed it on Usâmah, showing his blessing on him.[56]

CHAPTER EIGHTEEN

The Last Days of the Prophet (ﷺ)

The sickness

The Prophet (ﷺ) became sick shortly after his arrival in Madinah after fulfilling the farewell pilgrimage. A few days before the end of Ṣafar or the beginning of Rabee' I 11 H, towards the end of May 632 CE,[1] he began to suffer from illness. Bukhari narrated that in the course of his illness, the Prophet (ﷺ) told his wife 'Â'ishah (رضي الله عنها) about the poisoned repast which was brought to him by a Jewish woman during the Khaybar invasion and how it had affected him and reduced his strength.[2] Apparently, he experienced a constant headache and acute fever, so that his family thought him stricken with pleurisy, which he was not.[3]

Visiting al-Baqee' cemetery

One night, at midnight, he summoned his page, Abu Muwayhibah, to prepare for a short ride in response to some instructions he had received concerning seeking Allah's forgiveness for the deceased buried in al-Baqee' cemetery. When they arrived at the site of the graves, he addressed a few sentences to the departed, comparing their calmness with the consecutive tribulations which would afflict the people, tribulations in which each one would be worse than the one before. He turned to his servant and notified him of two options that he had been given: to posses the keys of the bounties of the world, be perpetuated and eventually admitted to paradise, or to meet his Lord and go to paradise. He (ﷺ) chose the second option. Finally, he asked for Allah's forgiveness for the deceased and went home to await his final period of illness.[4]

'Âi'shah's house is chosen

Despite his illness, the Prophet (ﷺ) continued to deal justly with his wives and continued to visit each of them on their appointed days. He was at the home of his wife Maymoonah (رضي الله عنها) when his condition suddenly worsened and prevented him from visiting the others. His wives hurried to assemble around him and unburden him of the need to go from house to house.[5] He (ﷺ) looked as if he would prefer to stay at 'Â'ishah's house. Without expressing this desire, he asked: «Where I will be tomorrow?»[6]

His wives realised what he hoped for and permitted him to go wherever he wished; so he moved to Â'ishah's house, where he stayed until he passed away.[7]

Last Testaments

The Prophet (ﷺ) was aware that his death was approaching, and there remained the significant question of how public affairs would be managed after he was gone. A verse of the Noble Qur'an had already been revealed concerning this matter; it described the believers as those,

﴿who [conduct] their affairs by mutual consultations.﴾

(Qur'an 42: 38)

So, the Prophet (ﷺ) did not openly recommend anyone as his successor as leader of the Muslim community, but implied that Abu Bakr (رضي الله عنه) should hold this authority by praising Abu Bakr during his last days[8] and enjoining Abu Bakr to lead the prayers when he (ﷺ) was unable to do so due to illness.[9] Several accounts clearly refer to the precedence of Abu Bakr to bear this responsibility. Muslim, the great scholar of Hadith, also reported that 'Â'ishah (رضي الله عنها) said that the Prophet (ﷺ) advised her to call her father, Abu Bakr, and her brother, 'Abdur-Raḥmân (رضي الله عنه). The reason behind calling them was to provide her father with written confirmation that he would assume power, lest someone else might try to claim it «while Allah and the believers do not want anyone but Abu Bakr.»[10]

On the last Thursday of his life, the Prophet (ﷺ) was in absolute agony. He told his Companions: «Come here, and I will have you write you something after which you will never go astray.»[11]

His Companions (may Allah be pleased with them) felt pity for his condition and thought it better to let him rest rather than fatigue him. They, therefore, expressed their contentment and satisfaction with what had already been revealed in the Qur'an. As a result, nothing further was put into writing, and the Companions were asked to leave.[12]

Later, he (ﷺ) called his family to pour seven skins of water over him so that he could go out and give the people some final advice. They executed his direction until he was refreshed. Then he went to the mosque, led a prayer and delivered an important speech.[13] Ibn Katheer was inclined to believe that this speech was a substitute for the letter, which he had intended to write.[14] He spoke of several issues:

- He (ﷺ) reminded the people of the battle of Uḥud and sought Allah's forgiveness for the Muslim soldiers who had been there.
- He (ﷺ) clarified the position of the Anṣâr, the supporters and hosts in Madinah. In this connection, he addressed his speech to the Muslims who had immigrated to Madinah. The immigrants increased every day, due to the conversion of many people to Islam and their preference for settling in Madinah, while the numbers of the Anṣâr, the original inhabitants of Madinah, remained as they were. In order to avoid any negative impact from this fact, he (ﷺ) distinguished the position of the Anṣâr and instructed the other Muslims to treat them well. About the Anṣâr, he (ﷺ) said: «They were my privacy and my shelter in which I harboured, so confer honour upon their nobility as well as upon their kind and respectable people, and absolve the wrongdoers among them.»[15]
- He (ﷺ) alluded to his death by telling a story of a servant of Allah who was allowed to choose between the splendour of this world or being with Allah. He chose being with Allah.[16] Abu Bakr (رضي الله عنه) was the only man who realised the true meaning of this story and burst into tears, saying: "We sacrifice our parents for your sake."[17]
- The Prophet (ﷺ) praised Abu Bakr (رضي الله عنه).
- He (ﷺ) instructed his followers to expel the polytheists from the Arabian Peninsula.[18]
- He (ﷺ) warned the Muslims not to imitate people of other religions who went astray by using the graves of their prophets as places to be worshipped.[19]
- He (ﷺ) asked the people to avenge him by word or deed if he had wronged any one of them, and asked them to demand their

riches back from him in cases where he had taken from them, if any. He inspired them to recover their rights without fear. Moreover, he elucidated that the dearest person to him is the one who recuperates his or her right from him, if any, or alternatively, exonerates him from it, so that he meets Allah free from being saddled with grievance because of anyone.

❖ He (ﷺ) enquired about extortion from the public rights, and said that if there were any, they should be returned to the treasury.

❖ He asked if anyone would like particular mention in his supplication and said that he would be sure[20] to pray for them. Then he left the rostrum and returned home.

Despite the religious and moral importance of the points he mentioned, they do not fully square with the sense of preventing Muslims from going astray. It is most likely that the core of what he had intended to have written in a letter, or at least a part of it, is the following advice on which he intensively focused during his last three days:

❖ He (ﷺ) advised the Muslims to have a good opinion of Allah as well trust as in His mercy and forgiveness.[21]

❖ He (ﷺ) charged them with being steadfast in observing prayers and dealing gently with slaves. He concentrated on this matter so much that he continued to say it until his venerable soul was in his throat.[22]

❖ Ibn Katheer, quoting from other scholars, also added that the Prophet (ﷺ) also counselled them to remember the importance of giving alms.[23]

Abu Bakr leads the prayers

As frailty impeded him from joining the collective prayers at the mosque, the Prophet (ﷺ) implemented the prayers at his home, following his final speech until he breathed his last. Neverthcless, he resolved that Abu Bakr (رضي الله عنه) should lead the Muslims in their prayers and refused to commission anyone else with this task.[24] Thus, Abu Bakr led the prayers before the death of the Prophet (ﷺ) seventeen or twenty times.[25] Only once, the Prophet (ﷺ) felt capable of participating in the collective prayer and stepped out to join the congregation, with his relatives' help. As soon as Abu Bakr (رضي الله عنه) perceived his approach, he made a move to leave the prayer niche but he was signalled to remain. The Prophet (ﷺ) sat on his left side and the verses were recited by Abu Bakr (رضي الله عنه) who remained standing. Abu Bakr followed the Prophet (ﷺ) in that prayer, and the people in turn followed Abu Bakr.[26]

Over the next few days, the Prophet's condition deteriorated and he was compelled to remain at home. In describing his critical condition, one of his visitors declared that even touching his body was unfeasible because of his high fever.[27] When his daughter Fâṭimah (رضي الله عنها) visited him, she too was distressed at his condition, but he told her that he would no longer suffer from any future pain.[28] He was aware of the severity of his illness and likened it to an illness that befell two men at once,[29] and hoped that the gravity of the illness would be a cause for more reward from Allah.[30] He could feel the end creeping towards him and confided this to his daughter secretly, so that she cried, and then he informed her in secret that she would be the first member of his family who would follow him, so that she laughed, as she would be happy to rejoin him.[31]

A farewell glimpse

In the course of performing the dawn prayer on Monday the 12th of Rabee‘ I 11 H, probably the 8th of June 632 CE,[32] the Prophet (ﷺ) moved aside the curtain that was between his room and the prayer hall and looked smilingly at the worshippers. Abu Bakr (رضي الله عنه), who was leading the prayer, thought that he intended to come out and wanted to step back so that the Prophet (ﷺ) might join in the prayer and lead it, and the other Muslims were on the point of leaving their prayers by his appearance. However, the Prophet (ﷺ) signalled to them to continue their duty, lowered the curtain and entered his room.[33] He (ﷺ) appeared before them in such good form that the Muslims believed him as hale and hearty as he was before his illness.[34] This was clear from ‘Ali’s (رضي الله عنه) reply when he was questioned about the Prophet’s health. He said, “Thanks to Allah, he has become well.”[35] Additionally, Abu Bakr (رضي الله عنه) felt the same and returned home to his wife in as-Sunuḥ, a place just outside of Madinah, while the other people became engrossed in their business.[36]

The agony of death

Contrary to the Muslims’ expectations, the Prophet’s (ﷺ) emergence was just a valediction and his condition had worsened considerably. To gain relief, he moistened his hand with water from a goblet, wiped it across his face, and said: «O Lord! Help me in the agonies of death!»[37]

His wife ‘Â’ishah (رضي الله عنها) was grieving at his situation and supplicated to Allah with the words that he used to utter when he was well. She started wiping his body with his hand, but he pulled it away[38] and requested Allah to forgive him as well as admit him to paradise.[39]

During this time, 'Â'ishah heard him say: «O Lord! I prefer to be with You.»[40]

She associated this sentence with the frequent information he used to state about the prophets, prior to their deaths, being given the options of immortality or demise,[41] and realised that his uttering of such words revealed his rejection of immortality.

The final minutes

A few moments before his death, he was visited by 'Abdur-Raḥmân (رضي الله عنه), the brother of Â'ishah (رضي الله عنها), who was cleaning his teeth with a siwâk, a small twig used for this purpose. The Prophet (ﷺ) glanced at it eagerly and Â'ishah (رضي الله عنها) comprehended his desire. She took it from her brother, trimmed it and softened it in her mouth then gave it to him. He (ﷺ) brushed his teeth properly with it and straightaway passed on to the next life[42] in the afternoon of that Monday, when he was sixty-three or sixty-five years old.[43] This is why she said proudly that the Prophet (ﷺ) leaned his head on her chest and that Allah mixed her saliva with his just before he died.[44]

Disbelief

The sad tidings created uproar. Groups of the faithful simply could not believe that their beloved Prophet (ﷺ) had died. Some of them thought that he was in a state similar to that which befell him when he was receiving the Revelation. 'Umar ibn al-Khaṭṭâb (رضي الله عنه) swore that he was still alive and would return to lop off the appendages of the hypocrites who claimed he had died![45] The people as a whole were shocked and confused about the occurrence.

Shortly afterwards, Abu Bakr (ﷺ) arrived from his house and entered the room of his daughter 'Â'ishah (ﷺ), where the Prophet (ﷺ) was lying. He uncovered him, kissed him and wept for him.[46] At that crucial moment, he imperturbably stepped into the mosque and delivered an address about the Prophet's (ﷺ) fate. He said, "He who worshiped Muhammad (ﷺ) (should know that) he has died, but he who worships Allah, (should remember) that Allah is Ever-living, never dies." Then, he strengthened his speech with a few verses of the Noble Qur'an relevant to the death of the Prophet (ﷺ):[47]

﴿Muhammad is no more than a Messenger, and indeed [many] Messengers have passed away before him. If he dies or is killed, will you then turn back on your heels [as disbelievers]? And he who turns back on his heels, not the least harm will he do to Allah, and Allah will give reward to those who are grateful.﴾

(Qur'an 3: 144)

Electing a leader

As soon as the death was announced, the Muslim people split into three groups. The first consisted of 'Ali, az-Zubayr ibn al-'Awâm and Ṭalḥah ibn 'Ubaydillâh (may Allah be pleased with them), who assembled in Fâṭimah's home (ﷺ). The second was formed by the people who emigrated from Makkah with the Prophet (ﷺ) and some of the Anṣâr, who took sides with Abu Bakr (ﷺ); and the third party included the rest of the Anṣâr who inclined towards Sa'd ibn 'Ubâdah (ﷺ).[48] These assemblies, formed out of desire to determine who would assume the position as leader of the Muslims, produced a suspicion that the Muslims would be scattered and thus exposed to external enemies, such as those who alleged prophecy before the Prophet (ﷺ) died, like Musaylimah and al-Aswad al-'Ansi.[49]

Due to this fear, the burial of the Prophet (ﷺ) was postponed and priority was given to protecting the Islamic body politic, as this appeared the most judicious and practical move. So, on Monday and for part of the next day, the Muslims were engaged with the affair of who would become caliph and lead the community.[50] Immediately after solving this problem and electing Abu Bakr (رضي الله عنه) as their ruler, the Muslims made preparations to bury the Prophet (ﷺ).

The end

Washing the body of the Prophet (ﷺ) according to Islamic funeral rituals was performed by a few of his family members, in agreement with the desires expressed in his will.[51] 'Ali held him to his chest and helped his uncle al-'Abbâs, who was also the uncle of the Prophet (ﷺ), and al-'Abbâs' sons Faḍl and Qutham to turn him over. The Prophet's adopted grandson, Usâmah ibn Zayd, and his servant, Ṣâliḥ, (may Allah be pleased with them all), poured the water. In addition, Aws ibn Khawli al-Anṣâri (رضي الله عنه) watched the others as they washed the Prophet (ﷺ). In the course of performing this duty, they did not disrobe him nor did they notice in him what is usually observed in the departed. They covered him in three winding-sheets[52] and laid him on a bed in his home.

The people were organised to enter collectively, according to their gender and age. So, the men went first, followed by the women and then the children. Then they were asked to individually perform the special prayer for the deceased.[53] Abu Ṭalḥah (رضي الله عنه), the gravedigger of Madinah, dug the grave of the Prophet (ﷺ) on the spot inside 'Â'ishah's room where he died, based on the saying of the Prophet (ﷺ): «When a prophet dies he is buried in the place where he died.»[54]

The Prophet (ﷺ) was quietly interred on the eve of Wednesday, the 13th of Rabee' I 11 H,[55] likely corresponding to the 9th of June 632 CE.

Conclusion

It is evident from this summarized journey through the life of the Prophet (ﷺ) that the emergence of the message of Islam was a turning point in the world and represented one of the greatest changes to its spiritual, political and social facets. Prior to the rise of Islam, much of life was led by doctrines that were either idolatrous, meaning invented by humans, or close to heathenism, wherein previous divine teachings were stripped of their values to comply with individual desires. People had changed the stamp of religion to suit themselves and to obtain others' obedience and compliance. Under the domination of worldly interests, people had lost their identities and instead of occupying their positions on the grounds of being mutually human, they were classified as masters and servants due to their race or financial standing. The spirit that imbued this type of life was the sense of superiority of the masters over those whom they despised for their lower social status. The latter had to adapt to this and demonstrate submissiveness and ignobility, despite feeling that their treatment was unfair. This reality resulted in oppression, discrimination and the suspension of people's creative power. Even in religious supplication, the 'highest' classes of people alleged to have the power of mediating with the Lord, or their invented worldly gods, and thus they had to be followed in their approaches and asked to make spiritual intercessions.

This was the general case around the world, including the Arabian Peninsula in which Bedouin tribal customs and values prevailed. The Prophet Muhammad (ﷺ) had grown up in such an environment, but his nature was pure enough to reject that reality. As an individual, he was distinguished by sincerity, truthfulness and justice, and he became the one whom others agreed unanimously to trust. Even those who refused to believe in his prophesy entrusted him with their possessions.

When approaching forty years of age, Muhammed (ﷺ) started receiving divine revelation, and thus his religious task became to guide people to the Right Way. He conveyed his message in a wise manner from his homeland, but his success was limited due to the severe opposition he and his Companions faced, despite his reputation as a shining example of excellent conduct. More tangible success commenced after the immigration of the Muslims to Madinah, where he (ﷺ) constructed an Islamic society that dispersed the darkness, liberated the people from slavery and extolled the values of humanity, justice and equality.

The key that opened the way for achieving this goal was the acknowledgment of the Oneness of Allah and acceptance of the prophecy of His Messenger Muhammad (ﷺ). Believing and acting upon this statement meant rejecting the created worldly gods and consequently leaving behind the system of life which centred around those beliefs. The Prophet (ﷺ) was absolutely alert to the conflict that might be caused by this, and therefore, he chose to pass the message in two different stages while he was in Makkah: first quietly and privately, later openly and publicly. However, the oppression that he and his Companions experienced from the pagans for about thirteen years of preaching the message obliged the Prophet (ﷺ) to go further afield. This was a further cause of suffering for Muhammad (ﷺ) until he met a small group of people from Madinah who believed in his message and offered shelter to the Muslims.

The corrupt powers of the day realised the potential danger to themselves of letting Islam propagate, and this increased their determination to destroy the Muslims. They drew up many plans to eradicate them, joined in alliances and provoked many battles. With regard to such hostile movements, the Prophet (ﷺ) had only the choice of defending the religion and the new community, despite the enemy's being much greater in number and in possession of superior armaments. Nevertheless, victory mostly fell on the side of the Muslims and the population of Muslims grew continuously. At the same time, the enemy was dwindling and failing until Islam was completely victorious in the Arab lands. From here, Islam was ready to radiate throughout the whole world.

The Prophet (ﷺ) had started calling people to believe in the Oneness of Allah singlehandedly, and by the time he passed away, the majority of Arabs were following his religion. As a role model, he possessed all the qualities that the Noble Qur'an had stated for the ideal and exemplary Muslim. Therefore, the strength of his message coupled with his shining practical example of true faith began to penetrate the hearts of the people. The following points represent a small bouquet of lessons taken from his life:

❖ Human beings must have a clear vision and understanding of the fundamental values of their faith, and they must be enthusiastic and take serious responsibility for this earthly life and balance it with the hereafter.

❖ People should consider the wellbeing of others as they would consider their own and treat other people on this basis by sympathising with them, caring for their safety and conducting them to the Right Path. The Muslim preaches a balanced and settled life and aspires to guide humankind to ultimate success by instructing them in the Oneness of Allah and explaining the purpose of its creation. In short, this entails the realisation of the Almighty, worshiping Him alone and practicing the teachings and directives that He gives us.

The Prophet (ﷺ) supplicated to Allah on many occasions to lead the disbelievers to the way of the truth. With the subsequent spread of Islam and his governance of the new Islamic State, the Prophet (ﷺ) initiated many changes and set an example for all. He released his opponents if they fell in capture and forgave them if they turned to pay him homage. He (ﷺ) supported justice but never sought vengeance, only highlighting the spirit of indulgence and tolerance that is inherent in Islam.

- Peace has priority in Islam. The teachings of the Noble Qur'an and the Prophet (ﷺ) clearly illuminated this fact; however, this does not mean that the tools of power should be ignored in the face of an enemy who desires one's subservience.
- Spreading the principle of equality between people is integral to Islam, as all people spring from the same parents, Adam and Eve. Thus, everyone is related in humankind, and they are brothers and sisters if they hold to the religion of Islam. This norm cements societies and supports cooperation as opposed to continuous clash and conflict. No human being should be subjected to persecution and injustice. Therefore, there is no room for discrimination in Islam on whatever basis. The only ground for distinguishing people in the sight of Allah the Almighty is through a person's piety, and then every person has the potential to be qualified for any status in his or her society.
- The notions of justice and loyalty are further concepts that the Prophet (ﷺ) circulated among the people. These attributes are crucial in dealing with others as well as in managing personal, family and social matters and even issues concerning one's

enemies. Each individual, male or female, free or slave, has the responsibility to uphold justice and loyalty; and Islam demands that a person should administer it rightly to acquire the pleasure of Allah.

❖ Consultation and dialogue are key components to the upholding of a successful society. These ways of dealing with others contribute through the enrichment gained from personal ideas and also offer a safety valve within the decision-making process or adoption of particular stances.

Numerous other values emerged via the religion of Islam. The Prophet (ﷺ) and the Muslims applied them in their own personal relationships with God and in their external relationships with other people. The positive, moral conduct of the Muslims attracted the peoples of different nations and opened their hearts and minds to the ideal life that is achievable within the shade of Islam. The efficacy of the Prophet (ﷺ) and those that followed him (may Allah be pleased with them) is evident by considering that within just a few decades that the Light of the Truth radiated even in distant lands.

May Allah send His peace, mercy and blessings upon Prophet Muhammad and upon his family and followers until the Day of Resurrection.

Notes

Preface

[1] Right Way: the 'Right Way' or 'Straight Path' (*aṣ-Ṣirâṭ al-Mustaqeem*) is a Qur'anic expression which means Islamic monotheism and all that Islam endorses as means of living a life that is pleasing to Allah (*Subḥânahu wa Ta'âlâ* — Glorified and Exalted is He).

Chapter One

[1] Abu Shuhbah, *As-Seerah an-Nabawiyah*, vol. 1, pp. 60-61
[2] Ibid., vol. 1, p. 93
[3] Ibid; Ibn al-Atheer, *Al-Kâmil fee at-Târeekh*, vol. 1, p. 312
[4] *ibn*: son, son of
[5] aṭ-Ṭabari, *Târeekh ar-Rusuli wal-Mulook*, vol. 4, p. 108
[6] al-Mubarakpuri, *Ar-Raheeq al-Makhtūm*, p. 40
[7] All the Qur'anic quotations in this book have been taken from *Interpretation of the Meanings of the Noble Qur'ân*, translated by Dr. Muhammad Muhsin Khân and Dr. Muhammad Taqî-ud-Dîn Al-Hilâlî, Riyadh: Dârussalâm, 1996.
[8] Abu Shuhbah, vol. 1, p. 88; al-Mubarakpuri, p. 40; aṣ-Ṣallâbi, *As-Seerah an-Nabawiyah*, vol. 1, p. 36
[9] wife of the Prophet (ﷺ)
[10] Bukhari, *Al-Jâmi' aṣ-Ṣaḥeeḥ*, hadith no. 5127
[11] Ibn Ḥajar, *Fatḥ al-Bâri*, vol. 9, p. 150
[12] Abu Shuhbah, vol. 1, p. 90
[13] Qal'aji, *Dirâsat Taḥleeliyah li Shakhṣiyah ar-Rasool*, p. 25
[14] Abu Dâwood, *Sunan Abi Dâwood*, hadith nos. 2074-2075
[15] Ibn Hishâm reviewed the biography of the Prophet (ﷺ) compiled by a scholar named Ibn Is-ḥâq and produced it in a new form. His scholarly revise was highly regarded and widely circulated, and it is the oldest

existing biography of the Prophet (ﷺ). According to some reports, Ibn Hishâm died in 218 H/ 833 CE.

16 Ka'bah: the House of Allah in Makkah, originally built by Prophets Ibrâheem and Ismâ'eel, and which Muslims face wherever they pray; also called the Sacred House

17 Ibn Hishâm, *As-Seerah an-Nabawiyah*, vol. 1, pp. 77-78

18 Ibid., vol. 1, p. 76

19 Ibid., vol. 1, p. 78

20 Ibn Katheer, *As-Seerah an-Nabawiyah*, vol. 1, p. 163; Abu Shuhbah, vol. 1, p. 80

21 CE: Common Era; the current Western system of calendar years; CE is an alternative to the use of 'AD' (*Anno Domini*)

22 Ḥamzah, *Qalb Jazeerah al-'Arab*, p. 151; al-Mubarakpuri, p. 36

23 al-Mubarakpuri, p. 36

24 banu/bani: lit. 'children (of)'; *usu.* referring to a tribe that claims a common ancestor

25 Ibid.

26 Ibn Hishâm, vol. 1, pp. 33-34; aṭ-Ṭabari, vol. 2, pp. 111-113

27 Ibn Hishâm, vol. 1, p. 43; aṭ-Ṭabari, vol. 2, pp. 118-119

28 al-'Aqqâd, *Maṭla' an-Noor*, pp. 41-42; al-Mubarakpuri, p. 37

29 http://www.makkahedu.gov.sa/Makkah/mak_his.asp (accessed May 1, 2005)

30 http://www.mekkaoui.net/Islam/ArkanislamAR/make.htm (accessed May 1, 2005)

31 Ibn al-Atheer, vol. 1, p. 80

32 Ibn Hishâm, vol. 1, p. 7

33 Ibid., vol. 1, p. 117

34 http://www.mekkaoui.net/Islam/ArkanislamAR/make.htm (accessed May 1, 2005)

35 Ibn Hishâm, vol. 1, pp. 123-126

36 a right known as *ḥijâbah*

37 a service known as *siqâyah*

38 a service known as *rifâdah*

39 Ibid., vol. 1, pp. 135-136

40 Ibid., vol. 1, pp. 125, 130

41 Ibid., vol. 1, pp. 131-132

42 Ibid., vol. 1, p. 132

43 Bukhari, hadith no. 3851; Ibn Hishâm, vol. 1, pp. 1-2

44 aṭ-Ṭabari, vol. 2, p. 202; al-Baghawi, *Sharḥ as-Sunnah*, vol. 13, p. 193; Ibn al-Qayyim, *Zâd al-Ma'âd*, vol. 1, p. 71; Ibn Sa'd, *Aṭ-Ṭabaqât al-Kubrâ*,

vol. 1, p. 58; Ibn al-Atheer, vol. 1, p. 565
[45] Muslim, *Ṣaḥeeḥ Muslim*, hadith no. 2776
[46] Ibn Hishâm, vol. 1, p. 136; aṭ-Ṭabari, vol. 2, p. 190
[47] Ibn Hishâm, vol. 1, p. 136
[48] bint: daughter, daughter of
[49] Ibid., vol. 1, p. 137
[50] Ibid., vol. 1, pp. 137-138
[51] Ibid., vol. 1, p. 142
[52] Ibid., vol. 1, pp. 148-150
[53] Ibid., vol. 1, p. 150
[54] Ibid., vol. 1, pp. 142-147; aṭ-Ṭabari, vol. 2, p. 190
[55] Ibn Hishâm, vol. 1, pp. 151- 155
[56] Ibn Hishâm, vol. 1, pp. 43, 45
[57] aṭ-Ṭabari, vol. 2, p. 123
[58] Ibid., vol. 1, p. 50
[59] Ibid.
[60] Ibn Hishâm, vol. 1, p. 54
[61] Ibid., vol. 1, pp. 57-61
[62] an-Nadawi, *As-Seerah an-Nabawiyah*, p. 82
[63] aṭ-Ṭabari, vol. 2, p. 186
[64] Khaleel, *Dirâsat fee as-Seerah*, p. 37
[65] Ibn Hishâm, vol. 1, p. 158
[66] aṭ-Ṭabari, vol. 2, p. 139
[67] Ibn Hishâm, vol. 1, p. 168; aṭ-Ṭabari, vol. 2, p. 139

Chapter Two

[1] Ibid., vol. 1, p. 158
[2] Ibid., vol. 1, pp. 158, 160
[3] Ibid., vol. 1, pp. 162-164
[4] Muslim, hadith no. 413
[5] Ibn Hishâm, vol. 1, pp. 164-165; aṭ-Ṭabari, vol. 2, p. 136
[6] Ibn Hishâm, vol. 1, p. 168; aṭ-Ṭabari, vol. 2, p. 139
[7] Ibn Hishâm, vol. 1, pp. 168-169; aṭ-Ṭabari, vol. 2, p. 139
[8] abu/abi: father, father of
[9] Ibn Hishâm, vol. 1, p. 179; aṭ-Ṭabari, vol. 2, p. 140
[10] al-Booṭi, *Fiqh as-Seerah an-Nabawiyah*, p. 46
[11] Ibn Ḥanbal, *Al-Musnad*, vol. 5, p. 262; al-Haythami, *Majma' az-Zawâ'id*, vol. 8, p. 222

[12] Ibn Hishâm., vol. 1, p. 163

[13] Ibid., vol. 1, pp. 165, 168

[14] aṭ-Ṭabari, vol. 2, p. 137

[15] Ibn Hishâm, vol. 1, pp. 180-183; aṭ-Ṭabari, vol. 2, p. 206

[16] ‘Ali, *Ṭâreekh al-‘Arab Qabl al-Islâm*, vol. 1, p. 106; Khaleel, p. 40

[17] Ibn Hishâm, vol. 1, p. 231

[18] Ibid., vol. 1, p. 233

[19] al-‘Ali, *Ṣaḥeeḥ as-Seerah an-Nabawiyah*, pp. 30-31; al-‘Umari, *As-Seerah an-Nabawiyah aṣ-Ṣaḥeeḥah*, vol. 1, p. 122

[20] Bukhari, hadith no. 4838

[21] Ibn Taymiyyah, *Al-Jawâb aṣ-Ṣaḥeeḥ*, vol. 1, p. 340

[22] Bukhari, hadith no. 2262

[23] aṣ-Ṣallâbi, *As-Seerah an-Nabawiyah*, vol. 1, p. 71

[24] al-Booṭi, p. 50

[25] aṭ-Ṭabari, vol. 2, p. 207; al-‘Ali, p. 57

[26] Khaleel, p. 41

[27] sacred months: the months in the Islamic (and pre-Islamic) calendar in which no warfare or hostilities are permitted

[28] Ibn Hishâm, vol. 1, p. 184

[29] Ibid., vol. 1, p. 186; Khaleel, p. 41; aṣ-Ṣallâbi, *As-Seerah an-Nabawiyah*, vol. 1, p. 78

[30] Ibn Hishâm, vol. 1, p. 186

[31] Ibid., vol. 1, p. 134; al-Atheer, vol. 1, p. 570

[32] Ibn Hishâm, vol. 1, p. 134

[33] Ibid., vol. 1, p. 188

[34] Ibid., vol. 1, pp. 188-189

[35] Ibid., vol. 1, p. 191

[36] Ibid.; aṭ-Ṭabari, vol. 2, p. 208

[37] al-Atheer, vol. 1, p. 570

[38] aṭ-Ṭabari, vol. 2, pp. 208-209; Some biographers mentioned that her father, Khuwaylid ibn Asad, had married her off to the Prophet (ﷺ), based upon the narration of Ibn Hishâm (see Ibn Hishâm, vol. 1, p. 190), but aṭ-Ṭabari (vol. 2, pp. 208-209) quoted al-Wâqidi’s criticism of this narration which includes a reference to the death of her father in the al-Fijâr War, which occurred five years prior to the marriage. Aṭ-Ṭabari therefore adopted the narration which I have chosen in the text.

[39] Ibn Hishâm, vol. 1, p. 190; aṭ-Ṭabari, vol. 2, p. 208; al-Atheer, vol. 1, p. 569

[40] Khaleel, p. 44; al-Mubarakpuri, p. 58; aṣ-Ṣallâbi, *As-Seerah an-Nabawiyah*, vol. 1, p. 82

[41] Bukhari, hadith nos. 3815-3821
[42] Ibid., vol. 1, pp. 194-195
[43] Ibn Hishâm, vol. 1, pp. 192-193
[44] Bukhari, hadith no. 3829
[45] Black Stone: a sacred relic from the time of Adam and Eve, and associated with the Ka'bah since before Islam (Editor)
[46] Ibn Hishâm, vol. 1, p. 197
[47] Ibid.
[48] Ibn Hishâm, vol. 1, p. 197

Chapter Three

[1] hajj:
[2] Ibn Hishâm, vol. 1, p. 199
[3] Ibid., vol. 1, p. 204
[4] Ibid., vol. 1, p. 236
[5] al-Booṭi, p. 60
[6] Ibid., pp. 61-62
[7] Ibn Hishâm, vol. 1, pp. 234-235
[8] Muslim, hadith no. 5939
[9] Bukhari, hadith no. 3
[10] Bukhari, hadith no. 138
[11] Ibn Mâjah, *Sunan Ibn Mâjah*, hadith nos. 3893, 3894, 3907, 3914, 3917. In a further two hadiths there is a reference to being one of seventy parts of prophecy, see hadith nos. 3895, 3897.
[12] Bukhari, hadith no. 3
[13] Ibid.; Muslim, hadith no. 403; aṭ-Ṭabari, vol. 2, p. 217 (a similar narration with slight variation)
[14] Ibn Hishâm, vol. 1, pp. 236-238
[15] an-Nadawi, p. 116; al-Mubarakpuri, p. 63
[16] an-Nadawi, p. 117
[17] Bukhari, hadith no. 3
[18] Ibn Hishâm, vol. 1, p. 241
[19] al-Mubarakpuri, p. 66
[20] Bukhari, hadith no. 4
[21] Ibn Hishâm, vol. 1, pp. 240-247; aṭ-Ṭabari, vol. 2, pp. 222-223
[22] Abu Shuhbah, vol. 1, p. 284
[23] Ibn Hishâm, vol. 1, p. 249

[24] Ibid., vol. 1, p. 250
[25] Ibid., vol. 1, pp. 250-252
[26] al-Ghaḍbân, *Al-Manhaj at-Tarbawee lis-Seerah an-Nabawiyah,* vol. 1, pp. 191, 195
[27] Salâmah, *Dawlah ar-Rasool*, pp. 225-233
[28] Ibn Hishâm, vol. 1, pp. 243-244
[29] al-Ghaḍbân, vol. 1, p. 465
[30] Ibid., vol. 1, p. 191
[31] aṣ-Ṣallâbi, *As-Seerah an-Nabawiyah*, vol. 1, p. 135
[32] Ibn Hishâm, vol. 1, pp. 250-262, where he mentioned all the converts at that period along with their pedigrees
[33] al-'Umari, vol. 1, p. 133
[34] al-Ghaḍbân, vol. 1, p.193
[35] Ibid., vol. 1, p. 192
[36] Ibn Hishâm, vol. 1, pp. 246-247, for an example
[37] al-Ghazâli, *Fiqh as-Seerah*, p. 76
[38] Ibn Hishâm, vol. 1, p. 264
[39] al-Mubarakpuri, p. 76
[40] the 26th chapter of the Noble Qur'an
[41] al-Balâdhiri, *Ansâb al-Ashrâf*, vol. 1, pp. 118-119
[42] Ibn Katheer, *Al-Bidâyah wan-Nihâyah*, vol. 3, p. 41
[43] al-Ghaḍbân, vol. 1, p. 210
[44] Bukhari, hadith no. 4770; Ibn Katheer, *Al-Bidâyah wan-Nihâyah*, vol. 3, p. 38
[45] al-Booṭi, p. 74
[46] Ibn Hishâm, vol. 1, p. 264
[47] Ibid., vol. 1, pp. 264-265
[48] Ibid., vol. 1, pp. 265-266
[49] Ibid., vol. 1, p. 266
[50] Ibn Hishâm, vol. 1, pp. 266-268
[51] Ibn Sa'd, vol. 3, p. 117
[52] Ibid., vol. 3, p. 248; Ibn Katheer, *Al-Bidâyah wan-Nihâyah*, vol. 3, pp. 58-59 and according to him the stab was in her heart; al-Wâḥidi, *Asbâb Nuzool al-Qurân*, p. 289; as-Suwayqit, *Miḥnah al-Muslimeen fee al-'Ahd al-Makki*, pp. 98-99
[53] Ibn Katheer, *Al-Bidâyah wan-Nihâyah*, vol. 3, pp. 57-58
[54] Ibid., vol. 3, p. 59; Ibn Hishâm, vol. 1, p. 320
[55] Ibn Katheer, *Al-Bidâyah wan-Nihâyah*, vol. 3, p. 59
[56] Ibn Hishâm, vol. 1, p. 289
[57] Abu Shuhbah, vol. 1, p. 293

58 Ibn Hishâm, vol. 1, pp. 291-292

59 Ibn Hishâm, vol. 1, pp. 293-294. Ibn Katheer narrated this event in a different way; see *Al-Bidâyah wan-Nihâyah*, vol. 3, pp. 62-63.

60 Ibn Hishâm, vol. 1, p. 294. Something similar happened to al-Waleed ibn al-Mugheerah; see Ibn Katheer, *Al-Bidâyah wan-Nihâyah*, vol. 3, pp. 60-61. This similarity possibly indicates the frequency of sending great individuals to the Prophet (ﷺ) to dissuade him from preaching his mission.

61 the 41st chapter of the Noble Qur'an

62 Ibn Hishâm, vol. 1, p. 294

63 Ibid., vol. 1, pp. 294-298

64 Ibid., vol. 1, p. 362

65 Ibid., vol. 1, pp. 300-302; Ibn Katheer, *Al-Bidâyah wan-Nihâyah*, vol. 3, pp. 52-53

66 al-Wâḥidi, p. 468

67 Ibn Hishâm, vol. 1, pp. 321-322; Ibn Katheer, *Al-Bidâyah wan-Nihâyah*, vol. 3, p. 66

68 aṭ-Ṭabari, vol. 2, p. 233

69 Ibn 'Abdil-Barr, *Ad-Durar fee Ikhtiṣâr al-Maghâzi was-Siyar*, p. 27

70 Sayyid Qutub, *Fee Dhilâl al-Qurân*, vol. 1, p. 29

71 aṣ-Ṣallâbi, *As-Seerah an-Nabawiyah*, vol. 1, pp. 330-331 mentioned some of these indications

72 Ibn Katheer, *Al-Bidâyah wan-Nihâyah*, vol. 3, p. 78

73 Jazli, *Al-Ḥijrah fee al-Qurân al-Kareem*, p. 316

74 aṣ-Ṣallâbi, *As-Seerah an-Nabawiyah*, vol. 1, pp. 349-350; al-Booṭi, p. 94

75 Ibn Taymiyyah, *Majmoo' al-Fatâwâ*, vol. 22, p. 30

76 Ibn Hishâm, vol. 1, pp. 322-323

77 Ibid., vol. 1, p. 330

78 Ibid., vol. 1, p. 335

79 Ibid., vol. 1, pp. 335-336

80 Ibid., vol. 1, pp. 337-338

81 Ibid.

82 Ibid., vol. 1, p. 341

83 Bukhari, hadith nos. 3877, 3878, 3879, 3880, 3881

84 Ibn Hishâm, vol. 1, p. 342

85 Ibid., vol. 1, p. 350

86 Bukhari, vol. 2, p. 323; al-Ghaḍbân, *At-Tarbiyah al-Qiyâdiyyah*, vol. 1, p. 375, quoted in al-Haythami, vol. 6, p. 17

87 Ibn Hishâm, vol. 1, pp. 364, 369

Chapter Four

[1] 'Ali al-Ḥalabi, *As-Seerah al-Ḥalabiyyah*, vol. 1, p. 474, quoted in al-Ghaḍbân, vol. 1, pp. 375-376

[2] Ibn Katheer, vol. 3, p. 84

[3] Ibn Hishâm, vol. 1, pp. 350-351; Ibn Katheer, vol. 3, p. 84; al-Atheer, vol. 1, p. 604

[4] Ibid.

[5] Ibn Katheer, vol. 3, p. 84

[6] Ibn Hishâm, vol. 1, p. 353

[7] al-Mubarakpuri, pp. 107-108; aṣ-Ṣallâbi, *As-Seerah an-Nabawiyah*, vol. 1, p. 314

[8] Ibn Katheer, vol. 3, p. 84

[9] Ibid., vol. 3, p. 97, on page 85 he gave another narration about the details that the white ants left behind; Ibn Hishâm, vol. 1, p. 377

[10] Ibn Hishâm, vol. 1, p. 377

[11] Ibid., vol. 1, p. 376; Ibn Katheer, vol. 3, pp. 95-97

[12] 'Abdul-Wahhâb Kaḥeel, *al-Ḥarb an-Nafsiyah Ḍidd al-Islâm*, p. 101, referred to by aṣ-Ṣallâbi, *As-Seerah an-Nabawiyah,* vol. 1, p. 321

[13] al-Booṭi, p. 88

[14] Ibn Katheer, vol. 3, p. 98

[15] Ibid., vol. 3, p. 127

[16] Bukhari, hadith nos. 3883-3885; Ibn Katheer, vol. 3, p. 123

[17] Bukhari, hadith no. 3884

[18] al-Booṭi, p. 97

[19] al-Mubarakpuri, pp. 114-115; aṣ-Ṣallâbi, *As-Seerah an-Nabawiyah*, vol. 1, pp. 359-360; 'Abdul-Qâdir, *Qiṣṣat al-Bayt al-Ḥarâm*, p. 151

[20] al-Booṭi, p. 99

[21] al-'Umari, vol. 1, p. 184

[22] Ibn Katheer, vol. 3, p. 134

[23] Ibid.

[24] Bukhari, hadith no. 3854

[25] Ibid., hadith no. 3856

[26] Muslim, hadith no. 2797

[27] aṣ-Ṣallâbi, *As-Seerah an-Nabawiyah*, vol. 1, pp. 361-362

[28] Ibn Hishâm, vol. 2, p. 419; aṭ-Ṭabari, vol. 2, p. 241; Ibn Katheer, vol. 3, p. 135

[29] al-Mubarakpuri, p. 124; aṣ-Ṣallâbi, *As-Seerah an-Nabawiyah*, vol. 1, p. 364

[30] Ibn Hishâm, vol. 2, pp. 419-420; Ibn Katheer, vol. 3, p. 135

[31] Bukhari, hadith no. 3231
[32] Ibn Hishâm, vol. 2, p. 421; Ibn Katheer, vol. 3, p. 136
[33] Ibn Hishâm, vol. 2, p. 421. Al-'Umari mentioned that this story was not attributed to a Companion of the Prophet (ﷺ), see vol. 1, pp. 186-188.
[34] Bukhari, hadith no. 3231
[35] Ibn Katheer, vol. 3, p. 137
[36] Abu Dâwood, hadith no. 4811; at-Tirmidhi, *Al-Jâmi' aṣ-Ṣaḥeeḥ*, hadith no. 1954
[37] Bukhari, hadith no. 4024
[38] Ibn Hishâm, vol. 1, pp. 396-398; Ibn Katheer, vol. 3, pp. 109-112; Bukhari, hadith no. 3887
[39] Ibn Hishâm, vol. 1, pp. 399-400; Ibn Katheer, vol. 3, p. 112; see also Ibn Ḥajar, vol. 7, pp 136-137; an-Nawawi, *Sharḥ Ṣaḥeeḥ Muslim*, vol. 2, p. 39
[40] Ibn Katheer, vol. 3, p. 112
[41] Ibn Hishâm, vol. 1, p. 402; Ibn Katheer, vol. 3, p. 113
[42] Ibn Hishâm, vol. 1, p. 399
[43] Bukhari, hadith no. 3886
[44] Ibn Katheer, vol. 3, p. 113
[45] Ibn Hishâm, vol. 1, pp. 402-403
[46] Ibid., vol. 1, p. 398
[47] Khaleel, p. 122
[48] Bukhari, hadith nos. 4864-4868
[49] al-Ghaḍbân, vol. 1, p. 451
[50] Ibid., vol. 1, p. 459

Chapter Five

[1] Ibn Hishâm, vol. 2, pp. 423-428
[2] Ibid., vol. 2, pp. 425-428
[3] Ibid., vol. 2, pp. 427-428
[4] Ibid., vol. 2, pp. 424-425
[5] Bukhari, hadith no. 335; Muslim, hadith no. 1167
[6] Ibn Hishâm mentioned that this group was from the Khazraj (vol. 2, p. 428) and in vol. 2, p. 441, explained that the Arabs called all the people of Yathrib 'the Khazraj', regardless of whether they are from the Khazraj tribe itself or belong to the Aws tribe. Khazraj, therefore, is a name used for both tribes, but biographers did not notice this point and claimed that the whole group was from the tribe of Khazraj and attributed this claim to Ibn

Hishâm. The reality is that the first group consisted of people from both tribes, although the majority was from the Khazraj. For example, Abul-Haytham ibn aṭ-Ṭayḥân was from the Aws tribe (see Ibn Katheer, vol. 3, p. 149). This understanding is also more appropriate, given the desire of the two tribes to solve their internal hostility.

7 Ibn Hishâm, vol. 2, pp. 428-429; Ibn Katheer, vol. 3, pp. 148-149

8 Ibn Hishâm, vol. 2, p. 430; Ibn Katheer, vol. 3, p. 150

9 Ibid., vol. 2, pp. 431-434; Ibn Katheer, vol. 3, p. 150

10 Bukhari, hadith no. 3892

11 Ibn Hishâm, vol. 2, pp. 435-437; Ibn Katheer, vol. 3, pp. 152-153

12 Ibn Hishâm, vol. 2, p. 438; aṭ-Ṭabari, vol. 2, p. 248; Ibn Katheer, vol. 3, p. 158

13 Ibn Hishâm, vol. 2, p. 441; aṭ-Ṭabari, vol. 2, p. 250, and he mentioned that the number was seventy males.

14 Ibn Hishâm, vol. 2, p. 438; aṭ-Ṭabari, vol. 2, p. 248; Ibn Katheer, vol. 3, p. 158

15 Ibn Hishâm, vol. 2, p. 441; aṭ-Ṭabari, vol. 2, pp. 249-250; Ibn Katheer, vol. 3, p. 160

16 Ibn Hishâm, vol. 2, pp. 447-448.

17 Ibn Katheer, vol. 3, p. 163

18 Ibn Hishâm, vol. 2, pp. 446-447; aṭ-Ṭabari, vol. 2, pp. 250-251; Ibn Katheer, vol. 3, pp. 159-160, 163

19 Ibn Hishâm, vol. 2, p. 442

20 al-Booṭi, pp. 124-125

21 Ibn Hishâm, vol. 2, p. 447-448

22 Ibid., vol. 2, p. 443; Ibn Katheer, vol. 3, p. 161

23 aṣ-Ṣallâbi, *As-Seerah an-Nabawiyah*, vol. 1, p. 419

24 Ibn Hishâm, vol. 2, pp. 476-480

25 Ibid., vol. 2, p. 468

26 Ibn Hishâm, vol. 2, pp. 468-470

27 Ibid., vol. 2, pp. 474-476

28 Ibid., vol. 2, p. 477

29 Ibid., vol. 2, pp. 480-482

30 Ibn Hishâm, vol. 2, p. 484; aṭ-Ṭabari, vol. 2, p. 256; Ibn Katheer, vol. 3, p. 177

31 Ibid.; a part of this picture had been narrated by Bukhari, hadith no. 3905

32 Ibn Hishâm, vol. 2, p. 485; aṭ-Ṭabari, vol. 2, pp. 256-257; Ibn Katheer, vol. 3, p. 179

33 the 36th chapter of the Noble Qur'an

34 Ibn Hishâm, vol. 2, p. 483; Ibn Katheer, vol. 3, p. 177

35 Ibn Katheer, vol. 3, p. 177

36 Bukhari, hadith no. 3906

[37] Ibn Hishâm, vol. 2, p. 486; Ibn Katheer, vol. 3, p. 180

[38] Ibn Katheer, vol. 3, p. 181

[39] Ibid., vol. 3, pp. 181-182

[40] Bukhari, hadith no. 3653

[41] Ibn Katheer, vol. 3, p. 184

[42] Bukhari, hadith no. 3906

[43] Ibn Katheer, vol. 3, p. 185; Ibn al-Qayyim, vol. 2, p. 53

[44] Ibn Katheer, vol. 3, p. 192

[45] Ibid., vol. 3, pp. 191-196

[46] Ibid., vol. 3, p. 194

[47] Ibn Hishâm, vol. 2, p. 493; Ibn Katheer, vol. 3, p. 197

[48] Bukhari, hadith no. 3932. However, Ibn Hishâm said that he stayed there for only four days and left on the fifth day, Friday, and performed the Friday prayer with the children of Sâlim ibn 'Awf in a valley before Madinah (see vol. 2, p. 494). For the comments of other scholars regarding this, see al-Ghaḍbân, vol. 2, p. 215. Al-'Umari (vol. 1, pp. 218-219) neglected all the narrations except that of Bukhari. This discrepancy remains, however, since the narration of Ibn Hishâm is further weakened by his reference to how the sons of Sâlim ibn 'Awf asked the Prophet (ﷺ) to reside with them. He remained on his camel and ordered them to set it free to find its own way as it was directed by Allah to the place that He had predestined for His Messenger (see vol. 2, p. 494). So, if he had prayed there on Friday, he would have dismounted from his camel, while he ordered the people to leave it until it knelt down by itself.

[49] Ibn Hishâm, vol. 2, p. 493

[50] Bukhari, hadith no. 3932

[51] al-Ghaḍbân, vol. 2, pp. 122-124

[52] Anṣâr: 'helpers'; the Muslim citizens of Madinah who gave refuge to the Prophet (ﷺ) and the other Muslim emigrants from Makkah

[53] Ibn Katheer, vol. 3, p. 197; al-'Umari, vol. 1, p. 218

[54] Bukhari, hadith no. 3932

[55] Bukhari, hadith no. 3925; Ibn Katheer, vol. 3, p. 197; al-'Umari, vol. 1, pp. 218-219

[56] Ibn Hishâm, vol. 2, pp. 494-495; Ibn Katheer, vol. 3, p. 198; al-'Umari, vol. 1, p. 219

[57] Ibn Hishâm, vol. 2, p. 499

[58] al-Booṭi, pp. 140-141

Chapter Six

[1] Ibn Katheer, vol. 3, p. 214; al-'Umari, vol. 1, p. 220

[2] Ibn Katheer, vol. 3, p. 220

[3] Bukhari, hadith no. 3932; Ibn Hishâm, vol. 2, p. 496, and he commented on the participation of the Prophet (ﷺ) as he wished to awaken the Muslims' desire for working on it; Ibn Katheer, vol. 3, p. 215; al-'Umari, vol. 1, p. 222

[4] aṣ-Ṣallâbi, *As-Seerah an-Nabawiyah*, vol. 1, p. 502

[5] Ibn Katheer, vol. 3, pp. 220-221

[6] al-Booṭi, p. 143

[7] an-Nadawi, pp. 186-187

[8] Bukhari, hadith no. 3926; Ibn Katheer, vol. 3, pp. 221-223

[9] al-'Umari, vol. 1, p. 242

[10] Ibn Katheer, vol. 3, p. 224

[11] Ibn Hishâm, vol. 2, pp. 505-507

[12] Ibid.

[13] al-'Umari, vol. 1, p. 244

[14] Bukhari, hadith no. 3937; Ibn Katheer, vol. 3, p. 228

[15] Bukhari, hadith no. 6747

[16] al-'Umari, vol. 1, p. 247

[17] al-'Umari, vol. 1, pp. 276, 281, 285. He quoted the whole text; see vol. 1, pp. 282-285.

[18] Ibid., vol. 1, pp. 282-284

[19] In interpreting the text in this way, I depended upon al-Qâsim ibn Sallâm, *Kitâb al-Amwâl*, p. 265.

[20] al-'Umari, vol. 1, p. 282

[21] aṣ-Ṣallâbi, *Fiqh at-Tamkeen*, pp. 463, 466; al-Booṭi, p. 153

[22] al-'Umari, vol. 1, p. 297

[23] Ibn Sallâm, pp. 263-264

[24] Ibn Sallâm, p. 266

[25] This poll tax would be in lieu of the *zakâh* (poor due) required of Muslims and in lieu of military duty which was obligatory upon Muslims when the State required it.

[26] The Qur'an refers to the Jews, Christians and other people of the previous scriptures as the 'People of the Book'.

[27] Khaleel, p. 325

[28] al-'Umari, vol. 1, p. 291

[29] Khaleel, p. 326

[30] Ibn Hishâm, vol. 2, pp. 428-429
[31] Ḥameedullâh, *Majmoo'ah al-Wathâ'iq as-Siyâsiyah*, p. 65
[32] as-Suhayli, *Ar-Rawḍ al-Ânif*, vol. 5, p. 43; aṣ-Ṣallâbi, *As-Seerah an-Nabawiyah,* vol. 1, p. 614
[33] Bukhari, hadith no. 7231
[34] Bukhari, hadith no. 3519; Muslim, hadith no. 6583
[35] Ibn Hishâm, vol. 2, p. 528
[36] Ibid., vol. 2, pp. 519-529
[37] Abu Dâwood, hadith no. 3004
[38] Bukhari, hadith no. 3950
[39] Ibn Hishâm, vol. 2, p. 590
[40] Ibid., vol. 2, p. 591
[41] Bukhari, hadith no. 3949
[42] Ḥameedullâh, p. 220. There is another document similar to this that had been concluded with Juhaynah: "They are guaranteed security to themselves and their properties and help against those who wrong or fight them unless they fight the Religion (of Islam) and the relatives. Their devoted and faithful desert people have the same (rights) as their urbanites."
[43] Ibn Hishâm, vol. 2, pp. 591-606
[44] Ibid., vol. 2, pp. 602-604

Chapter Seven

[1] Hijrah: the emigration of the Muslims from Makkah to Madinah, also the starting point of the Islamic Hijri calendar
[2] Ibn Hishâm, vol. 2, pp. 606-607; Ibn Katheer, vol. 3, p. 256
[3] Ibid.
[4] Bukhari, hadith nos. 3951, 3956-3959
[5] Ibn Hishâm, vol. 2, p. 607
[6] Ibid., vol. 2, p. 618
[7] Ibid., vol. 2, pp. 618-619; aṭ-Ṭabari, vol. 3, pp. 20-21; al-'Umari, vol. 2, p. 357
[8] Ibid., vol. 2, p. 615
[9] al-'Umari, vol. 2, pp. 361-362
[10] Khaṭṭâb, *Ar-Rasool al-Qâ'id*, pp. 111-115
[11] Bukhari, hadith nos. 3984-3985
[12] Bukhari, hadith no. 3992
[13] Ibid., hadith no. 3995; see also Ibn Hishâm, vol. 2, pp. 633-634
[14] aṭ-Ṭabari, vol. 3, p. 21; and in vol. 3, p. 39, he referred to only forty four

captives; Ibn Katheer, vol. 3, p. 279

15 Ibn Katheer, vol. 3, p. 301

16 al-'Umari, vol. 2, pp. 366-367

17 aṭ-Ṭabari, vol. 3, p. 39; Ibn Katheer, vol. 3, p. 305

18 as-Samarqandi, *Tuḥfah al-Fuqahâ'*, vol. 3, pp. 301-302

19 al-'Umari, vol. 2, pp. 368-369

20 Ibid., vol 2, pp. 369-370

21 Abu Shuhbah, vol. 2, p. 176; aṣ-Ṣallâbi, *As-Seerah an-Nabawiyah,* vol. 2, p. 711

22 Ibn Hishâm, vol. 2, pp. 647-648; aṭ-Ṭabari, vol. 3, pp. 41-42

23 Ibn Hishâm, vol. 2, p. 661; aṭ-Ṭabari, vol. 3, pp. 46-47

24 Bukhari, hadith no. 3989

25 aṭ-Ṭabari, vol. 3, p. 50

26 Ibid.

27 al-'Umari, vol. 2, p. 371

28 al-Booṭi, p. 160

29 aṭ-Ṭabari, vol. 3, p. 51

30 Ibid; Ibn Hishâm, vol. 3, pp. 43-44

31 Ibid.

32 Ibid., vol. 3, p. 46; al-'Umari, vol. 2, pp. 374-375

33 al-'Umari, vol. 2, p. 375

34 Ibn Hishâm, vol. 3, p. 46

35 Ibid., vol. 3, p. 45

36 al-'Umari, vol. 2, pp. 375-376

37 Ibn Hishâm, vol. 3, p. 50

Chapter Eight

1 Ibn Hishâm, vol. 3, pp. 60-61; see also Ibn Katheer, vol. 4, p. 10

2 al-Mubarakpuri, p. 246, who mentioned that the Prophet's uncle al-'Abbâs (رضي الله عنه) had sent him a message telling him that the troops were beginning to advance on Madinah. However, this information is not reliable since it was neither documented nor has its source been singled out.

3 Ibn Hishâm, vol. 3, pp. 61-62

4 aṭ-Ṭabari, vol. 3, p. 63; Ibn Katheer, vol. 4, p. 13, who mentioned that they only had one hundred horses

5 Ibn Katheer, vol. 4, p. 12

6 aṭ-Ṭabari, vol. 3, p. 62

[7] aṣ-Ṣallâbi, *As-Seerah an-Nabawiyah,* vol. 2, pp. 772-773
[8] Ibn Hishâm, vol. 3, p. 63; Ibn Katheer, vol. 4, p. 13
[9] Ibn Hishâm, vol. 3, p. 65; aṭ-Ṭabari, vol. 3, p. 64
[10] aṭ-Ṭabari, vol. 3, pp. 63-64
[11] Ibn Hishâm, vol. 3, p. 66
[12] aṭ-Ṭabari, vol. 3, pp. 63-64
[13] Ibn Katheer, vol. 4, p. 13
[14] Bukhari, hadith no. 4051
[15] Ibn Katheer, vol. 4, p. 14
[16] aṭ-Ṭabari, vol. 3, p. 62
[17] Ibn Hishâm, vol. 3, pp. 65-66; aṭ-Ṭabari, vol. 3, p. 65; Bukhari, hadith no. 4043
[18] Ibn Hishâm, vol. 3, p. 70
[19] aṭ-Ṭabari, vol. 3, p. 65
[20] Ibn Katheer, vol. 4, p. 24; al-'Umari, vol. 2, p. 385
[21] aṭ-Ṭabari, vol. 3, p. 68
[22] Ibid.; Bukhari, hadith nos. 4073-4076; Ibn Katheer, vol. 4, pp. 22-23
[23] Ibn Katheer, vol. 4, p. 23
[24] Ibn Katheer, vol. 4, pp. 25, 34
[25] Ibid.
[26] Bukhari, hadith no. 4078
[27] aṭ-Ṭabari, vol. 3, p. 74
[28] Ibn Hishâm, vol. 3, p. 94
[29] aṭ-Ṭabari, vol. 3, p. 76
[30] Ibn Katheer, vol. 4, pp. 48-49
[31] Ibid.
[32] aṭ-Ṭabari, vol. 3, p. 79
[33] Ibid., vol. 3, pp. 80-81; Ibn Katheer, vol. 4, pp. 49-50
[34] a sound hadith recorded by Ibn Mâjah and Abu Dâwood
[35] Bukhari, hadith no. 2809
[36] al-Booṭi, p. 178
[37] Ibn Hishâm, vol. 3, p. 90
[38] Ibn Katheer, vol. 7, p. 5
[39] Ibid., vol 7, p. 65
[40] al-Booṭi, p. 182
[41] Bukhari, hadith no. 4079
[42] Ibid.
[43] Bukhari, hadith nos. 4064, 4071; Muslim, hadith nos. 4642, 4684, 4690
[44] Bukhari, hadith no. 4075

Chapter Nine

[1] al-'Umari, vol. 2, p. 398
[2] Ibid.
[3] Ibn Hishâm, vol. 3, pp. 169-179; aṭ-Ṭabari, vol. 3, pp. 81-82
[4] Bukhari, hadith nos. 4085-4086
[5] Bukhari, hadith nos. 4085-4086
[6] Ibn Hishâm, vol. 3, pp. 183-185; aṭ-Ṭabari, vol. 3, pp. 85-86
[7] Bukhari, hadith no. 4089
[8] Ibid., hadith nos. 4087-4096
[9] Ibn Hishâm, vol. 3, p. 209
[10] aṭ-Ṭabari, vol. 3, p. 94; al-'Umari, vol. 2, p. 401
[11] Ibn Hishâm, vol. 3, pp. 209-210; aṭ-Ṭabari, vol. 3, pp. 93-94
[12] al-'Umari, vol. 2, p. 402; Khaleel, p. 208
[13] aṭ-Ṭabari, vol. 3, p. 116
[14] al-'Umari, vol. 2, p. 405
[15] Ibn Hishâm, vol. 3, p. 290; aṭ-Ṭabari, vol. 3, p. 116
[16] Bukhari, vol. 3, p. 39
[17] al-Booṭi, pp. 202-203; al-'Umari, vol. 2, p. 406
[18] Ibn Hishâm, vol. 3, pp. 290-291
[19] al-Ghaḍbân, vol. 3, p. 375
[20] Ibn Hishâm, vol. 3, p. 291
[21] Ibn Hishâm, vol. 3, p. 293
[22] Bukhari, hadith nos. 4141-4146; Ibn Hishâm, vol. 3, pp. 297-303
[23] al-Booṭi, p. 211
[24] Ibn Mâjah, hadith no. 2567
[25] al-Qayyim, vol. 2, p. 115; al-Booṭi, p. 212
[26] al-Booṭi, pp. 188-189
[27] Ibn Hishâm, vol. 3, pp. 172-173
[28] Ibid.

Chapter Ten

[1] Bukhari, hadith no. 4097
[2] Ibn Hishâm, vol. 3, p. 214; aṭ-Ṭabari, vol. 3, p. 96; Ibn Katheer, vol. 4, p. 93
[3] al-'Umari, vol. 2, p. 418
[4] aṭ-Ṭabari, vol. 3, p. 96
[5] Ibn Hishâm, vol. 3, pp. 214-215; aṭ-Ṭabari, vol. 3, pp. 96-97

[6] al-'Umari, vol. 2, p. 419

[7] Ibn Hishâm, vol. 3, pp. 219-220

[8] aṭ-Ṭabari, vol. 3, p. 97; Ibn Hishâm, vol. 3, p. 216; al-'Umari, vol. 2, p. 420

[9] al-'Umari, vol. 2, p. 420; aṣ-Ṣallâbi, *As-Seerah an-Nabawiyah,* vol. 2, p. 943

[10] ell: unit of length approximately the length of a man's forearm; its exact measurement varied from area to area

[11] aṭ-Ṭabari, vol. 3, pp. 97-98; al-'Umari, vol. 2, p. 421

[12] Bukhari, hadith nos. 4104, 4106

[13] Ibn Hishâm, vol. 3, pp. 217-219; Bukhari, hadith no. 4101

[14] al-'Umari, vol. 2, p. 422

[15] Bukhari, hadith nos. 4099, 4100, 4101, 4102

[16] Allah described the situation in the *Noble Qur'an*, 33: 11-20; Ibn Hishâm, vol. 3, p. 216

[17] Ibn Hishâm, vol. 3, p. 220

[18] Ibid., vol. 3, p. 224

[19] Ibid., vol. 3, pp. 224-225

[20] Ibid., vol. 3, pp. 220-221; aṭ-Ṭabari, vol. 3, pp. 99-100

[21] Ibn Hishâm, vol. 3, p. 222

[22] al-'Umari, vol. 2, p. 426; aṣ-Ṣallâbi, *As-Seerah an-Nabawiyah,* vol. 2, p. 947

[23] Ibn Hishâm, vol. 3, pp. 217-219

[24] Bukhari, hadith nos. 4111, 4112

[25] Ibn Hishâm, vol. 3, p. 223; aṭ-Ṭabari, vol. 3, p. 100

[26] Ibid.

[27] Bukhari, hadith no. 4115; Ibn Katheer, vol. 4, pp. 111-112

[28] al-'Umari, vol. 2, p. 428; Ibn Hishâm, vol. 3, p. 223

[29] Ibn Katheer, vol. 4, p. 107

[30] Ibn Hishâm, vol. 3, pp. 229-231; aṭ-Ṭabari, vol. 3, pp. 103-104; Ibn Katheer, vol. 4, pp. 111-112

[31] al-'Umari, vol. 2, p. 430

[32] Ibn Katheer, vol. 4, p. 115

[33] Ibn Hishâm, vol. 3, pp. 232-233; aṭ-Ṭabari, vol. 3, p. 104; Ibn Katheer, vol. 4, p. 113

[34] Bukhari, hadith no. 4105

[35] Ibn Hishâm, vol. 3, pp. 232-233; aṭ-Ṭabari, vol. 3, pp. 104-105; Ibn Katheer, vol. 4, pp. 113-114

[36] Bukhari, hadith nos. 4109-4110

[37] al-Booṭi, p. 221

Chapter Eleven

[1] Ibn Hishâm, vol. 3, p. 308
[2] al-'Umari, vol. 2, p. 435
[3] Ibn Hishâm, vol. 3, p. 309
[4] Bukhari, hadith nos. 4178-4179
[5] Ibid., hadith nos. 4150-4153
[6] Ibid., hadith nos. 2731-2732; Abu Dâwood, hadith no. 2765; Ibn Hishâm, vol. 3, p. 310
[7] Ibn Hishâm, vol. 3, pp. 311-314
[8] Ibid., vol. 3, p. 314; aṭ-Ṭabari, vol. 3, p. 129
[9] Ibn Hishâm, vol. 3, p. 315; aṭ-Ṭabari, vol. 3, p. 130
[10] Ibn Hishâm, vol. 3, p. 315; Bukhari, hadith nos. 4169, 4186, 4187
[11] Ibn Hishâm, vol. 3, p. 316
[12] Ibn Hishâm, vol. 3, pp. 317-318; Ibn Katheer, vol. 4, pp. 168-169; al-'Umari, vol. 2, pp. 441-443
[13] Bukhari, hadith nos. 2731-2732, 4180, 4181, 4189
[14] Ibid., hadith nos. 2731-2732
[15] Ibid., hadith nos. 4180-4181. It is worth mentioning that only men were demanded to be sent back to Makkah, but not women. The Prophet (ﷺ) did not return the females who resorted to him nor did Quraysh request this. The main reason appears to derive from the fact that men in general formed the military power at that time and the intention was to weaken the Muslims in this respect.
[16] Ibid., hadith nos. 2731-2732
[17] Ibid., hadith no. 4424; Muslim, hadith no. 1773; Ibn Sallâm, p. 28-32. Al-'Umari discussed the authenticity of these letters on the basis of examining the authenticity of the Hadith and concluded that the Prophet's letter to Caesar is the only authentic text which can be considered in envisaging the other letters. See vol. 2, pp. 456-459.
[18] aṭ-Ṭabari, vol. 3, pp. 137-144
[19] Ibn Hishâm, vol. 3, p. 322
[20] The Prophet (ﷺ) also described the result of this agreement as a victory; see for example, Abu Dâwood, hadith no. 2736.
[21] Ibn Hishâm, vol. 4, p. 370
[22] aṭ-Ṭabari, vol. 3, p. 154
[23] Ibid., vol. 3, p. 154
[24] Ibn Hishâm, vol. 4, p. 370; aṭ-Ṭabari, vol. 3, p. 152

[25] Bukhari, hadith no. 4256
[26] Ibid., hadith no. 4255
[27] Ibn Mâjah, hadith no. 2953
[28] Ibid., hadith nos. 4256-4257; Ibn Hishâm, vol. 4, p. 371; aṭ-Ṭabari, vol. 3, p. 153
[29] al-'Umari, vol. 2, p. 464
[30] Ibn Katheer, vol. 4, p. 227
[31] Ibid., vol. 4, p. 229
[32] ash-Shawkâni, *Fatḥ al-Qadeer*, vol. 5, p. 546
[33] Ḥawwâ, *Al-Islâm*, p. 395
[34] Ibid., p. 341
[35] Ibn Mâjah, hadith nos. 936, 937, 938, 939
[36] Bukhari, hadith nos. 2731-2732
[37] Ibid.
[38] Ibid., hadith no. 846
[39] al-Booṭi, pp. 242-243

Chapter Twelve

[1] 'Ali, vol. 6, pp. 513-514; al-'Umari, vol. 1, pp. 227-229
[2] Ibn Hishâm, vol. 2, p. 519
[3] Ibid.
[4] Abu Dâwood, hadith no. 3000; al-Wâḥidi, p. 38
[5] Ibn Hishâm, vol. 2, p. 513
[6] Ibid., vol. 2, pp. 516-518
[7] Ibid., vol. 2, pp. 527-528
[8] Bukhari, hadith no. 3941
[9] al-Wâḥidi, p. 430
[10] Ibid., pp. 430-431
[11] Ibn Hishâm, vol. 3, pp. 51-56; Abu Dâwood, hadith no. 3000
[12] Abu Dâwood, hadith no. 3000
[13] Ibid.
[14] Ibid., hadith no. 3001
[15] Ibn Hishâm, vol. 2, p. 571
[16] Ibn Hishâm, vol. 2, pp. 571-572
[17] al-Wâḥidi, pp. 32-34
[18] Ibn Hishâm, vol. 2, p. 571
[19] Ibid., vol. 2, p. 567

[20] aṣ-Ṣallâbi, *As-Seerah an-Nabawiyah,* vol. 1, pp. 570-573
[21] Ḥawwâ, *Al-Asâs fee as-Sunnah,* vol. 2, p. 537
[22] Ibn Hishâm, vol. 3, p. 55; Bukhari, hadith no. 4037
[23] Ḥawwâ, *Al-Asâs fee as-Sunnah,* vol. 2, pp. 537-538
[24] al-'Umari, vol. 1, p. 304
[25] Bukhari, hadith nos. 4038-4040
[26] aṭ-Ṭabari, vol. 3, p. 50
[27] Ibn Hishâm, vol. 3, pp. 47-48; Ibn Katheer, vol. 4, pp. 3-4
[28] Ibid.
[29] aṭ-Ṭabari, vol. 3, p. 50
[30] al-'Umari, vol. 1, p. 301
[31] aṭ-Ṭabari, vol. 3, p. 50
[32] Ibn Hishâm, vol. 3, p. 48; aṭ-Ṭabari, vol. 3, p. 51
[33] al-Booṭi, p. 171
[34] Bukhari, vol. 3, p. 17
[35] Ibn Hishâm, vol. 3, p. 190; aṭ-Ṭabari, vol. 3, pp. 88-89
[36] al-'Umari, vol. 1, pp. 306-307
[37] Abu Dâwood, hadith no. 3004
[38] al-'Umari, vol. 1, p. 307
[39] Ibn Hishâm, vol. 3, pp. 190-191; aṭ-Ṭabari, vol. 3, p. 89; Ibn Katheer, vol. 4, p. 75
[40] aṭ-Ṭabari, vol. 3, pp. 52-53
[41] Ibn Hishâm, vol. 3, p. 191; Bukhari, hadith nos. 4031-4032
[42] Ibn Hishâm, vol. 3, p. 191
[43] Bukhari, hadith no. 4117
[44] Ibid., hadith no. 4119
[45] al-'Umari, vol. 1, p. 314
[46] Ibn Hishâm, vol. 3, p. 235; aṭ-Ṭabari, vol. 3, p. 106; Ibn Katheer, vol. 4, p. 120
[47] Ibn Hishâm, vol. 3, pp. 236-237; Ibn Katheer, vol. 4, p. 120
[48] Ibn Hishâm, vol. 3, pp. 239-240; Bukhari, hadith nos. 4121-4122. Ibn Hishâm mentioned that there were between six and seven hundred men, and stated that 'the exaggerators' mentioned eight to nine hundred, see vol. 3, p. 241. However, Ibn Katheer said clearly that the number was just four hundred, see vol. 4, p. 122.
[49] al-'Umari, vol. 1, p. 318
[50] Ibn Hishâm, vol. 3, p. 192
[51] Ibid., vol. 3, p. 191
[52] Ibid., vol. 3, p. 220
[53] Bukhari, hadith no. 4205

[54] Ibid., hadith nos. 4197, 4200
[55] al-'Umari, vol. 1, p. 321
[56] Ibn Hishâm, vol. 3, p. 330
[57] Ibid., vol. 3, pp. 330-331
[58] al-'Umari, vol. 1, pp. 324-325
[59] Bukhari, hadith no. 4200
[60] Ibn Hishâm, vol. 3, p. 337; Abu Dâwood, hadith no. 3018
[61] Ibn Hishâm, vol. 3, p. 337
[62] Abu Dâwood, hadith nos. 3011-3015
[63] Bukhari, hadith no. 4200
[64] aṭ-Ṭabari, vol. 3, p. 150
[65] Ibid.
[66] Abu Dâwood, hadith no. 3016
[67] an-Nadawi, pp. 318-319
[68] Bukhari, hadith no. 4216
[69] Ibid., hadith nos. 4244-4255
[70] Ibid., hadith no. 4210
[71] al-Booṭi, p. 246

Chapter Thirteen

[1] al-'Umari, vol. 2, p. 467
[2] aṣ-Ṣallâbi, *As-Seerah an-Nabawiyah,* vol. 2, p. 1137
[3] Ibn Hishâm, vol. 4, p. 373
[4] Ibid., vol. 4, pp. 374-375
[5] Ibid., vol. 4, pp. 374-377
[6] Ibid., vol. 4, pp. 378-379; aṭ-Ṭabari, vol. 3, p. 162
[7] Ibn Katheer, vol. 4, p. 247; al-'Umari, vol. 2, p. 468
[8] Ibn Katheer, vol. 4, pp. 247-248
[9] Ibn Hishâm, vol. 4, pp. 388-389
[10] Bukhari, hadith no. 4262; Ibn Hishâm, vol. 4, p. 380; aṭ-Ṭabari, vol. 3, p. 163; Ibn Katheer, vol. 4, pp. 246-467
[11] Ibn Hishâm, vol. 4, p. 380
[12] al-'Umari, vol. 2, p. 468; aṣ-Ṣallâbi, *As-Seerah an-Nabawiyah,* vol. 2, pp. 1143-1144
[13] al-'Umari, vol. 2, p. 471
[14] al-Booṭi, pp. 261-262
[15] Ibn Katheer, vol. 4, p. 244

[16] Bukhari, hadith no. 4262
[17] al-'Umari, vol. 2, p. 472

Chapter Fourteen

[1] Ibn Hishâm, vol. 4, p. 390; aṣ-Ṣallâbi, *As-Seerah an-Nabawiyah,* vol. 2, p. 1158
[2] Ibn Hishâm, vol. 4, p. 395; Ibn Katheer, vol. 4, pp. 278-279
[3] Ibn Hishâm, vol. 4, p. 395
[4] Ibn Hishâm, vol. 4, pp. 396-397; aṭ-Ṭabari, vol. 3, p. 166
[5] Ibid.; Ibn Katheer, vol. 4, p. 282
[6] Ibn Hishâm, vol. 4, p. 400; Ibn Katheer, vol. 4, p. 285
[7] aṭ-Ṭabari, vol. 3, p. 167
[8] Bukhari, hadith nos. 4275-4279
[9] Ibn Hishâm, vol. 4, p. 400
[10] Ibid.
[11] Ibn Hishâm, vol. 4, p. 400
[12] Ibid., vol. 4, p. 402; Abu Dâwood, hadith no. 3022
[13] Bukhari, hadith no. 4280
[14] Ibn Hishâm, vol. 4, p. 403; Abu Dâwood, hadith nos. 3021, 3022
[15] Ibn Hishâm, vol. 4, pp. 403-405
[16] Ibid., vol. 4, pp. 407-408; Bukhari, hadith no. 4280; al-'Umari, vol. 2, pp. 478-479
[17] Ibn Hishâm, vol. 4, pp. 409-410
[18] Bukhari, hadith no. 4302
[19] Ibid., hadith nos. 4305-4311
[20] Ibid., hadith no. 4312
[21] Ibn Hishâm, vol.. 4, p. 405
[22] al-'Umari, vol. 2, p. 481
[23] Muslim, hadith nos. 4622, 4624
[24] Bukhari, hadith no. 4298
[25] Ibid., hadith no. 4287
[26] Ibid., hadith no. 4288
[27] al-'Umari, vol. 2, p. 485
[28] Bukhari, hadith nos. 4295, 4313
[29] Ibid., hadith no. 4296
[30] Ibid., hadith no. 4304
[31] Ibid., hadith no. 4299
[32] Ibid., hadith no. 4279

[33] al-'Umari, vol. 2, pp. 481-482
[34] see also the verse of the Noble Qur'an found at 9: 28
[35] al-Booṭi, p. 276-277
[36] the 48th chapter of the Noble Qur'an
[37] Bukhari, hadith no. 4281
[38] al-Booṭi, p. 275-276
[39] an-Nawawi, vol. 14, p. 81; al-Booṭi, p. 280
[40] Ibid., p. 283

Chapter Fifteen

[1] aṭ-Ṭabari, vol. 3, p. 179
[2] Khaleel, p. 250
[3] Ibn Hishâm, vol. 4, p. 437; aṭ-Ṭabari, vol. 3, p. 179; Ibn Katheer, vol. 4, p. 323
[4] Ibn Hishâm, vol. 4, pp. 437-438; aṭ-Ṭabari, vol. 3, p. 180; Ibn Katheer, vol. 4, p. 323
[5] The valley of Ḥunayn is situated between Makkah and Ṭâ'if, close to the place known as Dhil-Majâz. It is about thirteen miles from Makkah on the side of Mount of Arafât; see as-Sindi's comments on *Ṣaheeḥ Bukhari*, vol. 3, p. 68.
[6] al-'Umari, vol. 2, p. 494
[7] Ibn Ḥajar, vol. 8, p. 29; al-'Umari, p. 494
[8] Bukhari, vol. 3, p. 68
[9] Ibid., vol. 4, pp. 439-440; Ibn Katheer, vol. 4, pp. 324-325
[10] Ibn Hishâm, vol. 4, p. 440; aṭ-Ṭabari, vol. 3, p. 181; Ibn Katheer, vol. 4, p. 324
[11] Ibn Hishâm, vol. 4, p. 444
[12] Ibn Katheer, vol. 4, p. 322
[13] Bukhari, vol. 3, p. 68
[14] Ibn Hishâm, vol. 4, pp. 442-443; aṭ-Ṭabari, vol. 3, p. 181; Ibn Katheer, vol. 4, p. 326
[15] Ibn Hishâm, vol. 4, p. 443; Ibn Katheer, vol. 4, p. 326
[16] Bukhari, hadith nos. 4315, 4316, 4317
[17] Ibn Hishâm, vol. 4, p. 445; aṭ-Ṭabari, vol. 3, pp. 182-183; Bukhari, hadith nos. 4317, 4333; Abu Dâwood, hadith no. 2658; Ibn Katheer, vol. 4, pp. 326-327
[18] al-'Umari, vol. 2, p. 497
[19] al-'Umari, vol. 4, p. 453
[20] Ibn Hishâm, vol. 4, pp. 453-455; Bukhari, hadith no. 4323; aṭ-Ṭabari, vol. 3, pp. 184-185
[21] aṭ-Ṭabari, vol. 3, p. 186

[22] al-'Umari, vol. 2, p. 504
[23] Ibn Hishâm, vol. 4, p. 478; aṭ-Ṭabari, vol. 3, p. 186; al-'Umari, vol. 2, p. 507
[24] Ibn Hishâm, vol. 4, p. 482; aṭ-Ṭabari, vol. 3, p. 187; al-'Umari, vol. 2, p. 507
[25] Ibn Hishâm, vol. 4, pp. 482-483
[26] Ibid., vol. 4, p. 483; Ibn Katheer, vol. 4, p. 348
[27] Ibn Hishâm, vol. 4, p. 485; Bukhari, hadith nos. 4326-4327
[28] aṭ-Ṭabari, vol. 3, p. 187
[29] Bukhari, hadith no. 4325
[30] Ibn Hishâm, vol. 4, p. 488
[31] Bukhari, hadith nos. 4318-4319
[32] Ibid., hadith nos. 4330-4337
[33] Ibid., hadith no. 4331
[34] Ibid., hadith nos. 4330, 4332-4334; Ibn Hishâm, vol. 4, pp. 498-501
[35] Ibn Hishâm, vol. 4, p. 488
[36] Ibid., vol. 4, pp. 488-490; Bukhari, hadith nos. 4318-4319
[37] Ibn Hishâm, vol. 4, p. 491
[38] Ibid., vol 4, p. 500
[39] Abu Dâwood, hadith no. 4488
[40] Ibn al-Qayyim, vol. 3, p. 479; al-'Umari, vol. 2, p. 521
[41] Ibn Hishâm, vol. 4, pp. 457-458
[42] al-Booṭi, p. 292
[43] Bukhari, hadith nos. 4321-4322
[44] al-Booṭi, p. 291
[45] Ibid., p. 293

Chapter Sixteen

[1] Ibn Katheer, vol. 4, p. 374
[2] Ibn Katheer, vol. 5, p. 2
[3] Khaleel, p. 301; al-'Umari, vol. 2, p. 522
[4] Ibn Hishâm, vol. 4, p. 516; aṭ-Ṭabari, vol. 3, p. 196
[5] aṭ-Ṭabari, vol. 3, p. 196
[6] Bukhari, hadith no. 2778
[7] Ibn Hishâm, vol. 4, p. 518; Ibn Katheer, vol. 5, p. 4
[8] Ibn Hishâm, vol. 4, p. 517
[9] Ibid., vol. 4, p. 516
[10] Ibn Hishâm, vol. 4, p. 519
[11] Ibid., vol. 5, p. 7

[12] aṣ-Ṣallâbi, *As-Seerah an-Nabawiyah,* vol. 2, p. 1244
[13] Ibn Hishâm, vol. 4, pp. 523-525; aṭ-Ṭabari, vol. 3, pp. 199-200
[14] Ibn Hishâm, vol. 4, pp. 518-519; aṭ-Ṭabari, vol. 3, p. 197; Bukhari, hadith no. 4418
[15] Ibn Hishâm, vol. 4, p. 519
[16] Bukhari, hadith no. 4416
[17] Ibn Katheer, vol. 5, p. 9
[18] Ibid., vol. 5, p. 10
[19] Ibn Hishâm, vol. 4, pp. 520-521, 524
[20] See the following verses of the Qur'an: 7: 73-79; 11: 61-68; 26: 141-159; 54: 23-33; 91: 11-15
[21] Ibn Katheer, vol. 5, pp. 10-11
[22] Bukhari, hadith nos. 4419-4420
[23] Ibn Hishâm, vol. 4, p. 525
[24] Ibid., vol. 4, pp. 525-526. Ibn Katheer quoted the letter that was given to the people of Jarbâ' and Adruḥ according to which they had to pay in every Rajab one hundred dinârs and one hundred oke (ounce) of scent in addition to giving sincere advice and help to Muslims in return for their safety; see Ibn Katheer, vol. 5, pp. 16-17.
[25] Ibn Hishâm, vol. 4, p. 526
[26] Ibn Hishâm, vol. 4, p. 527; aṭ-Ṭabari, vol. 3, p. 200; Ibn Katheer, vol. 5, p. 18
[27] Ibn Hishâm, vol. 4, p. 527; aṭ-Ṭabari, vol. 3, p. 201
[28] Ibn Katheer, vol. 5, pp. 21-22
[29] Bukhari, hadith no. 4423
[30] aṭ-Ṭabari, vol. 3, pp. 201-202
[31] Bukhari, hadith no. 4418; Ibn Hishâm, vol. 4, p. 531; Ibn Katheer, vol. 5, pp. 23-27
[32] Bukhari, vol. 2, p. 298
[33] at-Tirmidhi, hadith nos. 3700-3701
[34] al-Booṭi, p. 306
[35] Ibid., p. 307; Ibn al-Qayyim, vol. 3, p. 20; Abu Dâwood, hadith no. 2773
[36] Muslim, hadith nos. 952-953; Ibn Ḥanbal, hadith no. 1665

Chapter Seventeen

[1] Ibn Hishâm, vol. 4, pp. 538-539
[2] Ibid., vol. 4, p. 540
[3] Ibid.; Abu Dâwood, hadith no. 3026

[4] Ibn Katheer, vol. 5, p. 30
[5] Ibid.; Ibn Hishâm, vol. 4, p. 540
[6] Abu Dâwood, hadith no. 3025
[7] Ibid.
[8] Bukhari, hadith no. 4365
[9] Ibid., hadith nos. 4368-4369, 4371
[10] Ibn Katheer, vol. 5, pp. 71-72
[11] Ibid., vol. 5, pp. 75-77
[12] Ibid., vol. 5, pp. 88-89
[13] Bukhari, hadith nos. 4373-4375
[14] Ibn Hishâm, vol. 4, pp. 559-560; Ibn Katheer, vol. 5, p. 40
[15] Bukhari, hadith nos. 4373, 4378
[16] Ibn Katheer, vol. 5, pp. 52-56
[17] Bukhari, hadith nos. 4341-4348; Ibn Katheer, vol. 5, pp. 99-103
[18] Bukhari, hadith nos. 4349-4354; Ibn Katheer, vol. 5, pp. 104-108
[19] Bukhari, hadith no. 4347
[20] Ibid., hadith nos. 4344-4345
[21] Abu Dâwood, hadith no. 3094
[22] Ibid; Bukhari, hadith nos. 4670-4672
[23] Ibn Katheer, vol. 5, p. 35
[24] Abu Shuhbah, vol. 2, p. 534
[25] aṣ-Ṣallâbi, *As-Seerah an-Nabawiyah,* vol. 2, pp. 1307-1308
[26] Bukhari, hadith no. 4363
[27] Ibn Hishâm, vol. 4, p. 546
[28] Ibn Katheer, vol. 5, pp. 37-39
[29] Ibid., vol. 5, p. 109
[30] Ibid.
[31] Ibn al-Qayyim, vol. 3, p. 595
[32] Ibn Hishâm, vol. 4, p. 603
[33] Bukhari, hadith nos. 1739-1742
[34] Ibn Hishâm, vol. 4, p. 603
[35] Ibid., vol. 4, pp. 603-604
[36] Ibn Hishâm, vol. 4, p. 604
[37] Ibid.
[38] Ibid.
[39] Ibid.
[40] Bukhari, hadith nos. 1561, 1562, 1566, 1568, 1570, 1572, 1638
[41] Ibid., hadith nos. 1605-1606
[42] Ibid., hadith nos. 1610-1611

[43] Ibid., hadith no. 1612
[44] Ibid., hadith nos. 1721-1723, 1734-1737
[45] Ibid., hadith no. 1604
[46] Ibid., hadith no. 1650
[47] Ibid., hadith nos. 1755, 1757
[48] Ibid., hadith nos. 1655-1657
[49] Ibid., hadith no. 1658
[50] Ibid., hadith nos. 1676-1681
[51] Ibid., hadith nos. 1685-1687
[52] Ibn Hishâm, vol. 4, p. 606
[53] Khaleel, p. 315
[54] Ibn Hishâm, vol. 4, p. 650; Bukhari, hadith nos. 4468- 4469
[55] Ibn Hishâm, vol. 4, p. 650
[56] Ibid., vol. 4, p. 651; at-Tirmidhi, hadith no. 3817
[57] Ibn Hishâm, vol. 4, p. 642
[58] Bukhari, hadith no. 4428
[59] Ibn Katheer, vol. 5, pp. 224-225
[60] Ibid.
[61] Ibn Katheer, vol. 5, p. 225
[62] Bukhari, hadith no. 4450; Muslim, hadith no. 6292
[63] Bukhari, hadith no. 4450
[64] Ibn Hishâm, vol. 4, pp. 649-650; Bukhari, hadith nos. 3654-3658; Muslim, hadith nos. 6170-6176
[65] Ibn Hishâm, vol. 4, p. 652; Ibn Katheer, vol. 5, pp. 232-233
[66] Muslim, hadith no. 6181; Ibn Katheer, vol. 5, p. 228 cited similar positions from Aḥmad ibn Ḥanbal.
[67] Bukhari, hadith no. 4432
[68] Ibid.
[69] Ibid., vol. 3, p. 95, hadith no. 4442
[70] Ibn Katheer, vol. 5, p. 228
[71] Ibn Katheer, vol. 5, p. 229
[72] Muslim, hadith no. 6170
[73] Ibid.
[74] Bukhari, hadith no. 4431
[75] Ibid., hadith no. 4441
[76] Ibn Katheer, vol. 5, p. 231
[77] Muslim, hadith nos. 7229, 7231
[78] Ibn Mâjah, hadith nos. 1625, 2697, 2698
[79] Ibn Katheer, vol. 5, pp. 238-239

[80] Bukhari, hadith nos. 712-713
[81] Ibn Katheer, vol. 5, p. 235
[82] Bukhari, hadith nos. 712-713; Ibn Katheer, vol. 5, p. 233
[83] Ibn Katheer, vol. 5, p. 237
[84] Bukhari, hadith no. 4462
[85] Ibn Katheer, vol. 5, p. 237
[86] Ibid.
[87] Bukhari, hadith nos. 4433-4434; Ibn Mâjah, hadith no. 1621, with some contrasts in the details.
[88] This is the most famous narration. There is a consensus that his death was on a Monday, which does not correspond with the 12th of Rabee' I or the 10th. Many scholars determined the second of this month (see Ibn Katheer, vol. 5, p. 255) which sounds more accurate for it coincides with that day of the week. If this date is adopted, then it falls on 29 May 632 CE.
[89] Bukhari, hadith no. 4448; Ibn Mâjah, hadith no. 1624; Ibn Katheer, vol. 5, p. 235
[90] aṭ-Ṭabari, vol. 3, p. 252; Ibn Mâjah, hadith no. 1624
[91] Bukhari, hadith no. 4447
[92] aṭ-Ṭabari, vol. 3, p. 252
[93] Ibn Mâjah, hadith no. 1623
[94] Ibid., hadith no. 1619; Bukhari, hadith no. 4439
[95] Bukhari, hadith no. 4440
[96] Ibid., hadith no. 4437
[97] Ibid., hadith no. 4463; Ibn Mâjah, hadith no.1620
[98] Bukhari, hadith nos. 4438, 4451
[99] Ibid., hadith no. 4466. Ibn Katheer, vol. 5, pp. 254, 258-259
[100] Bukhari, hadith nos. 4450-4451
[101] Ibn Mâjah, hadith no. 1627
[102] Bukhari, hadith nos. 3667, 4452-4453
[103] Ibid., hadith nos. 3668, 4454; Ibn Mâjah, hadith no. 1627
[104] Ibn Hishâm, vol. 4, pp. 656-660
[105] Ibid., vol. 4, pp. 599-601
[106] Ibn Katheer, vol. 5, p. 260
[107] Ibid., vol. 5, p. 264
[108] Ibid., vol. 5, pp. 260-261
[109] Ibn Mâjah, hadith no. 1628
[110] Ibid.
[111] Ibid.; Ibn Katheer, vol. 5, pp. 270-271

References

‘Abdul-Qâdir, ‘Abdul-‘Azeez Ghunaym. *Qiṣṣah al-Bayt al-Harâm* [The story of the Sacred House], vol.1 of *Silsilah al-Buḥuth al-Islâmiyah*. Egypt: Maktabah al-Azhar ash-Shareef, 2001.

Abu Dâwood *Sunan Abi Dâwood*. Edited by ‘Izzatud-Da‘âs. Damascus: NP, 1971.

Abu Shuhbah, Muḥammad. *As-Seerah an-Nabawiyah fee Ḍaw‘ al-Qur’ân was-Sunnah* [The Prophet’s biography according to the Qur’an and the Sunnah], 3rd ed. Damascus: Dâr al-Qalam, 1996.

al-‘Ali, Ibrâheem. *Ṣaḥeeḥ as-Seerah an-Nabawiyah* [The Prophet’s biography according to authentic sources], 3rd ed. Beirut: Dâr an-Nafâ’is, 1998.

‘Ali, Jawâd. *Al-Mufaṣṣal fee Târeekh al-‘Arab Qabl al-Islâm* [History of the Arabs before Islam]. Baghdad: Maktabah az-Za‘eem, 1961.

al-‘Aqqâd, ‘Abbâs Maḥmood *Maṭla‘ an-Noor* [An emanation of light]. Cairo: Dâr Nahḍah Miṣr, nd.

al-Baghawi. *Sharḥ as-Sunnah* [Explanation of the Sunnah], 1st ed. Edited by ‘Ali Muḥammad Mu‘awwaḍ and ‘Âdil Aḥmad ‘Abdul-Majd. Beirut: Dâr al-Kutub al-‘Ilmiyah, nd.

al-Balâdhiri. *Ansâb al-Ashrâf* [The noblest lineages]. Edited by Muḥammad Ḥameedullâh. Cairo: Dâr al-Ma‘ârif, nd.

al-Booṭi Muḥammad Sa'eed Ramaḍân. *Fiqh as-Seerah an-Nabawiyah ma'a Moojaz li Târeekh al-Khilâfah ar-Râshidah* [Understanding the Prophet's biography, with a brief summary of the history of the Rightly-guided Caliphate], 6th ed. Cairo: Dâr as-Salâm li aṭ-Ṭṭibâ'ati wan-Nashri wat-Tawzee', 1999.

al-Bukhâri. *Al-Jâmi' aṣ-Ṣaḥeeḥ* [The authentic collection]. Edited by 'Imâd Zaki al-Bârdi. Egypt: Al-Maktabah at-Tawfeeqiyah, nd.

adh-Dhahabi. *As-Seerah an-Nabawiyah* [The Prophet's biography]. Beirut: Dâr al-Kutub al-'Ilmiyah, nd.

al-Ghaḍbân, Muneer. *Al-Manhaj at-Tarbawi li as-Seerah an-Nabawiyah* [An educational methodology from the Prophet's biography], 1st ed. al-Manṣoorah (Egypt): Dâr al-Wafâ' li at-Ṭṭibâ'ati wan-Nashri wat-Tawzi', 1998.

al-Ghazâli, Muḥammad. *Fiqh as-Seerah* [Understanding the Life of the Prophet], 2nd ed. Egypt: Dâr al-Kitâb al-'Arabi, 1955.

Ḥameedullâh, Muḥammad. *Majmoo'ah al-Wathâ'iq as-Siyâsiyah* [A collection of political documents], 5th ed. Beirut: Dâr an-Nafâ'is, 1985.

Ḥamzah, Fu'âd. *Qalb Jazeerah al-'Arab* [The heart of Arabia]. Egypt: al-Maṭba'at as-Salafiyah, 1923.

Ḥawwâ, Sa'eed. *Al-Asâs fee as-Sunnah* [Fundamentals of the Sunnah]. Cairo: Dâr as-Salâm, 1989.

——. *Al-Islâm*, 4th ed. Cairo: Dâr as-Salâm, 2001.

al-Haythami, 'Ali ibn Abi Bakr. *Majma' az-Zawâ'id wa Manba' al-Fawâ'id* [A gathering of provision and a source of benefit]. Beirut: Dâr al-Kitâb al-'Arabi, 1982.

Ibn 'Abdil-Barr. *Ad-Durar fee Iikhtiṣâr al-Maghâzi was-Siyar*. Cairo: Lajnah Iḥyâ' at-Turâth, 1994.

Ibn al-Atheer. *Al-Kâmil fit-Târeekh* [A complete history], 3rd ed. Edited by Abu l-Fidâ' 'Abdullâh al-Qâḍi. Beirut: Dâr al-Kutub al-'Ilmiyah, 1998.

Ibn Ḥajar. *Fatḥ al-Bâri fee Sharḥ Ṣaḥeeḥ al-Bukhâri* [Commentary on *Ṣaḥeeḥ al-Bukhâri*]. Beirut: Dâr al-Ma'rifah, nd.

Ibn Ḥanbal, Aḥmad. *Al-Musnad*. Edited by Aḥmad Muḥammad Shâkir. Cairo: Dâr al-Ma'ârif, 1950.

Ibn Hishâm. *As-Seerah an-Nabawiyah* [The Prophet's biography]. Edited by Muṣṭafa as-Saqqâ, Ibrâheem al-Ibyari, and 'Abdul-Ḥafeedh Shalabi. Beirut: al-Maktabah al-'Ilmiyah, nd.

Ibn Katheer. *Al-Bidâyah wan-Nihâyah* [The beginning and the end], 2nd ed. Beriut & Riyadh: Maktabah al-Ma'ârif and Maktabah an-Naṣr, 1978.

——. *As-Seerah an-Nabawiyah* [The Prophet's biography], 2nd ed. Edited by Muṣṭafâ 'Abdul-Wâhid. Beirut: Dâr al-Fikr, 1978.

Ibn Mâjah. *Sunan Ibn Mâjah*. Edited by Muḥammad Fu'âd 'Abdulbâqi. Egypt: Dâr Iḥyâ' al-Kutub al-'Arabiyah, nd.

Ibn al-Qayyim. *Zâd ul-Ma'âd fee Hadyi Khayr al-'Ibâd* [The provision of the traveller: a gift from the best of people], 1st ed. Edited by Shu'ayb al-Arnâ'oot. Damascus: Dâr ar-Risâlah, 1979.

Ibn Sa'd. *Aṭ-Ṭabaqât al-Kubrâ*, NE. Lebanon: Dâr Ṣâdir and Dâr Beirut, 1957.

Ibn Sallâm, al-Qâsim (Abu 'Ubayd). *Kitâb al-Amwâl* [Finance], 2nd ed. Edited by Muḥammad Khaleel Haras. Beirut: Dâr al-Fikr, 1988.

Ibn Taymiyah. *Majmoo'ah al-Fatâwâ* [Compendium of Religious Verdicts], 2nd ed. Edited by 'Ameer al-Jazzâr and Anwar al-Bâz. al-Manṣoorah (Egypt): Dâr al-Wafâ' li aṭ-Ṭibâ'ati wan-Nashri wat-Taand Riyadh: Maktabah al-'Ubaykân, 1998.

——. *Al-Jawâb aṣ-Ṣaḥeeḥ liman Baddala Deen al-Maseeḥ* [An apt answer to those who changed the religion of the Messiah]. NP: al-Majd, nd.

Jazli Aḥzami. *Al-Hijrah fil-Qurân al-Kareem* [The migration according to the Noble Qur'an], 1st ed. Riyadh: Maktabah ar-Rushd, 1996.

Khaleel, 'Imâdud-Deen. *Dirâsat fee as-Seerah* [Lessons from the Prophet's biography], 3rd ed. Beirut: Mu'assasat ar-Risâlah & Dâr an-Nafâ'is, 1978.

Khaṭṭâb, Maḥmood Sheet. *Ar-Rasool al-Qâ'id* [The Commander Messenger], 2nd ed. Baghdad: Maktabah an-Nahḍah, 1960.

al-Mubarakpuri, Safi-ur-Rahman. *Ar-Raheeq al-*Makhtûm [The sealed nectar]. Cairo: Dâr al-Ḥadeeth, nd.

Muslim. *Ṣaḥeeḥ Muslim*, 1st ed. Edited under the supervision of Shaykh Ṣâliḥ ibn 'Abdul 'Azeez. Riyadh: Dâr as-Salâm li Nashr wat-Tawzee', 1999.

an-Nadawi, Abu l-Ḥasan. *As-Seerah an-Nabawiyah* [The Prophet's biography], 12th ed. Damascus & Beirut: Dâr Ibn Katheer, 2001.

an-Nawawi. *Sharḥ Ṣaḥeeḥ Muslim* [Commentary on *Ṣaḥeeḥ Muslim*].

Qal'aji, Muḥammad. *Dirâsat Taḥleeliyah li Shakhṣiyah ar-Rasoo*[Investigative studies in the personality of the Messenger], 1st ed. Beirut: Dâr an-Nafâ'is, 1988.

Quṭub, Sayyid. *Fee Dhilâl al-Qurân* [In the shade of the Qur'an].

Salâmah, Kâmil. *Dawlah ar-Rasool min at-Takween ila at-Tamkeen* [The Messenger's state: from foundation to viability], 1st ed. Amman: Dâr Ammâr, 1994.

aṣ-Ṣallâbi, 'Ali Muḥammad. *As-Seerah an-Nabawiyah* [The Prophet's biography], 1st ed. Sharjah: Maktabah as-Saḥâbah and Cairo: Maktabah at-Tâbi'een, 2001.

——. *Fiqh at-Tamkeen fee al-Qur'ân al-Kareem* [Understanding viability from the Noble Qur'an], 1st ed. Amman: Dâr al-Bayâriq, 1999.

as-Samarqandi, 'Alâ'ud-Deen. *Tuḥfah al-Fuqahâ'* [Treasure of the scholars]. Beirut: Dâr al-Kutub al-'Ilmiyah, nd.

ash-Shawkâni, Muḥammad ibn 'Ali. *Fatḥ al-Qadeer* [Conquest of the Powerful]. NP: Dârul-Fikr, nd.

as-Suhayli, Abu l-Qâsim. *Ar-Rawḍ al-*Ânif. Edited by 'Abdur-Raḥmân al-Wakeel. Cairo: Dâr al-Kutub al-Ḥadeethah, nd.

as-Suwaykit, Sulaymân. *Miḥnah al-Muslimeen fee al-'Ahd al-Makki* [Careers of Muslims during the Meccan period]. Riyadh: Maktabah at-Tawbah, 1992. (pt one, p 41)

aṭ-Ṭabari. *Târeekh ar-Rusuli wal-Muloo*k [History of messengers and sovereigns], 1st ed. Revised by Ṣidqi Jameel al-'Aṭṭâr. Beirut: Dâr al-Fikr, 1998.

at-Tirmidhi. *Al-Jâmi' aṣ-Ṣaḥeeḥ* [Authentic collection], 1st ed. Edited by Kamâl Yoosuf al-Ḥoot. Beirut: Dâr al-Kutub al-'Ilmiyah, 1987.

al-'Umari, Akram. *As-Seerah an-Nabawiyah aṣ-Ṣaḥeeḥah* [The Prophet's biography according to authentic sources]. Madinah: Maktabah al-'Uloom wal-Ḥikam, 1992.

al-Wâḥidi, Abu l-Ḥasan 'Ali ibn Aḥmad an-Neesâboori. *Asbâb Nuzool al-Qurân* [Reasons for Revelation of the Qur'an]. Edited by Kamâl Baseeni Zaghlool. Beirut: Dâr al-Kutub al-'Ilmiyah, 1998.

Other sources and resources

al-Hilâli, Muḥammad Taqi-ud-Din and Khan, Muḥammad Muḥsin. *Interpretation of the Meanings of the Noble Qur'an* (English-Arabic). Riyadh: Darussalam, 1996.

www.makkahedu.gov.sa/Makkah/mak_his.asp (accessed May 1, 2005)

www.mekkaoui.net/Islam/ArkanislamAR/make.htm (accessed May 1, 2005)

http://abdurrahman.org/seerah/sirat_ibn_hisham.pdf (accessed Jan. 2010)

http://web.archive.org/web/20040625103910/http://www.hraic.org/hadith/ibn_ishaq.html (accessed Jan. 2010)

*Glossary of Islamic Terms**

abu (or abi)	أبو، أبي	father (of)
âmeen	آمين	O Allah, accept our invocation; amen
Anṣâr	أنصار	'helpers': the Muslim citizens of Madinah who gave refuge to the Prophet (ﷺ) and the other Muslim emigrants from Makkah
banu (or bani)	بنو، بني	lit. 'children (of)'; usu. referring to a tribe that claims a common ancestor
Baqee' Cemetery	البقيع	the cemetery located next to the Prophet's Mosque in Madinah in which many of the Prophet's (ﷺ) companions and family members are buried
Hadith (ḥadeeth)	حديث	the collected statements and actions of Prophet Muhammad (ﷺ) that with the Qur'an form the basis of Islamic law
hadith (ḥadeeth)	حديث	a statement or action of Prophet Muhammad (ﷺ) that was remembered

* The Arabic words are transliterated according to the conventions of the Transliteration Chart found in this book. If a word has become part of the English language (i.e. is found in a dictionary of Standard English), that spelling is used in this book and appears first in this Glossary, with the transliterated form in brackets after it.

		and recorded by his Companions and followers
Hajj (ḥajj)	حج	the major pilgrimage to the Sacred Mosque, site of the Ka'bah at Makkah, to be undertaken by every able Muslim once in his/her lifetime
Ḥijâz	حجاز	the Western region of the Arabian Peninsula that includes Makkah and Madinah
Hijrah	هجرة	migration: *esp*. the migration from Makkah to Madinah by Prophet Muhammad (ﷺ) and his Companions that marks the start of the Islamic calendar
jihad (jihâd)	جهاد	struggle or striving (in Allah's cause)
jinn (plural of jinni)	جن	non-human, rational beings created by Allah from fire, often referred to as 'demons' or 'devils'; They have free will like humans: some are Muslims, others disbelievers; some are obedient to Allah, others disobedient. Satan is a jinni.
jizyah	جزية	a tax levied on the people of the Scriptures when they are under the protection of a Muslim government; it is in lieu of the alms tax paid by Muslims
Kaaba (Ka'bah)	الكعبة	the House of Allah in Makkah, originally built by Prophets Ibrâheem

		and Ismâ'eel, and which Muslims face wherever they pray
al-Masjid al-Aqṣâ	المسجد الأقصى	the 'Farthest Mosque', mentioned in the Qur'an (17: 1)
al-Masjid al-Ḥarâm	المسجد الحرام	the Sacred Mosque in Makkah where the Kaaba is situated
Muhâjiroon (or Muhâjireen)	مهاجرون	the Muslims who migrated with Prophet Muhammad (ﷺ) from Makkah to Madinah
Ramadan (Ramaḍân)	رمضان	the ninth month in the Islamic calendar; the month of obligatory fasting; the month in which the first verses of the Qur'an were revealed
soorah or soorat	سورة	chapter of the Qur'an
Sunnah	سنّة	the practice and collected sayings of Prophet Muhammad (ﷺ) that together with the Qur'an forms the basis of Islamic law
'umrah	عمرة	a minor, non-obligatory pilgrimage to Makkah
'umrat al-qaḍâ	عمرة القضاء	a compensatory 'umrah, or minor pilgrimage
Yathrib	يثرب	pre-Islamic name of the town that became known as Madinah, where the Islamic state was established after the Hijrah

MAP OF THE HIJAZ

During the time of the Prophet Muhammad (ﷺ)

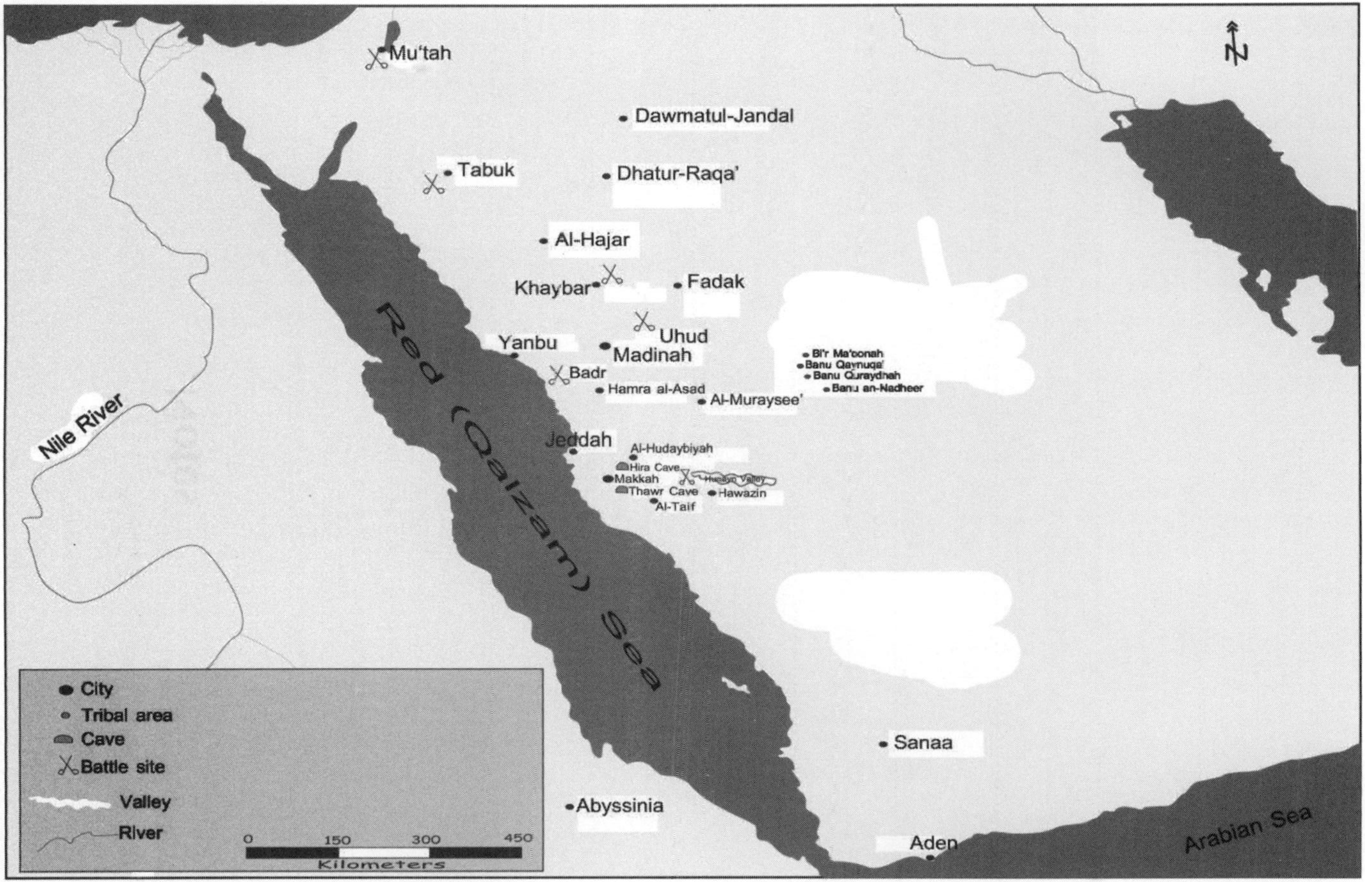

Mu'tah
Dawmatul-Jandal
Tabuk
Dhatur-Raqa'
Al-Hajar
Khaybar
Fadak
Uhud
Yanbu
Madinah
Badr
Hamra al-Asad
Al-Muraysee'
Bi'r Ma'oonah
Banu Qaynuqa'
Banu Quraydhah
Banu an-Nadheer
Nile River
Red (Qalzam) Sea
Jeddah
Al-Hudaybiyah
Hira Cave
Makkah
Thawr Cave
Hawazin
Al-Taif
Sanaa
Abyssinia
Aden
Arabian Sea
City
Tribal area
Cave
Battle site
Valley
River
0
150
300
450
Kilometers
N

Notes

Notes

Notes

Notes

Notes

Notes

Notes

Notes

Notes

Notes

....

....

....

....

....

....

....

....

....

....

....

Notes